Innovation Capabilities and Entrepreneurial Opportunities of Smart Working

Beatrice Orlando
Department of Economics and Management, University of Ferrara, Italy

A volume in the Advances in Logistics, Operations, and Management Science (ALOMS) Book Series

IGI Global
PUBLISHER of TIMELY KNOWLEDGE

Published in the United States of America by
IGI Global
Business Science Reference (an imprint of IGI Global)
701 E. Chocolate Avenue
Hershey PA, USA 17033
Tel: 717-533-8845
Fax: 717-533-8661
E-mail: cust@igi-global.com
Web site: http://www.igi-global.com

Library of Congress Cataloging-in-Publication Data

Names: Orlando, Beatrice, 1979- editor.
Title: Innovation capabilities and entrepreneurial opportunities of smart working / edited by Beatrice Orlando.
Description: Hershey, PA : Business Science Reference, [2023] | Includes bibliographical references and index. | Summary: "This knowledge gap poses a significant challenge for scholars and practitioners seeking to make informed decisions and drive meaningful change. Addressing this critical need for comprehensive understanding, Innovation Capabilities and Entrepreneurial Opportunities of Smart Working, edited by Beatrice Orlando from the University of Ferrara, Italy, serves as a resource that explores the multifaceted effects of the increasing and widespread use of SW and DL. It delves into crucial topics such as efficiency and effectiveness, knowledge management, impact on individuals, and the broader social, economic, and business implications"-- Provided by publisher.
Identifiers: LCCN 2023029593 (print) | LCCN 2023029594 (ebook) | ISBN 9781799887973 (hardcover) | ISBN 9781799887980 (paperback) | ISBN 9781799887997 (ebook)
Subjects: LCSH: Organizational change. | Organizational effectiveness. | Entrepreneurship.
Classification: LCC HD58.8 .I564 2023 (print) | LCC HD58.8 (ebook) | DDC 658.4/06--dc23/eng/20230719
LC record available at https://lccn.loc.gov/2023029593
LC ebook record available at https://lccn.loc.gov/2023029594

This book is published in the IGI Global book series Advances in Logistics, Operations, and Management Science (ALOMS) (ISSN: 2327-350X; eISSN: 2327-3518)

British Cataloguing in Publication Data
A Cataloguing in Publication record for this book is available from the British Library.

Advances in Logistics, Operations, and Management Science (ALOMS) Book Series

ISSN:2327-350X
EISSN:2327-3518

Editor-in-Chief: John Wang, Montclair State University, USA

MISSION

Operations research and management science continue to influence business processes, administration, and management information systems, particularly in covering the application methods for decision-making processes. New case studies and applications on management science, operations management, social sciences, and other behavioral sciences have been incorporated into business and organizations real-world objectives.

The **Advances in Logistics, Operations, and Management Science** (ALOMS) Book Series provides a collection of reference publications on the current trends, applications, theories, and practices in the management science field. Providing relevant and current research, this series and its individual publications would be useful for academics, researchers, scholars, and practitioners interested in improving decision making models and business functions.

COVERAGE

- Operations Management
- Organizational Behavior
- Services management
- Marketing engineering
- Political Science
- Finance
- Computing and information technologies
- Networks
- Decision analysis and decision support
- Production Management

IGI Global is currently accepting manuscripts for publication within this series. To submit a proposal for a volume in this series, please contact our Acquisition Editors at Acquisitions@igi-global.com or visit: http://www.igi-global.com/publish/.

The Advances in Logistics, Operations, and Management Science (ALOMS) Book Series (ISSN 2327-350X) is published by IGI Global, 701 E. Chocolate Avenue, Hershey, PA 17033-1240, USA, www.igi-global.com. This series is composed of titles available for purchase individually; each title is edited to be contextually exclusive from any other title within the series. For pricing and ordering information please visit http://www.igi-global.com/book-series/advances-logistics-operations-management-science/37170. Postmaster: Send all address changes to above address.

Titles in this Series

For a list of additional titles in this series, please visit:
http://www.igi-global.com/book-series/advances-logistics-operations-management-science/37170

Implementing Sustainable Development Goals in the Service Sector
Vipin Nadda (University of Sunderland, UK) Pankaj Kumar Tyagi (Chandigarh University, India) Rubina Moniz Vieira (St. Mary's University, London, UK) and Priyanka Tyagi (Chandigarh University, India)
Business Science Reference • copyright 2023 • 300pp • H/C (ISBN: 9798369320655) • US $275.00 (our price)

AI and Emotional Intelligence for Modern Business Management
Bhawana Bhardwaj (Central University of Himachal Pradesh, India) Dipanker Sharma (Central University of Himachal Pradesh, India) and Mohinder Chand Dhiman (Central University of Himachal Pradesh, India)
Business Science Reference • copyright 2023 • 415pp • H/C (ISBN: 9798369304181) • US $250.00 (our price)

Cases on Uncovering Corporate Governance Challenges in Asian Markets
Rashedul Hasan (Coventry University, UK)
Business Science Reference • copyright 2023 • 300pp • H/C (ISBN: 9781668498675) • US $235.00 (our price)

Global Perspectives on Soft Power Management in Business
Kannapat Kankaew (Burapha University International College, Thailand)
Business Science Reference • copyright 2023 • 536pp • H/C (ISBN: 9798369302507) • US $275.00 (our price)

Considerations and Characteristics of the Millennial Leader in Today's Global Society
Tymon M. Graham (TMGraham Consulting, LLC, USA)
Business Science Reference • copyright 2023 • 273pp • H/C (ISBN: 9781668447116) • US $240.00 (our price)

Integrating Intelligence and Sustainability in Supply Chains

For an entire list of titles in this series, please visit:
http://www.igi-global.com/book-series/advances-logistics-operations-management-science/37170

IGI Global
PUBLISHER of TIMELY KNOWLEDGE

701 East Chocolate Avenue, Hershey, PA 17033, USA
Tel: 717-533-8845 x100 • Fax: 717-533-8661
E-Mail: cust@igi-global.com • www.igi-global.com

Table of Contents

Detailed Table of Contents

With the onset of the Covid-19 pandemic, organizations in many sectors switched to the remote working system in order to maintain social distance among people. With the increase of home-office working in management literature, examining how useful the home-office working model as an example of smart working systems has gained importance to ensure the continuity of the systems. After the pandemic, some organizations did not return to their physical working environments and preferred completely online or hybrid business models. What kind of study is being executed is an important question for the realization of new research. In these studies, revealing how effective home-office research is and how much they can provide the expected benefit will be useful information for business human resources management in the strategy development processes. The purpose of this study is to investigate home office-related studies conducted during the Covid-19 pandemic and to reveal pros and cons of the home-office working in management literature.

COVID-19 crisis has enabled most tertiary institutions as well as business organizations worldwide to search for other means of imparting knowledge to students as well as carrying out business activities. This has given rise to both smart working and distance learning. This transformation process faces a number of complexities from both institutions and business organizations. Putting these aside, it has also generated opportunities for entrepreneurs to be innovative in pursuing infopreneurial activities by functioning maximally well within the distance learning domain. Distance learning has created opportunities to enhance the education system and prepare the learners for potential future emergencies. Smart working on the other hand, has enabled organizations to carry out businesses anywhere and everywhere. This chapter therefore, examined the entrepreneurial and innovative opportunities of smart working and distance learning within a developing country perspective with implications for practice, society and policies

The chapter on new and future trends in research explores the latest developments in research on innovation capabilities and entrepreneurial opportunities in the context of smart working. The chapter highlights emerging research trends, including the use of AI and machine learning for smart working, the impact of smart working on employee well-being, and the intersection of smart working with sustainability goals. The implications of these trends for innovation and entrepreneurship are explored, including challenges and opportunities such as keeping up with technological advancements, balancing benefits and drawbacks, and enhancing innovation capabilities while reducing environmental impact. Smart working research offers opportunities to improve work-life balance and contribute to sustainability goals by reducing commuting and associated emissions. By staying on the cutting edge of research, organizations can position themselves to capitalize on emerging opportunities and remain competitive in the future.

This chapter examines the use of virtual mentors in distance learning for entrepreneurship education. Virtual mentors establish a strong connection with students via sharing personal stories, overcoming the challenges of physical interaction in distance learning. The benefits of learning from global experts are discussed, along

in business operations during and after the Covid-19 outbreak will enable machine learning techniques to be used more in predicting uncertainty. This attempt will be beneficial in pointing out new research trends of machine learning in the business context for the future.

The rise of smart working has revolutionized the way organizations operate, presenting new strategies and courses of action for innovation and entrepreneurial growth. This book chapter proposes research into the strategies and management practices that organizations can employ within the framework of resilience, agility, and dynamic capabilities to unlock and harness innovation capabilities and entrepreneurial opportunities in the context of smart working. By examining the interplay between these concepts, this chapter seeks to uncover practical insights and provide guidance for organizations in maximizing the potential of smart working for innovation and entrepreneurship.

Preface

In today's rapidly changing world, our work and learning environments have experienced a significant transformation, largely driven by the profound impact of the Covid-19 pandemic. The outbreak prompted an unprecedented shift towards smart working and distance learning, which quickly became the norm for countless individuals and organizations worldwide. While the efficiencies of these digital modes of work and education are undeniable, they have brought forth a new set of challenges and opportunities that demand careful exploration.

Smart working and distance learning, with their undeniable merits, are not without their complexities. The increased adoption of these practices has raised questions about their long-term effectiveness, the potential for burnout among workers, and the limited circulation of informal knowledge. In an era marked by rapid technological advancements and shifting paradigms, it has become increasingly crucial to comprehensively understand the full spectrum of implications associated with smart working and distance learning.

In the pages of this edited reference book, aptly titled "Innovation Capabilities and Entrepreneurial Opportunities of Smart Working," we embark on a journey to investigate the multifaceted landscape of these digital transformations. I recognize that the significance of this theme is not confined to the immediate moment; rather, it is a topic that will exert a profound and enduring impact on both business and society as a whole.

My aim is to provide a comprehensive exploration of the positive and negative effects that stem from the growing prevalence of smart working and distance learning. I have endeavored to create a resource that will be valuable not only to scholars seeking a deeper understanding of this transformative shift but also to practitioners who are striving to make informed decisions in a rapidly evolving world.

This volume delves into a range of critical topics, including:

- **Interplay Between Tools and Smart Working/Distance Learning:** We analyze the dynamic relationship between technological tools and these new modes of work and education.

- **Impact on Cognitive and Social Capabilities of Individuals:** We examine how smart working and distance learning influence the personal and social development of individuals.
- **Real Impact at Social, Economic, and Business Levels:** We take a comprehensive look at the far-reaching effects on society, the economy, and businesses.
- **Short and Long-Run Negative Effects of Smart Working/Distance Learning:** We address concerns about potential drawbacks and long-term consequences.
- **Digital Innovation and Smart Working/Distance Learning:** We discuss how digital innovation intersects with these modes of work and learning.
- **New and Future Trends of Research:** We conclude by offering insights into promising avenues for future research in this evolving field.

I believe that this book will serve as a valuable resource for those seeking to navigate the complexities and opportunities inherent in the era of smart working and distance learning. The contributors have brought together a wealth of knowledge, insights, and expertise, making this a comprehensive reference work that I hope will inspire new ideas and drive informed decision-making.

ORGANIZATION OF BOOK

Chapter 1 delves into the world of home office working, a significant facet of smart working modes that gained prominence during the Covid-19 pandemic. With organizations adopting remote working to ensure social distancing, the chapter scrutinizes the effectiveness and benefits of this model. It explores the outcomes of home-office related studies conducted during the pandemic, shedding light on both the advantages and disadvantages documented in management literature. By examining these pros and cons, this chapter offers valuable insights for business human resources management and strategic decision-making.

Chapter 2 unravels the transformation brought about by the Covid-19 crisis, which compelled educational institutions and businesses to embrace distance learning and smart working. This transformation, although fraught with complexities, has also sparked entrepreneurial and innovative opportunities. The chapter explores how entrepreneurs have leveraged the distance learning and smart working domains to create and expand their ventures. It also discusses the broader implications for practice, society, and policy within the context of a developing country.

Chapter 3, "New and Future Trends in Research," provides a forward-looking perspective on the evolving landscape of innovation capabilities and entrepreneurial opportunities in the context of smart working. It delves into emerging research trends, including the role of AI and machine learning in smart working, the impact on employee well-being, and its intersection with sustainability goals. The chapter offers insights into the challenges and opportunities these trends present, with a focus on how organizations can stay competitive in an ever-changing environment.

Chapter 4 explores the use of virtual mentors in distance learning, particularly in the context of entrepreneurship education. It highlights the unique benefits of virtual mentorship, which transcends physical limitations and fosters a strong connection between mentors and students. The chapter underscores the value of learning from global experts and the role of parasocial interaction in creating meaningful engagement. Educators and practitioners alike will find practical strategies to enhance the distance learning experience by leveraging virtual mentors to provide real-world insights and facilitate networking.

Chapter 5 investigates the role of knowledge management systems (KMSs) in enhancing creativity among remote workers. In the wake of the Covid-19 pandemic, organizations have shifted to remote work, and KMSs play a crucial role in sharing knowledge and stimulating employee creativity. This chapter explores the factors that influence the relationship between KMS usage and creative performance, including absorptive capacity and motivation. Through an online survey, it offers insights into the impact of KMS usage on creative performance and the direct effects of absorptive capacity and motivation.

Chapter 6 delves into the transformative power of machine learning in the context of smart working. It explores the utilization of machine learning techniques to enhance decision-making in uncertain environments. The chapter emphasizes the role of artificial intelligence in processing data and its potential to predict uncertainty. As the business landscape evolves during and after the Covid-19 pandemic, machine learning emerges as a critical tool. This chapter provides an insightful view of the future research trends surrounding machine learning in the business context.

Chapter 7 is a strategic exploration of how organizations can harness innovation capabilities and entrepreneurial opportunities within the realm of smart working. It delves into the strategies and management practices that enhance resilience, agility, and dynamic capabilities. By examining the interplay between these concepts, the chapter aims to provide practical insights and guidance for organizations seeking to unlock the full potential of smart working for innovation and entrepreneurship.

I extend my heartfelt gratitude to all the authors, researchers, and contributors who have made this book possible. It is my sincere hope that the insights shared within these pages will be instrumental in shaping a brighter and more innovative future.

Beatrice Orlando
University of Ferrara, Italy

Chapter 1
A Systematic Review of Home-Office-Related Studies in the Business Context During the COVID-19 Pandemic Term

Isik Cicek
Necmettin Erbakan University, Turkey

ABSTRACT

With the onset of the Covid-19 pandemic, organizations in many sectors switched to the remote working system in order to maintain social distance among people. With the increase of home-office working in management literature, examining how useful the home-office working model as an example of smart working systems has gained importance to ensure the continuity of the systems. After the pandemic, some organizations did not return to their physical working environments and preferred completely online or hybrid business models. What kind of study is being executed is an important question for the realization of new research. In these studies, revealing how effective home-office research is and how much they can provide the expected benefit will be useful information for business human resources management in the strategy development processes. The purpose of this study is to investigate home office-related studies conducted during the Covid-19 pandemic and to reveal pros and cons of the home-office working in management literature.

1. INTRODUCTION

Working from home has a much longer history than working in offices outside. The

DOI: 10.4018/978-1-7998-8797-3.ch001

history of work from home dates back to the middle Ages, when craft and trade shops were set up within the living space (Radovic-Markovic, et, al. 2021).

Covid-19 pandemic brought unexpected changes in our daily life. During the current COVID-19 pandemic, most companies reduced office times and encouraged their employees to work from home in order to protect people from infection. Direct face-to-face communication was replaced by online meetings using video conferencing, chats, and cloud-based collaboration (Schmidtner et al, 2021). In the mean time, the pandemic has been causing negative socioeconomic effects throughout the world (Fujita, et al, 2021). A wide range of jobs in various industries can be done from home, including remote work. Namely, work from home, teleworking, remote office-it has several names, but no matter what you call it, it means working in an environment that is not the company's office, while ensuring that productivity does not suffer (Radovic-Markovic, 2021).

The term 'smart working' has been used to describe an evolutionary change taking place over a number of different dimensions in the world of work (Boorsma and Mitchell 2011). There has been a decline in the importance of place in work activities; greater scope for collaboration; employee autonomy and talent management; and an emphasis on innovation (Hamel and Breen, 2007). Much of the discussion around the concept of 'smart' working is focused on work traditionally performed in offices – administrative and managerial tasks. Personal life can be enhanced through smart homes that support advanced communication with devices via an Internet-of-Things (Carillo et al. 2017; Bednar and Welch, 2019). In this working mode, there are no specific constraints on the time or location of work. Due to the use of technology, smart workers may perform the same duties and activities as those of ordinary workers and achieve the same set targets and results while choosing a workplace and time schedule that are more convenient for both the activity to be performed and their personal needs (Angelici and Profeta, 2020)

A recent survey found that the majority (79%) of employees seeking flexibility in work are well educated and have managerial experience, while 73% felt that flexibility is a prerequisite for strong interpersonal relationships of employees (Ishay, 2019). According to Ishay (2019), the Gallup survey of good governance is a key factor in improving employee productivity and innovation. Remote employees require a different management style, so managers need to make sure they master the appropriate skills. Achieving these benefits requires strong, consistent leadership and constant communication. Founders and managers must set an example, be transparent and work to communicate the company's mission, values and goals. Some good starting points include (Freeport, 2020):

- Scheduling regular, comprehensive Zoom calls at least once a month to discuss the initiatives, present any new employment, and celebrate every victory, big or small.
- Organizing virtual activities to build a team, to encourage people to get to know the whole organization better

Most human resources experts agree that finding talent is getting harder and harder in their local markets. However, not only is the best staff difficult to secure, but existing staff can also look for work abroad or relocate for family reasons. Accordingly, some research shows that hiring remote workers reduces staff shortages. Certainly, by choosing the option of hiring geographically distant workers, the door is opened for hiring a far wider range of staff. Enabling employees to work from home also empowers them to be independent and disciplined. In addition, it provides a sense of trust. From the employee's point of view, their employer shows faith in them that they can reconcile work and private commitments while still being productive even though they are not under the watchful eye of management (Schiller, 2020; Radovic-Markovic, 2021).

Because of the several underlying success factor that can affect the efficiency of home-office working, the theoretical and practical studies depending on the field research gain importance to direct the researchers for conducting new studies. In this respect, in order to reveal the factors related to the extent to which home-office studies will provide the expected benefit, it will be useful to review the studies on this subject and to express the results with an inductive approach.

2. DESIGN/METHOD

For this study, qualitative research technique is used. Scopus database is searched using the keywords of "business", "Covid-19", "home-office" *for the date starting from Covid-19 outbreak. The date of all articles in the list are 2020, 2021, 2022, 2023,Theoretical, review or research types of articles included in the scope. The Price Rule can be asserted for the classification of the academic studies.*

A literature review of the research was carried out with bibliometric analysis. Laws such as Bradford's Law (1934) and Price Law (1976) can be used in biblimeotric analysis. Bradford's law works with the principle of grouping the journals containing the articles on the determined subject as numbers. It is used in the classification of journals for their articles rather than the article. The Bradford method could not be used since certain journals that specifically cover the articles of home-office working after covid-19 pandemic are not so many and varied to be classified in the 1/3 category. In Price's law, half of all scientific research papers are written by a number of authors equal to the square root of the total number of scientists. The square root of the total number of journals contains half of the total number of articles. Since the subject is home-office working after Covid-19 pandemic, it is expected that there will be more publications on this subject.

Firstly, 51 articles are listed. After reading carefully, 42 out of 51 articles are examined in the context. For the keywords determined, 461 sources registered in the Scopus database were reached in the categories of Business, Management and Accounting (miscellaneous) and General Business, Management and Accounting as subject. Source types covers journals, book series, and conference proceedings.

It can be stated that the value of 461, which is the number of resources accessed does not differ significantly from 441, which is the square of half of the examined resource in accordance with the Price rule.

The information in the sources are summarized at Table 1 in terms of the published journal, theme, sampling, method, theory, industry, and contextual variables. SciMat software is also utilized analysing the articles.

3. FINDINGS

All studies are investigated and the elements are reported as following order: General status and influential variables, favourable circumstances for home-office working, adverse circumstances for home-office working, technological perspective, and special cases.

3.1. General Status and Influential Variables

Starting with Covid-19 outbreak, home office, short-time work were enforced by governmental corona regulations. According to Airbnb study results, the employer and employees preferred to use their own house as an office instead of renting a new office to ensure social isolation during the Covid-19. Research results do not support a shift towards advertising listings for home-office or quarantine purposes.

The question of what work can be done from home has come to the fore. Job descriptions are an important point of view in deciding which jobs will be performed with the home-office system. Work from home friendly measure to evaluate whether the corresponding tasks can be performed from home is based on the descriptions from the International Standard Classification of Occupations 2008 (ISCO-08) standard. The Work from home friendly jobs can also be estimated by combining this measure with the labour statistics on occupational employments

Table 1. Home-office studies in business context studies during Covid-19 pandemic

No	Name of Journal	Theme	Sampling	Sector	Method	Theory	Other contextual variables	Authors, Year
1	the Future of Real Estate	Hotel		Tourism	Conceptual -Book Chapter		**Work from hotels: Is hybrid** people look for an alternative to working from home. This provides opportunities for coworking spaces and organizations that traditionally do not focus on providing workplace:hotels	van Sprang, H., Groen, B.(2021)
2	IEEE Engineering Management Review	methods of effective and efficient collaboration in distant work environments.	More than 170 people working in different job positions and from different branches and companies in Germany	General	Online survey	a scenario of the future of agile working in a post COVID-19 world is derived	Values and principles of agile working emphasize the benefits of personal communication and open team spaces with members sitting in close proximity	Schmidtner, M., Doering, C., Timinger, H. (2021)
3	Advances in Business Related Scientific Research Journal	managers' needs	900 Austrian, Czech and Slovak managers.		survey		how the managers approached the transition to e-working as well as their future perspectives after the epidemic. e-management, modern technology and business communication, informal communication, novel and innovative types of collaboration greatest fear of managers,	Beňo, M., Hvorecký, J., Cagáňová, D (2021)
4	International Journal of Entrepreneurship,				Theoretical		Many CEOs and senior managers have changed their minds about remote working equally in a short time. They soon realized that their teams were just as productive from home as they were in the office outside, and some even more productive	Radović-Marković, M., Stevanović, M., Milojević, N (2021)
5	International Journal of Culture, Tourism, and Hospitality Research	Airbnb and hotels	9 major European cities	hotel industry and Airbnb	empirical analysis data from STR and Inside Airbnb for the period January 2018–September 2020 ear-to-year changes in various performance metrics text-mining methods, signs for new use-cases are explored, including renting flats for home-office or quarantine.			Gyódi, K (2021)
6	Journal of Facilities Management, .	shift to teleworking during COVID-19 pandemic is going to diminish the need to procure/rent extensive office space	241 respondents		triangulation of Google search engine, survey and post hoc case study analysis.	The contingency theory	procuring office space and its price per square meter. Employee productivity	Naor, M., Pinto, G.D., Hakakian, A.I., Jacobs, A. (2021)

continued on following page

Table 1. Continued

No	Name of Journal	Theme	Sampling	Sector	Method	Theory	Other contextual variables	Authors, Year
7	Contributions to Management Science		in Turkey		Conceptual -Book Chapter		sickness-resilient digital employees, the software robots, became more apparent. Robot Process Automation (RPA) introduced the ultra-performing and fast-learning software robots into our lives. different applications of RPA robots around the world and in Turkey during the COVID-19 pandemic	Doğuç, Ö (2021)
8	Research for Development,		coworking managers		international survey		service workers move from traditional work in the office to work at home through remote or teleworking, which most coworkers of the coworking spaces belong effects of the Covid-19 pandemic on coworking spaces	Ceinar, I.M., Mariotti, I. (2021)
9	Asia-Pacific Journal of Business Administration		371 employees	IT		job demands and resources model	remote working and their impact on practical and psychological outcomes for the employee the role of certain job demands and resources on negative and positive outcomes through mediating role of strain and well-being , workload pressure, task interdependence, professional isolation and family interference in work lead to exhaustion and further stress, whereas the presence of autonomy and schedule flexibility and sufficient technology resources improve employee work-life balance and further better productivity and performance and job satisfaction.	Jamal, M.T., Anwar, I., Khan, N.A., Saleem, I (2021)
10	Management Research,		Mexican work environment 332 responses	General	Quantitative, exploratory based on primary and secondary sources, an online questionnaire was		stress and the aspects related to the arrival of COVID-19, well-being in the workplace,	Madero Gómez, S., Ortiz Mendoza, O.E., Ramírez, J., Olivas-Luján, M.R. (2020)
11	2020 3rd International Conference on Computer and Informatics Engineering,	Developmet of virtual office application					Prototype the company can provide online services to its customers/clients. The prototype of this application is developed using the prototyping method for an organization	Eriya, Yuly, A.R., Adila, R.N., Nugrahani, F., Waluyo, Y.S., Hammad, J.A.H (2020)
12	Journal of Innovation Management	the sentiments of the people regarding Work-from-Home concept	twitter activities posted on social media. Total 100,000 tweets	General			Work-from-Home concept was taken positively by the people. The emotions associated with most of the tweets were of trust and anticipation indicating that this concept is being welcomed by the people.	Dubey, A.D., Tripathi, S. (2020)

continued on following page

Table 1. Continued

No	Name of Journal	Theme	Sampling	Sector	Method	Theory	Other contextual variables	Authors, Year
13	Journal of Asian Finance, Economics and Business,	improve job performance during the Covid-19 pandemic at startup companies	in Indonesia managers of start-up companies in Jakarta, Banten, and West Java		Questionnaires quantitative study with primary data		job satisfaction, job innovation, Indonesian culture control, and job performance Increasing job performance is deemed necessary in facing the economic crisis caused by the Covid-19 pandemic Job innovation, job satisfaction, and culture control are deemed necessary in improving job performance. Before the Covid-19 pandemic, employees worked in offices for seven hours, but after this pandemic, they change work patterns, moving them to work from home. Working from home requires companies to exercise better control and leadership patterns so that employees can work comfortably	Muttaqin, G.F., Taqi, M., Arifin, B (2020)
14	Construction Economics and Building	Women workforce after Covid-19 term	80 Women workforce	Construaction	Open-enden questionnaire	-	(i) overworked; (ii) working space; (iii) social interactions; (iv) collaboration; and (v) parenting. The most cited strategies in addressing these challenges are: (i) increased visual communication; (ii) a dedicated workspace; (iii) self-scheduling; (iv) flexible working arrangements; and (v) breaking out work time and personal time	Oo, B.L., Lim, T.H.B., Zhang, Y. (2021)
15	Entrepreneul Business and Economic Review	how the form of remote work can be hindered in an institutional cultural context in non-Western countries.	data collection based on public report and news release in reference to the current academic literature of human resource management.	General	More than 100 000 results in Google news search, and I briefly checked the top 300 hits to examine institutional cultural influence on the execution of remote work in Japan	Cultural patterns	cultural context of non-Western countries, collectivism, high context, high power distance, and high uncertainty avoidance. Seniority-based HRM; long-term employment; processbased appraisal; teamwork; on-the-job training (OJT); overtime work; surveillance.	Iwashita H. (2021)
16	Journal for Labour Market Research, nn(j), m	Who and how many can work from home: evidence from task descriptions	For each occupation. Amazon Mechanical Turk (MTurk). descriptions from the International Standard Classification of Occupations kiiq (ISCO-iq) standard.	Amazon Mechanical Turk	proposes a method to estimate the share of these jobs. obtain a WFH friendly measure	-	share of WFH friendly jobs in an economy can then be estimated by combining these measures with the labor statistics on occupational employments.	Holgersen, H., Jia, Z., and Svenkerud, S. (2021)

continued on following page

Table 1. Continued

No	Name of Journal	Theme	Sampling	Sector	Method	Theory	Other contextual variables	Authors, Year
17	Zeitschrift fur Arbeits und Organisationpsychologie	the impact of telework and closure of educational and childcare facilities on working people during COVID-19. compare telework versus nontelework conditions and people with and without stay-at-home children.	465 working people in Germany	General	Quantitaive, survey	conservation of resources theory, selfregulation theory	stress, negative and positive affect, life satisfaction and trust in government, and loss of control over career success	Rieth, M., Hagemann, V. (2021)
18	Technology in Society	Is job performance conditioned by work-from	363 employees working from home due to Covid-19 restrictive measures	General	Quantitaive,	Job Demands-Resources theory,	employees' ICT (Information and Communication Technologies) anxiety and smartphone addiction can inhibit their work progress by provoking interruptions in the course and reducing the efficacy, further affecting performance.	Prodanova, J., Kocarev, L. (2021)
19	International Journal of Human Capital and Information Technology Professionals	the impact of mandatory work from home due COVID-jr on personal and professional lives of people with different demographics	237 employees	IT and non-IT	Quantitaive, Survey	-	Demographics, personal life dimensions—healthy lifestyle, family bonding, and physical stress. emotional well-being, Family size Professional dimensions related to work productivity and adopting new ways of working . occupational role. Dimensions related to new skill development and change in professional attitude	Pathak, D. Bharati, V.S., Mala, P. E. (2021)
20	Jahrbucher fur Nationalokonomie und Statistik	Working from Home, Wages, and Regional Inequality in the Light of COVID-19	20,018 individuals	general	Quantitaive, German Qualifications and Career Survey. BIBB/BAuA Employment Survey,	-	worker characteristics, the income, industry, occupation, and workplace properties substantial wage premium in a Mincer regression for workers performing their job from home	Irlacher, M., Koch, M. (2020)
21	International Journal of Production Economics.	examining the impact of COVID-jr's work implications on employees' performance (i.e. output quality and delivery).	106 employees	Different service organizations who have been working remotely during the pandemic	Quantitaive, survey		home office work environment, job insecurity and virtual connection, employee performance, I.4. technologies	Narayanamurthy, G. Tortorella, G

continued on following page

Table 1. Continued

No	Name of Journal	Theme	Sampling	Sector	Method	Theory	Other contextual variables	Authors, Year
22	Business Horizons,	Mindfulness and challenges of working from home in times of crisis. Approach that may help employees going through the challenges associated with working from home is mindfulness	-	-	Conceptual, Literature	-	mentally disconnect from work, individuals' attention to work tasks and thereby improve their performance; better manage screen fatigue. Work/Life Balance, well-being and productivity. Mindfullness techniques	Toniolo-Barrios, M. Pitt,L. (2021)
23	Internet research	impact of smart home applications by examining the factors that could contribute to perceived productivity and well-being whilst working from home. investigating the role of productivity and well-being in motivating the intention of remote workers to use smart home technologies in a home-work environment in the future.	528 smart home users working from home	General	Quantitative. cross-sectional research design. structural equation modelling	-	perceived productivity, service relevance, perceived usefulness, innovativeness, hedonic beliefs and control over environmental conditions. Well-being, task-technology fit, perceived ease of use, attitude to smart homes, . Intention to work from a smart home-office in the future .	Marikyan, D., Papagiannidis, S., F.Rana O. Ranjan, R. (2023)
24	Sustainability (Switzerland)	analysis of the attitudes of employees in pharmaceutical companies towards the business aspects of the pharmaceutical industry during and after the end of the pandemic	employees in pharmaceutical companies in the Republic of Serbia. 27 innovative and generic pharmaceutical companies.	medical drug industry	Quantitative. survey	-	coming to the office during the pandemic; the expectations of the employees to continue working from home after the outbreak of the COVID-19 pandemic. working from the home office have not been perceived as creating situations of endangering professional reputations, that is, they contribute to the sustainable economic success.	Milenkovic, J., Lakic, D., Bogavoc-Stanojevic, N. (2023)
25	Work	the more 'digitalized' and 'experienced with working from home (WFH),' the more positive peoples' perceptions are, explores how workers perceived WFH during the Œ COVID-19 lockdown from a psychosocial perspective	workers in Italy and Denmark	General	Quantitative. Survey. Ranking top and bottom respectively on the European Digital Economy and Society Index (DESI) and di‰erent pre-pandemic experiences of WFH	-	WFH perceptions and mental well-being. Home office constraints'	Ipsen, C., Kirchner, K., Bolisani, E., Scarso, E. (2023)

continued on following page

Table 1. Continued

No	Name of Journal	Theme	Sampling	Sector	Method	Theory	Other contextual variables	Authors, Year
26	Sustainability (Switzerland)	analyze changes in work-related mobility that occurred during the COVID-jr pandemic	multinational medium-sized chain. Situated in semi-rural Germany.	Retail Chain	Quantitatively. Case Study, expert interview	-	mobility behavior of the company's employees. frequency of commuting and business trips made by employees, framework conditions created by employers for the adoption of climate-friendly behavior.	Wilke, D., Rau, H., Hartling, J. W. (2022)
27	Medical Writing	if employees would like to return to a physical office or prefer to stay in the home office despite the lifting of most of the COVID-19 restrictions	353 US employees	Bioforum, Medical writers	Quantitaive Survey	-	Remote work and employee personality, Advantages of working from home, Overcoming disadvantages and difficulties of working from home, Remote work-life balance, Collaboration in the workplace, Support from manager(s) and colleague(s), Personal connections within the remote team	Daniela Kamir, Natalie Gavrielov, Cheryl Berkowitz (2022)
28	Academy of Journal of Interdisciplinary Studies	explore and understand the managers' perspectives of and attitudes towards face-to-display working, namely the reactions of managers working from home, their use of the home-office, views on future home-office development.	162 respondents from the Czech Republic	tertiary	Quantitative	-	productivity and satisfaction, work-life balance, physical human interaction, support from colleagues, having an at-home work space	
29	Journal of Asian and African Studies	relationship between COVID-19 pandemic and work outcomes of men and women in the case of Central Asia, region with under-established formal institutions, relatively poor social infrastructure, and mostly patriarchal society. T	Central Asia Men and Women Employees	General	Quantitative	-	medium-term employment level, short-term work productivity, gender	Tleubayeu, A., Kozhakhmet, S. (2022)

continued on following page

Table 1. Continued

No	Name of Journal	Theme	Sampling	Sector	Method	Theory	Other contextual variables	Authors, Year
30	International Journal of Culture, Tourism, and Hospitality Research	examine the impact of the COVID-19 pandemic on the traditional hotel industry and Airbnb in nine major European cities. examine the impact of the COVID-jr pandemic on the traditional hotel industry and Airbnb in nine major European cities.	data from STR and Inside Airbnb	Hotel Industry	Quantitative. Panel Data Regression Analysis. . Text mining	-	year-to-year changes in performance metrics, use cases, hotel supply, hotel prices, accommodation provision	Gyodi, K. (2022)
31	Jusletter IT	Digital workplace-challenges in labour law	-	-	Review (Literature)	-	location, working time, protection and insurance, protection of privacy, labor law, national legislation	Cosabic, J. (2022)
32	Frontiers in Sociology	Whether the pandemic will be a push factor for the acquisition of computer skills in late working life? he explanatory factors of the computer skills gained by older workers who were working from home during the COVID-jr pandemic	11402 employed persons aged 50 years and older In kq countries from the Survey of Health, Aging and Retirement in Europe (SHARE).	General	Quantitative	-	Worked only at home, worked at home and in usual workplace, computer skill, unemployment	König, R., Seifert, A. (2022)
33	Journal of Open Innovation,Technology, Market, Complexity	the effects of the business strategy (financial and market) and innovation management exerted on the economic indicators and business performances of SMEs in the south-central region of Sonora in Mexico, effect of the home office in the management of innovation and corporate performance	498 SMEs with between 6 and 250 employees	in the commerce sector	Quantitative Online questionnaire through the LimeSurvey Professional platform. PLS-SEM	Theory of competitive behavior, theory based on resources and capabilities	business strategy (financial and market), business performance, electronic commerce	Valdez-Juarez, L.E, Castillo-Vergara, M. Ramos-Escobar, E. A. (2022)

continued on following page

Table 1. Continued

No	Name of Journal	Theme	Sampling	Sector	Method	Theory	Other contextual variables	Authors, Year
34	Visual Review. International Visual Culture Review	The effect of The Home office and Tele-computing boosted by COVID-19 leading to a physical removal of workers on well-being	-	-	Case Study	-	Strategic Management of Internal Communication, business community	Mateus, A. F. (2022)
35	Proceedings of the European Conference on Knowledge Management, ECKM,	Challenges with work from home:	6 employees	General	Qualitative, semi-structured Interview, Case Study	Theory on Communities of Practice, Theory on tacit and explicit knowledge,Theory of Organizational Socialization, Motivation Theory	technology and digitalization as "hard core" skills, structures, culture and social interaction, development of loyalty to the company and quality of the production. Informal learning in the workplace, Relational development and maintenance	Ranglund, O.J., Haave, H., Vold, T. (2022)
36	Digital Challenges and Strategies in a PostPandemic World	how and to what extent female employees adapt to the "home" as both living and working space, how they experience the balance of work and non-work life, and how this situation affects their well-being	-	-	Qualitative Instagram Content Analysis netnographic approach	-	time interval, gender, positive-negative emotion-concept sharing, work and non-work life balance, workplace and institutionalism, seven themes mainly related to children and workspace arrangements. And the absence of males in the reŽected experiences of women	Vatansever, C., Özata, M.S., Ünsever, A. (2022)
37	Revista Juridica	the urban dimension of the social right of health and how this right and fundamental guarantee could be reconciled with the right of building and housing in the face of new requirements due to the e‰ects of the coronavirus pandemic (COVID jr) and also to turn to future needs.	-	-	Exploratory, deductive method. jurisprudential and doctrinal studies, Supreme Court, competence of Art.	principles of urbanism	social procedures or even other health measures, domestic infrastructure, local public administrators, land loation	Saleme,E. R. Bonavides, R. S., Michelucci, A. (2022)

continued on following page

Table 1. Continued

No	Name of Journal	Theme	Sampling	Sector	Method	Theory	Other contextual variables	Authors, Year
38	Studies in Big Data	Cybersecurity Risks and Their Mitigation for Work-From-Home Tools and Techniques	-	-	Conceptual (Literature)		utilizations of online stages as a home office, business's goal, home office safe.	Obaidullah, Y. M. (2022)
39	Revista de Gestao	influence of output control, autonomous motivation and controlled motivation on task performance of public servants at home office	236 public servants	Public institutions	Quantitative structural equation modeling (SEM)	Control Theory, Self-regulation Theory	autonomous motivation and output control.	Silva, C. A., Rosa, F. S. (2022)
40	Group and Organization Management	one's home working environment features salient signals of their social status that affect their performance.	304 remote workers from within the United States	General	Quantitative	sociocognitive theory of socioeconomic status (SES)	levels of SES report, sense of control over their environment, job performance, time an individual spends in their home office, pre-existing inequalities	Loignon, A.C., Johnson, M. A., Veestraeten, M., Boyd, T. L. (2022)
41	Studies in Systems, Decision and Control	In a changing business world companies need the ability to assess which trends and developments are essential to sustain own workforce and accomplish the goal of staying competitive, and of being connected to employees and customers	-	-	Conceptual (Literature)	-	Home office, short-time work, hygiene rules and social distancing were enforced by governmental corona regulations. Accomplishing goals requires personnel motivation, a process that is cross functional and goal directed while acting voluntary, moreover crisis requires motivation, based on consistency	Zöllner, K, Sulikova, R. (2022)
42	Sociedade e Estado	phenomenon of teleworking, which was driven by the context of the Covid-19 pandemic	-	-	Research paper bibliography and the analysis of secondary data on teleworking	Capitalism, modernization"	reformulating business gains, exploitation of human labor, intensifying working hours, appropriating the private space of workers' homes, making work and reproductive tasks compatible, especially by women, of isolation in relation to work groups and their political articulations, as well as psychological suffering and illness.	Duraes, B., Bridi, M.A.C, Dutra, R. Q (2021)

continued on following page

Some factors come to the fore in order for home working systems to provide the expected efficiency and effectiveness. Considering the research results about home-office, it is seen that work from home productivity is relative to working with commuting (WWC), emotional well-being, employee performance, personal life dimensions (healthy life style, family bonding, physical stress), gender, industry type, control over environmental conditions, ethnic diversity in the workplace, business communication, maintaining informal communication, novel and innovative types of collaboration, needing better support, co-working spaces especially for creative and innovative class of workers and coworking managers. Perceived well-being that are closely related to home-office productivity correlates with task-technology fit and attitude to smart homes. Intention to work from a smart home-office in the future is dependent on perceived well-being. The more time an individual spends in their home office, the stronger the relationship between their environment-based socio-economic status and their personal sense of control.

As a result of the analysis of the articles examined with the help of the Scimat program, two outputs were obtained.1. Strategic Diagram (Figure 1) 2. Cluster Network (Figure 2).

After the Covid-19 theme in the strategic diagram, the theme "time" appeared in the motor theme area. Studies with the theme of time draw attention to the time dimension of the work/life conflict variable. Performance dimension was determined as a low-development theme. The majority of studies have not focused on individual performance appraisal. When the cluster network is examined, it is seen that home-office is significantly related to the teleworking theme, productivity is examined relatively less, and the employee theme is less common.

3.2. Favourable Circumstances for Home-Office Working

In the realm of organizational theories, with a focus on the conservation of resources theory, the concept of working remotely from home can be interpreted as a valuable acquisition of resources. This interpretation aligns with the premises of the self-regulation theory, suggesting that working from home serves as a strategic approach to address challenges associated with home-office dynamics.

Numerous empirical studies have indicated that the practice of remote work yields several advantageous outcomes. These include diminished levels of stress, reduced negative emotions, heightened positive affect, increased life satisfaction, and a lesser sense of relinquishing control over one's career advancement. This positive outcome can be attributed to factors such as autonomy in decision-making, flexible scheduling, and adequate technological resources. These elements, in turn, engender favourable variables like the equilibrium between work and personal life,

Figure 1. Strategic diagram of themes

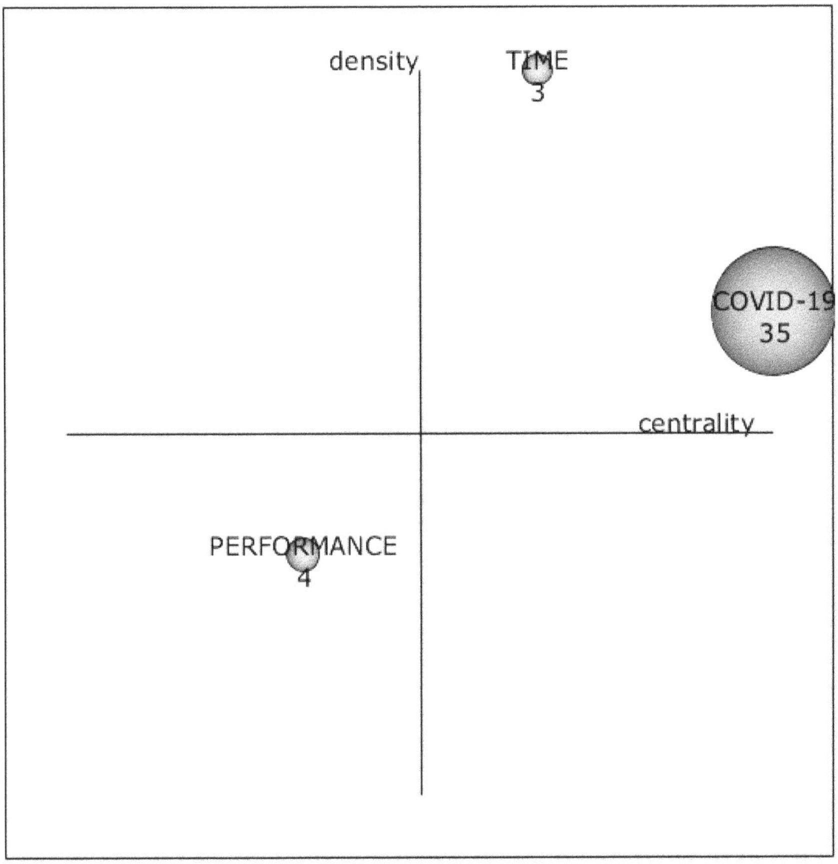

enhanced productivity, improved task performance, and heightened job satisfaction within home-office working systems.

A pivotal factor in achieving holistic well-being within the work environment is paramount for attaining optimal outcomes in the context of home-office arrangements, as the well-being of individuals directly influences the equilibrium between work and personal life.

The proficient management of internal communication stands as a pivotal determinant of productivity within home-office settings. Establishing employee engagement as a means to foster morale and trust is imperative in effectively addressing challenges inherent to remote work. Moreover, cultivating a heightened sense of control over one's immediate work environment significantly impacts the perceived efficacy of job performance within the home-office model. The presence

Figure 2. Network cluster diagram for 'Covid-19'

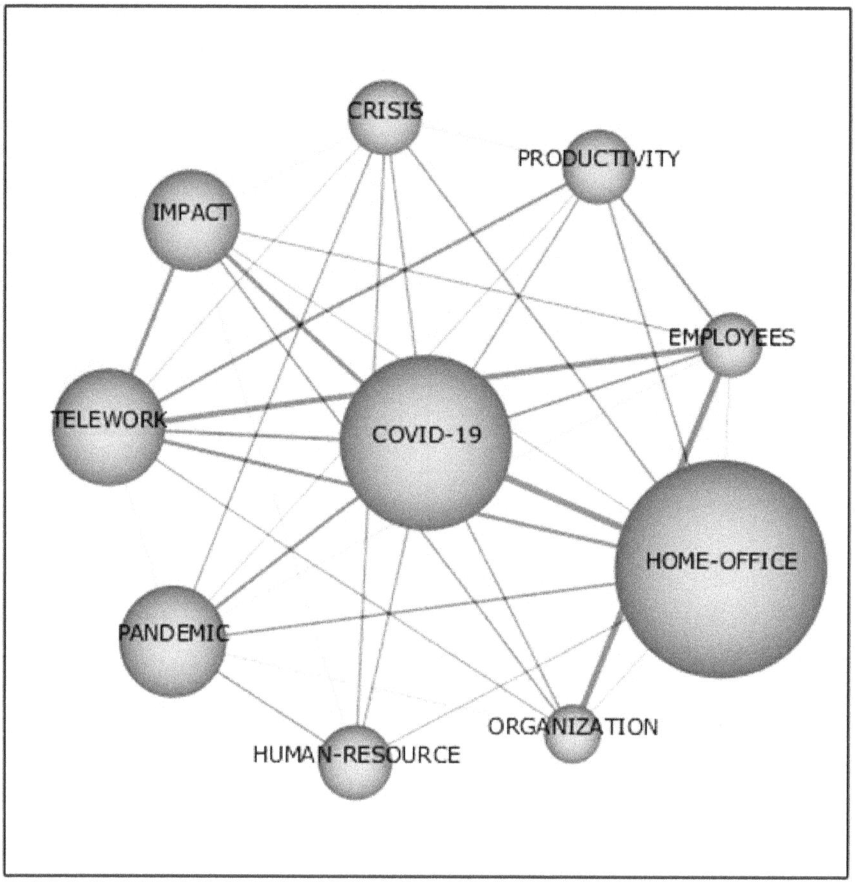

of autonomous motivation and stringent output control exhibits a robust and positive correlation with task performance within the realm of home-office work.

A fundamental precondition for favourable outcomes in home-based work systems is the motivation of personnel. The concept of working from a home office has not been associated with scenarios that jeopardize professional reputations.

From a compensation perspective, research findings suggest a robust and affirmative relationship between the proportion of job opportunities that facilitate remote work and the average income of workers. This underscores the notion that roles offering remote work options are relatively resilient in times of crisis.

One study revealed that management professionals held apprehensions regarding the impact of screen-mediated work on the balance between work and personal life, fearing a reduction in physical human interaction. Contrary to these apprehensions, the study found that decreased support from colleagues, gender differences, and the presence of a home-based workspace did not adversely affect productivity. In fact, screen-mediated work was identified as an efficient and time-saving tool that contributed to heightened productivity and satisfaction, particularly among younger professionals. This mode of work not only facilitated cost savings but also presented a viable option for future work models.

3.3. Adverse Circumstances for Home-Office Working

Taking into account the collective body of published literature, it is widely acknowledged that fatigue and stress can detrimentally impact employees, posing a challenge to ensuring seamless business continuity within home-office systems. Essential adverse factors associated with home-based work encompass heightened workload pressures, task interdependencies, a sense of professional isolation, and instances of work-family interference. Furthermore, the presence of ICT-related anxiety and an inclination towards smartphone addiction are identified as potential culprits that can impede individual performance within this working model.

Prominent among the challenges consistently highlighted in the realm of home-office work are: (i) excessive work demands; (ii) inadequacies in the designated work environment; (iii) limitations in social interactions; (iv) obstacles to collaborative endeavours; and (v) the intricacies of balancing work and parental responsibilities. The prevailing strategies cited for tackling these challenges involve: (i) an escalated utilization of visual communication tools; (ii) the establishment of a dedicated and conducive workspace; (iii) the implementation of personalized scheduling mechanisms; (iv) the adoption of flexible work arrangements; and (v) the deliberate demarcation of distinct boundaries between work and personal time. It is noteworthy that many of these challenges exhibit intricate interconnections, and the strategies adopted by both employees and employers are inherently multi-tiered and interdependent in nature.

In the initial stages, a multitude of employees encountered a dip in their work productivity, a waning of motivation, a surge in stress levels, and a deterioration in their mental well-being since the onset of the COVID-19 outbreak. It is noteworthy that prior exposure to remote work systems did not necessarily foster a positive perception of the home-based work paradigm. An avenue that holds promise for aiding employees navigating the intricacies associated with remote work challenges is the practice of mindfulness.

Of particular relevance, especially within the context of international human resource management, are the potential institutional and cultural impediments that may hinder the adoption of remote work practices in certain countries. Notably, non-Western nations could face hindrances due to prevalent factors such as heightened collectivism, substantial power distance, and a strong inclination towards uncertainty avoidance. These cultural nuances may significantly influence the feasibility and effectiveness of remote work arrangements.

3.4. Technology Perspective

A solid technological foundation is imperative for the successful implementation of home-office working systems. The advent of Industry 4.0 and the introduction of robotic process automation have heralded innovative solutions that bolster the efficiency of home-based work models. These technological advancements serve as pivotal instruments in preserving the streamlined functionality of home-office systems.

In the strategic realm of internal communication management, the incorporation of digital media emerges as a potent strategy to facilitate comprehensive system feedback. Leveraging digital platforms within this context proves to be an effective means of ensuring transparent and coherent communication flows.

A pivotal strategy in upholding the efficacy of remote work is the creation of a virtual office application. This virtual workspace serves as a cohesive hub where employees can collaborate, communicate, and engage in tasks, thereby fostering a sense of unity despite physical separation.

However, it is essential to be cognizant of the cybersecurity risks associated with the tools employed for remote work. Safeguarding sensitive information and ensuring the integrity of organizational operations should be paramount considerations in the implementation of work-from-home tools.

The expertise of smart home developers extends beyond the confines of domestic settings. Their technological prowess can be harnessed to enhance the functionality of applications in various contexts beyond the home environment. By harnessing the potential of technology, the smart home developers can contribute to the advancement of applications that transcend traditional boundaries.

3.5. Special Cases

Within the landscape of studies on home-office work, unique scenarios and circumstances have come to light. Notably, the personality traits exhibited by individuals have been identified as contributing factors in the assessment of the efficacy of home-office systems. An intriguing outcome from one study highlights that approximately 7.7% of employees identify as extroverts, and their experience of remote work occasionally intersects with feelings of solitude and isolation. Conversely, introverted employees express a sense of relief when engaged in smaller team settings, finding solace in reduced exposure to larger groups. Ambivert employees, characteristically adaptable, appear to navigate remote work with relative equanimity.

A prevailing and significant case pertains to the augmented caregiving and domestic responsibilities undertaken by women within the workforce. Women, especially mothers, and those operating from home offices, have exhibited diminished work productivity in response to the short-term impact of the COVID-19 pandemic. This phenomenon subsequently exerts a negative influence on the medium-term employment prospects for women. Interestingly, research suggests that women tend to exhibit greater resilience in adapting to e-working conditions compared to their male counterparts.

The unique circumstances faced by new employees recruited during the COVID-19 pandemic have also garnered attention. Despite the availability of robust technological solutions conducive to remote task execution, these individuals often express a desire for physical presence within the workplace. A sense of being valued and a yearning for personal and social connections that foster loyalty and quality are pivotal for new employees. These factors are frequently associated with informal learning dynamics in the workplace. The cultivation and maintenance of interpersonal relationships are crucial not only for proficiency in the digital realm but also for fostering a tangible presence within the physical workspace.

Moreover, it is noteworthy that certain employees who are already in a disadvantaged position are often less likely to hold roles that can be effectively carried out from a remote home-based setup. This underscores the inherent inequalities and disparities that can emerge when considering the feasibility of home-office work arrangements.

4. CONCLUSION

Overall, the concept of home-office emerged during the pandemic, leading to significant changes in employees' work patterns. CEOs and senior managers quickly shifted their views on remote work as teams proved to be just as, if not more, productive while working from home. The concept of home-office was widely embraced due to the trust it fostered among employees.

With the increasing preference for home-office work, there has been a decline in the demand for office space and a decrease in its price per square meter. Despite potential distractions at home, employee productivity remains relatively high while teleworking. Residences have become extensions of business activities, and the pandemic has resulted in the acquisition of valuable digital skills through remote work. Moreover, home-office has positive effects on innovation management, and lessons learned from remote work could potentially improve office work environments after the pandemic. However, for home-office to be beneficial, supportive working conditions at home are essential; otherwise, it might be perceived as a resource threat, particularly when dealing with stay-at-home children.

As workplaces become more digitalized, offering hybrid work options becomes critical, and the influence of national conditions on the success of these new working methods, including their impact on people's mental well-being, needs to be carefully considered. Companies must recognize that technology and digitalization are not isolated skills but intertwined with various aspects of organizational dynamics, such as structures, culture, and social interaction.

The rise of remote work has also influenced labour laws and urbanism. Home-office has the potential to alleviate traffic problems and reduce car pollution.

When all the studies on home-office are reviewed collectively, the majority (91%) indicate that employees welcome this working system, and it does not hinder achieving desired results. Overall, working from home has been perceived positively, with noted improvements in work productivity and work-life balance. The transition to remote work has yielded performance gains for many companies, and it is recommended to sustain these home-office systems in the post-pandemic period. People value digital tools and have found effective methods for collaboration in remote work environments. Home-office is no longer a mere alternative but is predicted to become increasingly common, with many jobs transitioning to hybrid working systems in the future.

Regarding managerial implications, companies need to exercise better control and leadership patterns to ensure employees can work comfortably from home. Remote work has proven to be a successful strategy in human resource management, providing better support to female employees. The adoption of new working methods varies across occupational roles, leading to skill development and changes in personal attitudes. Regulating home-office systems involves managing intensifying working hours and respecting workers' private spaces. Providing information to build management strategies that enhance employee performance in home-office settings is essential, and institutionalization is crucial for achieving the desired effectiveness of these systems.

Concerning the concept of smart working, the integration of smart homes that facilitate advanced communication with Internet-of-Things (IoT) devices has the potential to enrich individuals' personal lives (Carillo et al., 2017).

While acknowledging the potential for increased isolation, proponents of smart working propose that the adoption of collaborative and mobile technologies can offer enhanced support for team collaboration and innovation. This paradigm aligns with the emergence of Industry 4.0 and modern manufacturing systems (Lee et al., 2015), as well as the provision of services (Barile and Polese, 2010). Smart working entails a trade-off. On one hand, it offers the potential for flexible work locations and hours, surpassing the benefits associated with traditional telecommuting.

Telecommuting, which involves working from home, enables employees to reduce commuting costs and allows companies to optimize expenses. However, the cost reduction is more pronounced with smart working compared to telecommuting due to the latter requiring constant inspections and remote worker monitoring.

Four distinct models of smart work alternatives can be delineated: (1) the home office model, (2) the smart work center model, (3) flexible time arrangements (including discretionary work), and (4) mobile work. The home office model permits employees to work from their residences rather than commuting to a centralized office. This approach proves particularly advantageous for working mothers seeking a balance between professional and familial responsibilities. The smart work center model involves working from an office located in close proximity to one's residence, thus saving time, costs, and energy. Mobile work entails the flexibility for employees to conduct their tasks outside of the traditional office environment.

The adoption of smart working, particularly through the home office model, presents a spectrum of advantages, including time-saving benefits, heightened work efficiency, an improved quality of life, reduced commuting time, enhanced focus on tasks, increased family time, heightened personal well-being, and increased job satisfaction. Notably, the absence of face-to-face interactions in home office environments can foster heightened work concentration by minimizing unnecessary meetings and extraneous work requests during designated work hours. It is important to acknowledge that smart work, despite utilizing comparable amounts of resources like electricity, water, and energy at home, is not intrinsically tied to environmental considerations.

However, a noteworthy drawback of smart working is that several individuals reported a blurring of the boundaries between their work and personal lives. Despite this, the need for and relevance of smart working is anticipated to persist in the foreseeable future.

5. ORIGINALITY

Industry 4.0 and Industry 5.0 have significantly changed the way of executing jobs in organizations depending on technological advancement. The comfort that new technologies provide in human life, for example, home-office work, e-commerce, online work, and education change the business context for the employees. The Covid-19 pandemic has led individuals to social isolation due to closures and practices of maintaining a physical distance. In this circumstance, home-office working are commonly utilized. Reviewing of home-office studies is important in terms of revealing the next new research trend academically. In practice, it will be an input for the smart-working system strategies to be developed for the human resources management systems of the organization. With the onset of the pandemic, the interest in the effective use of resources by firms can play a role in ensuring sustainability, depending on the development of smart working systems on the home-office base.

REFERENCES

AngeliciM.ProfetaP. (2020). Smart-Working: Work Flexibility Without Constraints. (Working Paper No. 8165). CESifo. https://ssrn.com/abstract=3556304 doi:10.2139/ssrn.3556304

Barile, S., & Polese, F. (2010). Smart service systems and viable service systems: Applying systems theory to service science. *Service Science*, *2*(1–2), 21–40. doi:10.1287erv.2.1_2.21

Bednar, P. M., & Welch, C. (2020). Socio-Technical Perspectives on Smart Working: Creating Meaningful and Sustainable Systems. *Information Systems Frontiers*, *22*(2), 281–298. doi:10.100710796-019-09921-1

Boorsma, B., & Mitchell, S. (2011). Work-life innovation smart work—A paradigm shift transforming how, where, and when work gets done. *Cisco IBSG Point of View*. https://www. cisco.com/c/dam/en_us/about/ac79/docs/ps/Work- Life_ Innovation_ Smart_Work.pdf

Carillo, K., Scornavacca, E., & Za, S. (2017). The role of media dependency in predicting continuance intention to use ubiquitous media systems. *Information & Management*, *54*(3), 317–335. doi:10.1016/j.im.2016.09.002

Freeport, M. (2020). *Challenges of working remotely from a business perspective.*

Fujita, K., Inoue, A., Kuzuya, M., Uno, C., Huang, C. H., Umegaki, H., & Onishi, J. (2021). Mental Health Status of the Older Adults in Japan During the COVID-19 Pandemic. *Journal of the American Medical Directors Association*, *22*(1), 220–221. doi:10.1016/j.jamda.2020.11.023 PMID:33321080

Hamel, G. and Breen, B. (2007). The Future of Management. *Human Resource Management International, 16*(6)

Ishay, Y.B. (2019). *Revisiting "Work from Home" from an Organizational Perspective*. Research Gate.

Lee, J., Bagheri, B., & Kao, H. A. (2015). A cyber-physical systems architecture for industry 4.0-based manufacturing systems. *Manufacturing Letters*, *3*(1), 18–23. doi:10.1016/j.mfglet.2014.12.001

Price, D. (1976). A general theory of bibliometric and other cumulative advantage processes. *Journal of the American Society for Information Science*, *27*(5), 292–306. doi:10.1002/asi.4630270505

Radović-Marković, M., Stevanović, M., & Milojević, N. (2021) Remote Working in Terms of Covid-19. *International Journal of Entrepreneurship, 25* (1). ISSN 1939-4675

Schiller, R. (2020). *A perspective on working from home: The good and the bad (But mostly good)*. Benefits Pro.

Schmidtner, M., Doering, C., & Timinger, H. (2021). Agile Working During COVID-19 Pandemic. *IEEE Engineering Management Review*, *49*(2), 18–32. doi:10.1109/EMR.2021.3069940

Chapter 2
Entrepreneurial and Innovative Opportunities of Smart Working and Distance Learning

Oluwabunmi Bakare-Fatungase
https://orcid.org/0000-0002-4665-3969
Lead City University, Nigeria

Sudetu Oseni
Auchi Polytechnic, Nigeria

ABSTRACT

COVID-19 crisis has enabled most tertiary institutions as well as business organizations worldwide to search for other means of imparting knowledge to students as well as carrying out business activities. This has given rise to both smart working and distance learning. This transformation process faces a number of complexities from both institutions and business organizations. Putting these aside, it has also generated opportunities for entrepreneurs to be innovative in pursuing infopreneurial activities by functioning maximally well within the distance learning domain. Distance learning has created opportunities to enhance the education system and prepare the learners for potential future emergencies. Smart working on the other hand, has enabled organizations to carry out businesses anywhere and everywhere. This chapter therefore, examined the entrepreneurial and innovative opportunities of smart working and distance learning within a developing country perspective with implications for practice, society and policies

DOI: 10.4018/978-1-7998-8797-3.ch002

INTRODUCTION

As organizations and working culture evolves, so does the need to enable, engage and reward people in innovative ways. More reason businesses strive for sharper service, lower overhead costs and higher motivation that is translating into competition for the brightest and best staff; thus making the innovative ecosystem intense and highly competitive. However, organizations need to employ prospective staff more efficiently, keep them engaged and inspired to be best at what they do by embracing technological innovations cum entrepreneurial strategies. This can be achieved through appropriate human resource management so that organizational staff can fit into the contemporary discourse of entrepreneurial and innovative opportunities of smart working ushered in by the advent of the Covid-19 pandemic which has redefined all aspect of human existence of which the distance learning domain globally is not an exception.

Increasingly, smart working and the use of mobile technology is empowering staff to choose when and how to work which has been accentuated by the pandemic. To this end, smart working which are set of practices that add greater flexibility to work methods through innovative solutions has come to bare. Flexible location, schedule, hours worked and shared responsibility are some of the markers of smart working. Similarly, technology is transforming the way businesses are being done and impacting how values are being created, delivered and captured, most especially in the educational sector that the distance learning domain is domiciled which cannot dispute the indispensability of smart working in this fourth industrial revolution era (4^{th}IR). Therefore, there is expected to be a symbiotic relationship between the principles of smart working and distance learning which is aimed to provide uninterrupted educational benefits to whoever is interested remotely so that everyone have the requisite educational training which is the fundamental tenets of the Sustainable Development Goal 4 (SDG4) (Bakare & Okuonghae, 2022). This can connect students to universities worldwide, making it more accessible for students in different countries to interact on the global space seamlessly with University staff. It is also known to be more affordable, which is another factor that helps make education more accessible to many students around the world and in different socio-economic levels. However, despite the innovative opportunities of smart working which when embraced and entrenched within the domain of distance learning, brings out entrepreneurial opportunities as is being witnessed in the global north, the same cannot be said of countries in the global south of which Nigeria is not an exception. It is based on this premise that this chapter tends to explore the entrepreneurial and innovative opportunities of smart working and distance learning

Smart Working and Distance Learning

Smart working is a new model of work that uses the new technologies and the development of existing technologies to improve both the performance and the satisfaction that is obtained from the job. It should not be confused with the term co-working, which refers to a shared workspace, usually by self-employed professionals. Smart working can include working from home or anywhere because of technological ubiquity. This is due to the incorporation of new and sophisticated technology and a degree of trust; this type of agile working can also include technologically effective people who work from anywhere. This is due to the ubiquitous nature of these emerging technologies which is not inhibited by time, means and location (Bakare, 2023). Smart working means exactly what it sounds like as everything is smart these days such as telephones, clocks, vehicle etc. and is closely related to the concept of teleworking.

Smart working is a natural evolution of teleworking as it has added greater mobility and versatility to the features of the "traditional" distance work such as hourly flexibility or comfort. Teleworking moved the work from the office to the home, smart working takes it to almost any other place, from a park or a coffee shop to the waiting room of an airport, or anywhere (Bird, 2021). This process is accelerating with the rise of local, social and mobile technology. Technology today is improving our ability to innovate and grow as no organization, regardless of size, can compete without responding to this new digital age. As part of this digital age, employees are increasingly looking to their employers to provide flexible environments that is innovatively based so as to provide seamless services.

The study of Alrowwad et al., (2020), revealed that frequent feedback from employees on their given tasks had a substantial impact on organizational performance; while the study carried out by Soomro & Shah, (2019), claimed that smart working enhanced the level of affective attachment to their organization frequently resulting in high or enhanced performance within the organization. However, the findings of Mumu et al., (2021) in his study reported in the literature suggested that smart working practices, such as lower overhead costs or increased productivity for employees working from home during their busiest times, developed from conceptions of family-friendly organizational backing. This is to say that maintaining interest and efficiency will have a good impact on the success of the company. Transformational leadership style is thus important in encouraging smart working to continue working from home by giving workers all the support they need - mentally, financially, and in terms of feedback - and engaging in order to achieve higher productivity. Accessibility to technology may be related to greater affective commitment and improved growth rate of business performance as emphasized by Ahmad & Ismail (2021, p. 1272) who opined the "ability of the management to provide and practice a proper technology and online support practices such as fully utilize the technology communication network and modern equipment to increase the effectiveness of support in organization among employees may lead to increase employees' behavior". This is to say that there may be consequences for owners and managers of organizations in that they must demonstrate an accessible technology that is supportive of smart working in order to assure continual progress and dedication of their personnel.

This impact has also been felt within the educational ecosystem as due to the active development of Information and Communication Technologies (ICTs) as well as the 4^{th}IR technologies which has remodified in addition to providing ample opportunities for education. Today's media and interactive technologies provide a powerful platform for all those who want to learn, thereby strengthening the concept of "learning is for everyone" which is fundamental to the Sustainable development Goal 4 (SDG4). Advanced institutions focus on their flexibility and openness towards students as affirmed by Alfonso (2015) which implies smart work implies the educational institution care about the work process as much as students who are at the receiving end. This means prioritizing, delegating and improving the time management of both the staff and students to achieve the desired results at the click of a button which is a one of the fundamental principles of distance learning domain.

Distance learning is remotely based which is a method of studying specifically designed for students who are separated from teachers or assistants by physical distance. Distance learning is carried out by means of the Internet and web technologies (Dron & Anderson, 2014) which does not include any in-person interaction with an instructor or study peers. Students study at home on their own, and the learning is more individual and varies on speed and timeline according to each individual student and their availability. It relies on the educational tools of online learning which is corroborated by Webster (2020) which defines it as a method of study where teachers and students do not meet in a classroom but use the Internet, e-mail, mail, etc., to have classes. Simply put, distance learning is when students learning are done remotely and do not have face-to-face interactions with lecturers/instructors/teachers and/or other students.

Distance learning is sometimes confused with online learning. Online learning can be used as a supplement for teachers in their courses, while distance learning replaces teachers with instruction that is pre-set on the learning platform. Online learning is when teachers or students use educational tools which are accessible on the internet. This means that students can also use online tools even while they are physically in a classroom with their teacher and peers. Online learning can be used anywhere and anytime, so teachers may have students using them as tools in class or for preparation and assignments at home. Online learning tools are often used to create blended learning environments in the classroom. This helps keep students engaged in the class and immersed in the material (Kaplan & Haenlein, 2016; Samoylenko, Zharko, & Glotova, 2022).

Distance learning which is also known as distance education is the education of students who may not always be physically present at school or where the learner and the teacher are separated in both time and distance. Traditionally, this usually involved correspondence courses wherein the student corresponded with the school via mail. Distance education is a technology-mediated modality and has evolved with the evolution of technologies such as video conferencing, TV, and the Internet. Today, it usually involves online education and the learning is usually mediated by some form of technology and smart working strategies. A distance learning program can be completely distance learning, or a combination of distance learning and traditional classroom instruction (called hybrid or blended) such as the National Open University of Nigeria (NOUN) and the University of Ibadan School of Distance Learning (UIDLC). Other modalities include distance learning with complementary virtual environment or teaching in virtual environment (e-learning) (Anderson & Rivera, 2020).

Entrepreneurial Opportunities of Smart Working and Distance Learning

The entrepreneurial opportunities brought about by technology is innovatively having positive impact in unquantifiable ways, as these are opening doors that are beyond human comprehension within the business domain. Entrepreneurship usually starts as a small business but the long-term vision is much greater, to seek high profits and capture market share with an innovative idea. It is a business enterprise by an entrepreneur that usually disrupt the current market with a new product or service in order to make a profit. Entrepreneurs are often known as sources of new ideas or innovators, as they always bring new ideas and inventions into the market to extract economic values, bearing most of the risks and enjoying most of the rewards. For entrepreneurs to be successful they need to be risk takers and courageous as that is what starting any new business entails. Also, being creative and innovative in order to generate new business ideas capable of starting a firm and making gains, have the ability to be a forward thinking leaders in order to have a clear focus, be open-minded so as to gain trust, be capable of adjusting to any situation or condition that may arise, and having a good background knowledge of the product he/she is offering and the prevailing market trends of that product are core to their values (Gaddefors & Anderson, 2017)

The above is anchored on the different theoretical assumptions of entrepreneurship which are hinged on the nature of opportunity, the nature of entrepreneurs and the nature of decision-making which necessitates the functionalities of entrepreneurs within the entrepreneurial ecosystem. The radical change in working methods imposed by the Covid-19 pandemic has brought about a forced change that has allowed the world to discover the numerous benefits of remote working which underpins distance learning (from economic savings both for companies and employees, to the commuting reduction, up to the work-life balance). In all these, entrepreneurs' startups play an important role as promoters of technological and cultural revolutions destined to last over time.

From a futuristic benefit granted to a few, smart working has become a necessity first, and then an essential condition, increasingly requested by employees, especially by the new generation of workers as it is an environment they are comfortable with. In addition to the well-known benefits, a fundamental aspect for its diffusion is represented by the transformation of technology. Until a few years ago, technology was in a certain sense pursued by the workers, who had to keep constantly updating their skills. With the pandemic there has also been a radical change in the conception of technology itself: no longer pursued by the worker, but at the service of the worker as enablers (Bakare, 2023). This prompt response to the needs of the context and promotes time lines which is fundamental in our working life, thus displaying the efficiency, autonomy and freedom of the individual. To foster this evolution, the role of entrepreneurs is fundamental. Entrepreneurs, in fact, are born precisely to respond to the latest market needs or to take advantage of the opportunities and emerged trends. Many successful products and services that have depopulated during the pandemic were born from entrepreneurs startups contributing to the growth and improvement both technological and cultural of smart working. Entrepreneurs have several opportunities when it comes to smart working. This can be seen in the following ways:

1. Entrepreneurs can develop virtual 3D worlds for events, working and training to allow users to collaborate with their team remotely in a 3D virtual office space dedicated to smart working;
2. They can create platform dedicated to the wellbeing and team building, aimed at increasing and monitoring the psycho-physical wellbeing, harmony and productivity of workers;
3. They can also offer "smart working as a service" allowing users to organize "workation" (work-vacation) in places of interest, working in structures equipped with everything necessary for smart working (such as fast internet connection and adequate workstations) on the platform. It is possible to have access to a wide network of workspaces, services and experiences, aimed at both companies and freelancers.

Several studies have been carried out to look at the important part that smart working plays in raising firm performance (Adekoya et al., 2022; Jeske, 2022). Notwithstanding claims made in the literature that smart working improves organizational performance on both an individual and organizational level, many managers and business owners do not adopt it to the fullest extent. Although it is crucial to help employees strike a balance between their professional and personal obligations, some studies hypothesized that small and medium-sized businesses could find it more expensive and challenging to apply smart working practices than larger businesses (Pech & Vrchota, 2020). These studies, however, made the case that where there is a highly substantial correlation between smart working indicator data and business performance, there is potential for firm performance improvement.

Entrepreneurs create innovative businesses characterized by high flexibility and ability to adapt to the context in which they operate. In the case of smart working, they implement this change at the forefront, internalizing it and adopting it in their daily lives. By doing so, they have favoured its diffusion and contributed, from a cultural point of view, to making it become in effect a general standard for society. The affirmation of this new working paradigm has accelerated the birth of innovative solutions. Entrepreneurs have therefore, supported and accelerated the affirmation of smart working in organizations, playing a crucial role as promoters of technological and cultural revolutions destined to last over time.

The online learning market has witnessed a massive growth rate globally with the increased emphases on distance learning. To start a business in online education, the main task is to choose the direction of an e-learning business based on your own skills. One can start by providing educational services online, selling online courses, or by creating an online learning platform. After systematically analyzing the competition in online learning platforms, providing services is a better way to go. There are various fields to choose from in order to enter the vast market of e-learning. Various fields of e-learning like language learning, data and programming, marketing, graphics, design, and personal tutoring are some of the best options to choose from while opting for a suitable field.

In order to pursue the above listed options of distance education, it is expected that one has the ability to learn a new language online either by creating a platform for learning new language or as a tutor of different languages, be a private tutor as it is flexible as well as boosts skills, ability to know and teach data management and new languages in data programming as well as developing applications, ability to provide effective online marketing services and advice, be a good online graphic designer with a touch of professionalism in every aspects, ability to create eye-catching online content and designs and the provision of good services, and the ability to establish and run an online school as it thereby enhancing online courses to be created and running a new business (Thakur, 2020).

Starting a distance learning business could be a very good decision if one wants to take advantage of the business opportunity. E-learning is the future of education and must be well embraced as one can either go for customer development or hire a company to build the application in order to launch. Alternatively, one can use ready-made products that help to launch e-learning ventures within a short space of time. Educational domain globally opted for this remote learning space hinged on emerging technologies to curtail the spread of the virus amid the pandemic and at the same time disallow the discontinuity of academic activities. More reason, Bakare and Okuonghae (2023, p. 87) asserted that 'digital technologies like smartphones, social media, the Internet, software applications, websites, and e-books are redefining the educational landscape which was accentuated amid the Covid-19 pandemic'. Within the Nigeria space, higher institutions of learning most especially Private Universities were at the front burner in using online platforms for the provision of educational services to their students both at the Undergraduate and Postgraduate levels, while majority of Public Universities were found wanting in this space which could possibly be due to the lack of entrepreneurial skillset and unconducive technological terrain.

Bakare and Ademakinwa (2021) affirmed Lead City University Nigeria owned by an entrepreneur as one of the Private Universities within the Nigerian educational space that ensured that online platforms were harnessed so as not to cause disruption in the academic calendar as compared to most Federal and State Universities that had to cancel a session during the pandemic. Therefore, this exemplified the fact that the entrepreneurs who owned Private Universities in Nigeria amid the pandemic were innovative enough to employ smart working so as to work round the educational ecosystem without any hitch. This has gone a long way in entrenching entrepreneurship as a course in University curriculum knowing fully well that this is an ecosystem that was redefined by the pandemic and its exploration need not end with it. This is expected to bring out the creativity and innovation in Nigerian students who have been used to the traditional methods of face-to-face form of teaching methodology to the virtual domain laced with emerging technologies.

Innovative Opportunities of Smart Working and Distance Learning

Innovation is the process that transforms forward-looking new ideas into real world (commercial) products, services, or processes of enhanced value. The result of such a transformation can be incremental, evolutionary or radical in its impact on the status quo. In other words, it can represent a natural step forward in a concept's development, a leap to the next generation of that concept, or a completely new and different way of doing something altogether. Innovation relates to human ability to intentionally change to meet new opportunities. Thus, innovation describes an intended change including having a common direction or vision, recognizing and deciding opportunities related to the vision, intentionally and effectively moving in a direction to achieve the objective.

Kreiterling (2023) affirmed innovation as activities that adds value or creativity to a process of events or phenomenon. Similarly, Amidon (2010) opined it as a knowledge of creation, evolution, exchange of application of new ideas into marketable goods of an enterprise, the vitality of a nation's economy and the advancement of the society. Innovation can be explained as consisting of entrepreneurial, divergent, inventive, creative, exploratory, improvement, commonality shared, leadership, sharing and integrating differences, partnering and vision. The propounder of innovations are called innovators who can hold a situation in chaos for long periods of time without having to reach a resolution. They however often refuse to give up because they have a long-term commitment to their dream. Innovators introduce maximum tension into the thinking process, unifying concepts that often appear to be opposed, solving problems which appear impossible.

The gradual return to the office space does not mark the decline of smart working as this is bound to soar even in the post-pandemic. Smart working methods aim at a greater balance between the office space and remote work. Most large companies and some public administrations in Nigeria have modified spaces to adapt them to the new ways of smart working. Accordingly in large companies, the large-scale application of smart working favour the inclusion of people who live far from their workplace, parents and those who take care of the elderly and disabled. The ability to work an average of 2.5 days/week from home will lead to significant savings in time and money. This is significantly lesser for workers that use cars to go to the office.

Companies face unprecedented challenges in an economy dominated by globalization, rapid technological advances, demographic changes and fast-shifting consumer demands. The ability to reinvent products, services and processes continually is becoming essential for survival and success. Tackling these challenges cannot be done by senior teams alone as there is the need to harness the creativity, insights and engagement of the entire workforce. Leaders need to empower others to take the initiative, coaching and supporting them towards successful outcomes. They must become the champions of employee empowerment, participation and voice. The challenge for leaders is to take a systemic view of their own organizational structures and practices. Creating the culture of innovation and enterprise needed for twenty-first century challenges requires tenacity, inclusiveness and open mindedness to novel ideas. It means confronting deeply embedded attitudes and behaviours, asking difficult questions, and being open to experiences from a diverse range of other organizations (Kobia & Sikalieh, 2010).

Smart working encompasses new management styles, new ways of organizing and Human Resources Management (HRM). Examples are self-managed teams, flexible working hours and contracts and dynamic management as well as talent development. Most entrepreneurs believe that the benefits of smart working far outweigh its costs. Smart working has the best results when combined with technological innovations. The growth in productivity is always higher than with companies who only implement technological innovations. It is a Professional as well as Personal approach which yields the best results.

Smart working is the future we need today. For many employees, the ability to work from home, co-working spaces, or anywhere there is an internet connection, is a key part of balancing work and life, and getting the most out of each. However, remote working is not just about staying away from the office. Decoupling work from a specific place, time and device lets employees find working patterns that suit them and their lifestyle, helping them deliver their best. In a competitive recruitment landscape, multiple surveys show that offering remote working is key to attracting and retaining the best staff. With fewer employees on site, offices are smaller and cheaper to run in addition to staff being highly motivated and more productive. The business has more agility, and greater ability to flex with a changing world but at the same time does not just imply giving employees a free pass to the laze about. With less focus on a central workplace and time, the organization's identity and culture can become diluted. Without dynamic leadership, there is a danger that remote workers might not put in their best as it is expected thus leaving clienteles at their own mercy as the smart domain is a paradigm shift that both parties are migrating into.

The same can be said of educators and students as the move to remote learning has thrown the duo into a whole new world. Educators must understand potential roadblocks, challenges and then come up with creative solutions in order to help students. This was enunciated by Bakare et al., (2023) who affirmed the indispensable innovation and dynamism of ChatGPT and other Generative Artificial Intelligence (AI) tools within contemporary educational ecosystem in developed countries. But the bane of these technologies taking over academia is militating its adoption within the African space most especially within the Nigerian educational clime. To help with that, researchers have suggested ways to make distance learning effective for students so that the four learning basic needs of arousal, autonomy, relatedness and competence are met (Weinstein & Sumeracki, 2019; Wong, 2023).

1. Make Sure Students Understand the Tools Given Them

In the past few years, students have had to adjust to a whole new way of learning. This includes mastering new learning management systems and communication tools. Many of them are in entirely new territory which might take time for students to face these realities. They will not be able to learn effectively if they cannot navigate these new systems. Librarians who are the custodian of human knowledge should consider holding an orientation session to familiarize students with these systems as well as ensure that students can access support and documentation they might need to succeed.

2. Create Equity for Distance Learners

Not every distance learner is going to have access to the same resources. Educators must ensure that equitable distribution of resources is maximally ensured for a smooth sail in the learning process. Therefore, educators must consider taking the following actions which are to encourage schools to provide students in need with laptops, tablets and hot spots; provide off-line learning options; give multiple options for communication; make sure technologies are mobile friendly, and team up with community centers, libraries and organizations to help students have regular access to computers, tutors and other resources.

3. Connect Students with Independent Learning Tools

As distance learning progresses, students' needs will become more apparent as some will need extra help while others will need enrichment to stay engaged. Fortunately, so many organizations and corporations have stepped up to offer resources to help. Here are some great websites for students, whether they need assistance with writing, tutoring, or opportunities to pursue their interests. They are Khan Academy, National Geographic Kids, Cool Math, ABC mouse, Skill share, TED-Ed, Google Earth, NASA, Smithsonian, Google Arts and Culture etc. In addition to the above, educators should encourage students to find local sources of enrichment. Chances are local libraries, community colleges and museums have created programmes specifically for distance learners. Older students may be interested in sharing their discoveries with one another.

4. Maintain Live Connections during Distance Learning

It is important that educators maintain as much of a connection with their students as possible. That cannot be accomplished through prerecorded lessons or interactive worksheets. There is simply no replacement for live interactions. These help students connect to one another and their instructors. If possible, teachers should plan to do at least some live instruction. In addition to this, they should make time to connect with students individually. Something as simple as a weekly one-on-one Zoom meeting will allow educators to check in with each student. Use these meetings to assess students in ways that cannot be done through group learning interactions.

Finally, do not forget that a simple phone call is an easy, accessible way to connect with students. This is the kind of small effort that lets students and parents know that their instructors care enough to reach out to them individually.

5. Be Sensitive and Flexible

Even when accommodations are made to help students overcome barriers to connectivity and technical mastery, students may struggle. Not every student will have a dedicated place to work. They may even feel uncomfortable showing themselves and their living spaces during live classes. Some students may have taken on additional childcare responsibilities due to their parents' own work obligations. This is a good time to extend a bit more grace than usual for students who may not have perfect attendance or complete work on time. Also, consider factors such as bullying and family difficulties when establishing rules for group lessons. Students may appreciate having the ability to leave their cameras off or to share an avatar instead of a live feed. If students are struggling with keeping up academically, introduce them to resources such as Grammarly, All Top Reviews, and White Smoke.

Benefits of Smart Working and Distance Learning

As organizations and working culture evolves, so does the need to enable, engage and reward people in innovative ways. However, organizations need to employ their people more efficiently and keep them engaged and inspired to do their best work. Increasingly, remote working and the use of mobile technology is empowering staff to choose when and how to work. Smarter working helps to break down traditional silos, away from top-down hierarchical structures to a culture of collaboration, staff empowerment and flexibility. The following are the importance of smart working according to Kuzin (2018);

1. Smart working provides employees with the tools, culture and leadership, workspaces and technology to help them choose when, where and how they do their jobs.
2. Employees who feel in control of the variables in their working world are likely to have a heightened commitment to enhancing company results.
3. Smarter working contributes to a better work-life balance.
4. It improves staff satisfaction and retention which ultimately delivers value for money for organizations.
5. Smart working is a key way for organizations to stay ahead of disruption and cultural change. With innovation the lifeblood of business, discarding old

approaches for new ways that inspire employees can produce outstanding business results.

6. Smart working adds flexibility to where and when work is performed to increase productivity, reduce costs and improve brand reputation.
7. Smart work techniques rely on automated work processes and tools. As a result, a team can focus its attention on working together creatively, helping customers, developing new lines of business or other productive tasks.
8. Smart working can enable us to be more productive by doing more and/or better quality work for the same or reduced resource input; by reducing physical resources, better online systems and reduced travel costs; and by more effective working over distance.

There is no disputing the fact that there is a synergy in benefit of smart working to both the employers and employees as smart working improves workers innovative and creative thinking skills; improves productivity of the organization; teaches time management skills; results to increased free time to carry out other activities and encourages workers to fully concentrate on work because it demands mental presence.

On the other hand, distance learning can expand access to education and training for both general populace and businesses since its flexible scheduling structure lessens the effects of the many time-constraints imposed by personal responsibilities and commitments. Devolving some activities off-site alleviates institutional capacity constraints arising from the traditional demand on institutional buildings and infrastructure. As a result, more classes can be offered and enable students to enroll in more of their required classes on time and prevent delayed graduation (Anderson & Dron, 2011). Furthermore, there is the potential for increased access to more experts in the field and to other students from diverse geographical, social, cultural, economic, and experiential backgrounds. As the population at large becomes more involved in lifelong learning beyond the normal schooling age, institutions can benefit financially, and adult learning business courses may be particularly lucrative. Distance education programs can act as a catalyst for institutional innovation and are at least as effective as face-to-face learning programs, especially if the instructor is knowledgeable and skilled (Oblinger, 2020).

Distance education can also provide a broader method of communication within the realm of education. With the many tools and programmes that technological advancements have to offer, communication appears to increase in distance education amongst students and their professors, as well as students and their classmates (Masson, 2014). The distance educational increase in communication, particularly communication amongst students and their classmates, is an improvement that has been made to provide distance education students with as many of the opportunities as possible as they would receive an in-person education. The improvement being made in distance education is growing in tandem with the constant technological advancements (Wilson, 2023). Present-day online communication allows students to associate with accredited schools and programs throughout the world that are out of reach for in-person learning. By having the opportunity to be involved in global institutions via distance education, a diverse array of thought is presented to students through communication with their classmates. This is beneficial because students have the opportunity to combine new opinions with their own and develop a solid foundation for learning (Nguyen, 2015). One of the greatest advantages of distance learning is that it allows continuous learning and professional development. Students independently decide on time, place and pace of learning. Furthermore, students have at their disposal a large number of subjects and different study programmes. Fischer, Baker, Li, Orona and Warschauer, (2022) outlined the followings as the advantages of distance learning:

1. **Own pace**: Students can go through learning materials at their own pace and as many times they want. They can go faster through simple lessons and take more time for more complex and demanding lessons.
2. **Place for learning**: Depending on media used for distribution of learning materials through a distance learning system, students can learn in places that best suit them. Thus, students can be at home or at work and access information available via the Internet, send and receive e-mail messages, etc.
3. **Way of learning:** Everyone has their own way of learning. Some students prefer active, while others prefer passive learning. Lectures via distance learning allow different degrees of interaction between teachers and students and among students as well. Some students study independently by reading materials, making notes and performing required tasks. Some students learn better if they participate in discussions with other students by using e-mails, teleconferencing or video-conferencing. Some students prefer multimedia elements such as graphics, animation and sounds while learning. Thus, the most appropriate courses for them are the ones realized through the WWW services and the Internet.
4. **Practical work with various technologies:** Distance learning system relies on various technologies, such as computers, CD players, VCRs, etc. Therefore, students acquire knowledge and skills on the usage of these technologies as well.
5. **Independent learning:** In addition to all materials for learning, distance learning students are encouraged to independently explore new sources of information. They gather more information in order to gain knowledge in a particular area, or to successfully cope with a particular skill. Students are usually very motivated and want to solve tasks.

6. **Time:** The advantage of distance learning is studying in your own time. Students can study 24 hours a day, because they have access to teaching materials via distance learning system seven days a week.
7. **Communication with teachers and assistants:** New technologies enable high quality and fast communication with teachers and assistants, especially by means of audio and video recordings of lectures, e-mails, telephone, etc.

Challenges of Smart Working and Distance Learning

Amid the various advantages of smart working and distance learning, there are equally some challenges to both the employers and employee which include smart work may make workers lazy, as they get used to doing less work and get more output; mere smart work may not yield results as we cannot completely rely on smart work; to work smartly, knowledge about the work is needed, which comes only with hard work and experience, and Hard work cannot be taught to smart working persons if they are not willing to work hard.

Distance learning enables students to access and engage with quality educational content, all from the comfort and convenience of home. While it is easy to see both the benefits and relevance of distance education, such as increased flexibility, mobility and affordability, it is equally important to acknowledge the potential challenges with distance learning for students. From grade-schoolers to graduate students, e-learners at all age levels must overcome obstacles that are unique to virtual education, such as asynchronous communication and ever-present opportunities for time-wasting distractions. E-learners also face challenges that, while often present in the traditional classroom, can be amplified in a virtual setting, such as delayed or unclear instructor feedback. The following are some of the challenges of distance learning as identified in literature (Jedlicka, Brown, Bunch and Jaffe, 2002; Hwang, Shim and Cheon, 2023).

1. **Ineffective Time Management:** Research has proven that successful time management is associated with greater academic performance and lower levels of anxiety in students. Unfortunately, the same research also uncovered that many students find it hard to find a balance between their studies and their day-to-day lives; and worse, that ineffective time management was associated with outcomes like poor sleep patterns and increased levels of stress. Effective time management can be especially difficult in a distance learning environment, where students are challenged to pace themselves without the support from friends and peers that would help them stay focused in class.
2. **Lack of Instant Communication:** In an in-person setting, communication happens instantaneously, making it easy for students to get answers and

clarify points of confusion. In an e-learning setting, communication is often asynchronous, which means there is a gap between teacher and student. It is easy for misunderstandings to develop in these gaps - sometimes, allowing a problem to snowball before it can be corrected.

3. **Not Receiving Timely Feedback:** Providing feedback is one of the most important and meaningful ways that a teacher engages with a student. When feedback is delayed by additional days or weeks because of an online format, students can become confused or uncertain about the teacher's expectations, their progress and their performance in class.
4. **Not Receiving Clear Instructions or Expectations:** It is always crucial to set clear expectations for students. Otherwise, they can only guess at whether they are performing tasks and projects correctly. While setting clear standards is a challenge in any classroom, asynchronous communication can make it a greater obstacle.

Challenges Faced by Entrepreneurs in Smart Working and Distance Learning

Entrepreneurs have been greatly affected by the COVID-19 pandemic which resulted to smart working and distance learning. Studies carried out by Akpan, Soopramanien and Kwak (2020); Altowairiki (2021); and ElSaheli-Elhage (2021) showed that the business activities of the entrepreneurs were affected due to the difficulties faced during the COVID-19 pandemic periods that have led to a substantial decrease in their income. This made some of them to apply for financial assistance. The disruption of normal business activities had forced a majority of the entrepreneurs to find alternative sources of income. At the same time more than half of the entrepreneurs had turned to online platforms in conducting their businesses.

Some of the challenges faced by the entrepreneurs during those times were a significant decrease in their income, disruption of normal business activities forcing most of them to engage in alternative businesses, navigating to a digital clime they are not used to etc. However, amid the difficulties, entrepreneurs were more exposed to usage of ICT tools as they became necessary for doing business during the pandemic. Some of the online training modules were tailored to the specific needs of the participants who found it to be interesting and helpful. This is partly attributed to the combination of the medium used (online videos, Facebook, and WhatsApp), which provided participants with flexible learning time. However, there was mixed feelings of its significance as some participants found the smart working environment easy to navigate while those who are not used to the purely digital ecosystem fell out of various online activities. This was the case of Public institutions within the Nigerian space whose vast majority were absent amid the pandemic while the Private Universities like Lead City University, Bowen University, Covenant University etc owned by entrepreneurs were innovative and creative to use the challenges associated with the pandemic to improve their own productivity, create relevance, thus ensuring the sustainability of the Nigerian educational ecosystem.

SUMMARY

As a result of the Covid-19 pandemic, almost all the schools in the world were closed for physical learning. This gave room to many of the schools to move to online learning with the use of Zoom, Google Classroom, Google Meet etc. As leaders of most countries were trying everything in their powers to control the situation, many of the teachers, tutors and lecturers in developed countries adapted to online teaching but rate of adoption within the Nigerian clime was at a slow pace. This online teaching gave rise to distance learning which is still in place much after the Covid-19 pandemic. Distance learning is becoming more and more popular with students all over the world. As a result of the active development in Information and Communications Technology (ICT), ample opportunities have been provided for online education in the 21st century. This enabled most advanced institutions to focus on their flexibility and openness towards students. Businesses were not left behind during this pandemic as most businesses were inoperable as the pandemic led to a total lockdown of any form of activities. This gave rise to smart working as most businesses have to operate even during the pandemic on the cyberspace. As a result, video conferencing, commuting, online businesses etc. became the order of the day.

Entrepreneurship which is an innovative approach to the development of a new curriculum for all the universities is instilling the requisite skill-set in students graduate so that they can become employable instead of looking for white-collar jobs. Entrepreneurship spins about desire, invention/resourcefulness, knowhow, loss and incentives, confidence and containment. The 'entrepreneur' and 'entrepreneurship' are increasingly considered to be significant with regards to the production of goods and also for national development, especially in terms of economic growth and job creation. Entrepreneurship education at universities has become increasingly popular in the world, as traditional and established ways of doing business are being replaced by creative and innovative methods. Many advanced countries as well as developing countries including Nigeria believe that entrepreneurship is a key element in stimulating economic growth and development, which provides increased employment opportunities. Students not only develop core business knowledge and skills, but also improve core competencies that guarantee entrepreneurial success.

They are such competencies as creativity, initiative, perseverance, teamwork, risk awareness and responsibility.

Creativity and innovation are becoming increasingly important for the development of the 21st century knowledge society. They contribute to economic prosperity as well as to social and individual wellbeing and are essential factors for a more competitive and dynamic nation. Education is seen as central in fostering creative and innovative skills. This concept provides an overview of the theoretical foundations for creativity and innovation in the context of education. Innovation is applied in a process or product in order to benefit teaching. Therefore, innovative teaching is the process leading to creative learning, the implementation of new methods, tools and contents which could benefit learners and their creative potential. Educational actors need to have a clear vision, awareness and understanding of what creativity is and entails in order to fully comprehend how it can be enhanced. Judging the originality and value of an output entails seeing creativity as a relative attribute. Much has changed about innovation even though it is still very relevant. Competition has become very fierce and becoming even worse in the current climate. This trend has forced entrepreneurs and business owners alike to evolve their views on innovation. In today's world, Innovation demands that we retrain ourselves to find spaces within industries where we can create a more fulfilling experience for customers.

CONCLUSION

As customers and employees, our familiarity with devices and data is driving a fundamental shift in the way the world works. By supporting smart working, employers can drive efficiency, for example by saving costs such as office space and equipment. Furthermore, by freeing employees from their desks, businesses can reap the benefits of greater freedom, innovation and agility. Alongside freedom from the office, smart workers need the support to perform in their roles. As the workplace changes, companies need to lead that change. Rather than smart working being a concession to employees, it should form the basis of our modern working relationships. From the very top, there needs to be a clear vision for the importance of smart working within the organization as well as a plan to make its success a reality. As the workplace has gone modernized through digitalization, executives should be the exemplars of company culture. They should lead and inspire with their own passions and achievements. Creating an innovative business means championing the technologies of a smarter workplace. It means effective communication and knowledge-sharing throughout the organization.

Distance education is responsible for promoting quality information, resources and expertise. The three reasons for disseminating education to all societies are due to geographical isolation, social isolation and disadvantaged groups. Distance teaching techniques enable people to undertake a course of study in privacy. The advent of the Internet and the growth of WWW have now transformed distance teaching from a broadcast mode to an interactive mode. The Web, when combined with other network tools such as listservs, Usenet newsgroups and video teleconferencing, acts as a virtual classroom to bring together a community of learners for interactive education. The growth of television, telecommunication, videotape, audio tele-conferencing, audio graphics conferencing and video conferencing allowed bringing together the learners and instructors who are geographically separated. The use of innovative teaching methods helps to sustain students' interest and make the learning process more productive and interesting. The techniques that can be adopted are: computer-assisted learning (CD-ROMs), web-based learning, virtual laboratories, case studies, group discussion, brainstorming, audiovisual presentation, assignments, seminars, quiz and assigning project works.

Distance learning can expand access to education and training for both general populace and businesses since its flexible scheduling structure lessens the effects of the many time-constraints imposed by personal responsibilities and commitments. It creates an opportunity for the entrepreneurs who are well skilled and knowledgeable to delve into the business and offer some online training to those willing to undergo the training. Presently, a lot of students worldwide are learning from home. Given the right tools and support, students can thrive during distance learning. However, it does take an effort to ensure that students have what they need to succeed by having the right instructors. When instructors are sensitive to potential difficulties, work to ensure they make connections and use the many tools available, they are best able to help students adjust to this new reality.

Recommendations

The following recommendations are hereby made:

1. The Nigerian government needs to correct the drawbacks in its organization in order to increase the effectiveness of distance learning .
2. Instructors should be sensitive to potential difficulties of students and work to ensure that they make connections and use the many tools available to help students adjust to the new reality.
3. Management of organizations should show a clear vision for the importance of smart working to employees of such organizations together with a plan to make its success a reality.

4. Executive should lead by examples since the workplace has gone modernized through digitalization. This will encourage the workers to quickly adapt to smart working.
5. Management should create an innovative business by championing the technologies of a smarter workplace. This will improve effective communication as well as enhancing knowledge sharing.

Impact of the Study

The impact of this study is significant to the followings:

Practice: Through the combination of the best aspects of online and in-person learning, students have an element of control. This is incredibly flexible as well as improving communication. As a result, students acquire diverse knowledge that can make them independent and self-reliant. Smart working increases productivity of work and make engagement and services delivered more effectively. Environmental impacts are reduced as one does not need to think of space or when, where and how work is to be performed. Smart working adds flexibility to where and when work is performed to increase productivity, reduce costs and improve brand reputation.

Society: Distance learning/virtual courses provide a higher quality education at a lower cost for every member of the society. This makes it easy for all and sundry to acquire knowledge thereby increasing the literacy rate of the society. It helps one to get a degree from anywhere in the world at the click of a button. Apart from that, distance learning saves ones time and allows learning at one's own pace. The most important fact is that one can study without quitting ones job. Smart working and distance learning help a society to develop by building a strong workforce and blended learning environment which goes a long way in building a very strong intellectual nation. This promotes the acquisition of new skills which will unveil new opportunities and help find innovative solutions to societal problems.

Policy: It is expected that educational policies will be redefined within developing countries such as Nigeria so as to embrace the innovativeness brought to bear by the Covid-19 pandemic so as to ensure the infusion of smart working to the nitty-gritty of the educational ecosystem and the distance learning domain.

REFERENCES

Adekoya, O. D., Adisa, T. A., & Aiyenitaju, O. (2022). Going forward: Remote working in the post-COVID-19 era. Employee Relations. *International Journal (Toronto, Ont.)*, *44*(6), 1410–1427.

Ahmad, N. A., Sham, F. M., & Ismail, A. (2021). Technology-Based Support in Organizations and the Impact on Affective Commitment. *Social Sciences, 11*(8), 1263–1274.

Akpan, I. J., Soopramanien, D., & Kwak, D.-H. (2020). Cutting-edge technologies for small business and innovation in the era of COVID-19 global health pandemic. *Journal of Small Business and Entrepreneurship*, 1–11. doi:10.1080/08276331.2020.1799294

Alfonso, G. J. (2015). Olien and distance e-Learning: New dimensions in teaching, learning, research, and extension for higher education institutions. *The Internattonal Journal on Olien and Distance e-Learning, 1*(1-2), 2-4.

Alrowwad, A. A., Abualoush, S. H., & Masa'deh, R. E. (2020). Innovation and intellectual capital as intermediary variables among transformational leadership, transactional leadership, and organizational performance. *Journal of Management Development, 39*(2), 196–222. doi:10.1108/JMD-02-2019-0062

Altowairiki, N. (2021). Online Collaborative Learning: Analyzing the Process through Living the Experience. [IJTE]. *International Journal of Technology in Education, 4*(3), 413–427. doi:10.46328/ijte.95

Amidon, O. (2010). Undergraduate student online learning readiness. *International Journal of Education and Research, 5*(2), 44–54.

Anderson, T., & Dron, J. (2011). Three generations of distance education pedagogy. *International Review of Research in Open and Distance Learning, 12*(3), 80–97. doi:10.19173/irrodl.v12i3.890

Anderson, T., & Rivera, V. P. (2020). A critical look at educational technology from a distance education perspective. *Digital Education Review* (37): 208-229. . hdl: doi:10.1344/der.2020.37.208-229

Bakare, O. D. (2023). Emerging Technologies as a Panacea for Sustainable Provision of Library Services in Nigeria. In *Global Perspectives on Sustainable Library Practices* (pp. 1–21). IGI Global.

Bakare, O. D., & Ademakinwa, M. A. (2021). The Impact of Covid - 19 on Mentorship of Graduate Students in Nigerian Universities. *Journal of the Nigerian Pastoral Counselling Association, 1*(1), 15–19.

Bakare, O. D., & Okuonghae, N. (2022). Information Managers as Change Agents in achievingSustainable Development in the 21st Century. *Journal of Environmental Science and Economics, 1*(2), 68–78.

Bakare, O. D., & Okuonghae, N. (2023). Digital Technologies and Resources for Learning Under Lockdown. In *Impact of Disruptive Technologies on the Socio-Economic Development of Emerging Countries* (pp. 87–103). IGI Global. doi:10.4018/978-1-6684-6873-9.ch006

Bakare, O. D., Oladokun, T., Quadri, G. O., & Idowu-Davies, T. O. (2023). ChatGPT and Other Generative Artificial Intelligence (AI) Tools in Teaching and Learning as Integrative Pathways to Contemporary University Education. In *Creative AI Tools and Ethical Implications in Teaching and Learning* (pp. 168–180). IGI Global. doi:10.4018/979-8-3693-0205-7.ch009

Bird, L. (2021). The role of startups in improving smart working. Entrepreneur: What It Means to Be One and How to Get Started. Investopedia.

Dron, J., & Anderson, T. (2014). *Teaching Crowds: Learning and Social Media.* AU Press.

ElSaheli-Elhage, R. (2021). Access to Students and Parents and Levels of Preparedness of Educators during the COVID-19 Emergency Transition to e-Learning. [IJonSE]. *International Journal on Studies in Education, 3*(2), 61–69. doi:10.46328/ijonse.35

Fischer, C., Baker, R., Li, Q., Orona, G., & Warschauer, M. (2022). Increasing success in Higher Education: The relationships of online course taking with college completion and time-to-degree. *Educational Evaluation and Policy Analysis, 44*(3), 355–379.. ISSN 0162-3737. S2CID 244498785. doi:10.3102/01623737211055768

Gaddefors, J., & Anderson, A. R. (2017). Entrepreneurship and context: when entrepreneurship is greater than entrepreneurs. *International Journal of Entrepreneurial Behavior & Research. 23*(2), 267–278.. doi:10.1108/IJEBR-01-2016-0040

Hwang, N. K., Shim, S. H., & Cheon, H. W. (2023). Digital learning designs in occupational therapy education: A scoping review. *BMC Medical Education, 23*(1), 1–19. doi:10.118612909-022-03955-x PMID:36604723

Jedlicka, J. S., Brown, S. W., Bunch, A. E., & Jaffe, L. E. (2002). A comparison of distance education instructional methods in occupational therapy. *Journal of Allied Health, 31*(4), 247–251. PMID:12491955

Jeske, D. (2022). Remote workers' experiences with electronic monitoring during covid-19: Implications and recommendations. *International Journal of Workplace Health Management, 15*(3), 393–409. doi:10.1108/IJWHM-02-2021-0042

Kaplan, A. M., & Haenlein, M. (2016). Higher education and the digital revolution: About MOOCs, SPOCs, social media, and the Cookie Monster. *Business Horizons*, *59*(4), 441–450. doi:10.1016/j.bushor.2016.03.008

Kobia, M., & Sikalieh, D. (2010). Towards a search for the meaning of entrepreneurship. *Journal of European Industrial Training*, *34*(2), 110–127. doi:10.1108/03090591011023970

Kreiterling, C. (2023). Digital innovation and entrepreneurship: A review of challenges in competitive markets. *Journal of Innovation and Entrepreneurship*, *12*(1), 49. doi:10.118613731-023-00320-0

Kuzin, D. V. (2018). Global competences and challenges for entrepreneurship educators. *Journal of Entrepreneurship Education*, *21*(2S), 1–11.

Masson, M. (2014). Benefits of TED Talks. *Canadian Family Physician Medecin de Famille Canadien*, *60*(12), 1080. PMID:25500595

Mumu, J. R., Tahmid, T., & Azad, M. A. K. (2021). Job satisfaction and intention to quit: A bibliometric review of work-family conflict and research agenda. *Applied Nursing Research*, *59*, 151334. doi:10.1016/j.apnr.2020.151334 PMID:33947506

Nguyen, T. (2015). The effectiveness of online learning. *Journal of Online Learning and Teaching*, *11*(2), 309–319.

Oblinger, D. G. (2000). The Nature and Purpose of Distance Education. *Technology (Elmsford, N.Y.)*.

Pech, M., & Vrchota, J. (2020). Classification of small-and medium-sized enterprises based on the level of industry 4.0 implementation. *Applied Sciences (Basel, Switzerland)*, *10*(15), 5150. doi:10.3390/app10155150

Samoylenko, N., Zharko, L., & Glotova, A. (2022). Designing Online Learning Environment: ICT Tools and Teaching Strategies. *Athens Journal of Education*, *9*(1), 49–62. doi:10.30958/aje.9-1-4

Soomro, B. A., & Shah, N. (2019). Determining the impact of entrepreneurial orientation and organizational culture on job satisfaction, organizational commitment, and employee's performance. *South Asian Journal of Business Studies*, *8*(3), 266–282. doi:10.1108/SAJBS-12-2018-0142

Source. Michigan: Michigan Virtual University (March/April). Archived from the original on 18 July 2011. Retrieved 23 January 2011.

Thakur, S. (2020). *Profitable Business Opportunities in Online Education Digital Nomad who loves to read & write startup stories, and tech news.*

Webster, M. (2020). *Organizing Instruction and Study to Improve Student Learning. IES Practice Guide. NCER 2007-2004.* National Center for Education Research.

Weinstein, Y., & Sumeracki, M. A. (2019). Understanding how we learn: A visual guide. David Fulton, Routledge (p. 13).

Wilson, D. (2023). Distance/remote learning engagement. *Journal of Resourceful and Distribution*, *1*(1), 78–86.

Wong, R. (2023). When no one can go to school: Does online learning meet students' basic learning needs? *Interactive Learning Environments*, *31*(1), 434–450. doi:10.1080/10494820.2020.1789672

Chapter 3
Exploring the Frontier:
New and Future Trends in Research

Iris-Panagiota Efthymiou
https://orcid.org/0000-0001-9656-8378
University of Greenwich, London, UK

ABSTRACT

The chapter on new and future trends in research explores the latest developments in research on innovation capabilities and entrepreneurial opportunities in the context of smart working. The chapter highlights emerging research trends, including the use of AI and machine learning for smart working, the impact of smart working on employee well-being, and the intersection of smart working with sustainability goals. The implications of these trends for innovation and entrepreneurship are explored, including challenges and opportunities such as keeping up with technological advancements, balancing benefits and drawbacks, and enhancing innovation capabilities while reducing environmental impact. Smart working research offers opportunities to improve work-life balance and contribute to sustainability goals by reducing commuting and associated emissions. By staying on the cutting edge of research, organizations can position themselves to capitalize on emerging opportunities and remain competitive in the future.

INTRODUCTION

The business landscape is constantly evolving, with new technologies, changing customer needs, and market disruptions all playing a role in shaping the way companies operate. In this context, organizations need to remain agile and responsive to change, and this requires a deep understanding of the latest research trends and

DOI: 10.4018/978-1-7998-8797-3.ch003

insights (Betti & Sarens, 2021). In the field of smart working, staying up-to-date with new and emerging research trends is particularly important, as this can help organizations to unlock new opportunities for innovation and entrepreneurship.

Therefore, the purpose of this chapter is to highlight the importance of staying up-to-date with new and emerging research trends in the context of smart working and to provide an overview of some of the most promising new research directions in this area. We will explore some of the most exciting new research directions in smart working, and discuss the potential implications of these trends for innovation and entrepreneurship in this space. By staying on the cutting edge of research, organizations can position themselves to take advantage of emerging opportunities and stay competitive in the years to come.

Smart Working

Smart working, also known as telecommuting or remote work (Roberto et al., 2023), has been a growing trend in recent years, with the "COVID-19 pandemic" accelerating its adoption worldwide (Savić, 2020). As a result, there has been increased interest in researching the impact of smart working on "employee productivity and well-being," as well as the role of technology in enabling smart working and the challenges and opportunities associated with managing remote teams (Kelliher & Anderson, 2010).

One key finding from recent studies is that smart working can have a positive effect on employee productivity. It is important to note that the effectiveness of smart working may vary depending on the nature of the work, organizational culture, and individual preferences. However, the overall trend indicates that smart working can have a positive effect on employee productivity. A research by Stanford University found that "remote workers" were 13% more "productive" than their "office-based counterparts," likely due to the reduced distractions and time saved from not having to travel (Mishra, Agarwal & Agarwal, 2020). Additionally, a study by "Harvard Business Review" found that remote workers were more likely to work longer hours and were more productive during those hours (Moss, 2021).

However, there are also potential downsides to smart working, particularly when it comes to employee well-being (Soga et al., 2022). A study by the International Labour Organization found that "remote workers" reported higher levels of "stress and anxiety," as well as greater difficulty in maintaining work-life balance. Employers need to provide support and resources to remote workers to help mitigate these negative effects (Afonso, Fonseca, & Teodoro, 2022).

Technology plays a critical role in enabling smart working, and recent research has highlighted the importance of having the right tools and infrastructure in place (Oztemel & Gursev, 2020). Organizations need to invest in robust and reliable technology infrastructure to support smart working effectively. The availability of these tools and infrastructure can empower employees, streamline collaboration, and enhance productivity in a remote work environment. A survey by Buffer (2021) found that remote workers cited communication and collaboration tools as the most important factor in enabling them to be productive and successful. Additionally, research by Woods (2021) has highlighted that investing in technologies such as video conferencing and collaboration software can help remote teams stay connected and engaged.

According to Malhotra, Majchrzak, and Rosen (2007) managing remote teams also presents unique challenges and opportunities, particularly when it comes to building and maintaining trust. Building and maintaining trust in remote teams requires intentional efforts, clear communication, and opportunities for team members to connect and collaborate. By fostering a culture of trust, organizations can overcome the challenges of remote work and create an environment conducive to productivity and success. Some key ways in which organizations can foster a culture of trust in a remote work setting is effective communication, empowerment and autonomy, support and collaboration, acknowledge and appreciate the efforts and achievements of remote employees, Transparent Goal Setting, invest in remote-specific training and development programs to enhance employees' skills and knowledge, encourage work-life balance, promote mental health awareness, and provide access to counsellinf or wellness programs. Foster a culture that values employee well-being also, recognize the emotional challenges of remote work and provide support systems, and of course Lead by Example. By focusing on these aspects, organizations can build trust among remote employees, leading to increased engagement, higher productivity, and a positive work culture. It is important to adapt these principles to the unique needs and challenges of remote work and regularly evaluate their effectiveness to ensure ongoing success (Sorensen, C. 2004). A study by Harvard Business Review found that trust is a key to successful remote team collaboration and that managers can foster trust by setting clear expectations, communicating frequently, and providing support and recognition to remote workers. Additionally, research has shown that "remote work" can lead to greater flexibility and autonomy for employees, which can lead to higher levels of "job satisfaction and retention" (Moss, 2021).

OVERVIEW OF CURRENT TRENDS IN SMART WORKING RESEARCH

Technological Trends

One of the notable trends shaping smart working is the integration of "artificial intelligence (AI) and machine learning (ML)" technologies (Cioffi et al., 2020).

These advancements have the potential to automate repetitive tasks, facilitate data-driven decision-making, and foster collaboration between humans and machines (Himanen et al., 2019). Researchers will likely focus on developing customized algorithms tailored to the needs of smart workers and investigating the ethical and social implications of increased automation (Coombs et al., 2020).

Furthermore, the ethical and social implications of automation in smart working are expected to be a significant area of research. As AI and ML technologies become more prevalent in the workplace, concerns arise regarding the potential displacement of "human workers," leading to job losses and economic disruptions. This understanding can inform the development of policies, regulations, and strategies that ensure a balanced and inclusive approach to the integration of automation technologies in the workforce (Efthymiou, I. P., 2020). It is crucial to explore how these technologies can be utilized to benefit both workers and organizations while minimizing negative impacts (Autor, 2015).

Another prominent technological trend in smart working is the advancement of communication technologies. With the growing prevalence of remote work and distributed teams, effective communication tools have become paramount. Researchers will likely delve into the applications of "virtual reality, augmented reality, and mixed reality" to enhance communication and collaboration among smart workers (Daim et al., 2012).

For instance, virtual reality can create immersive workspaces that enable remote workers to experience a sense of being physically present together (Malik, Masood & Bilberg, 2020). Augmented reality can provide real-time guidance and support to workers who require assistance with complex tasks (Lukosch et al., 2015), while mixed reality can facilitate interactive simulations, allowing workers to practice and refine their skills in a safe environment (Moore & Gheisari, 2019).

Social and Cultural Trends

Social and cultural trends are playing a crucial role in shaping the future of smart working. Among these trends, the growing emphasis on mental health and well-being in the workplace is a significant factor. The "COVID-19 pandemic" has accelerated this trend, highlighting the importance of supporting workers' mental health and well-being as they navigate the challenges of remote work and increased screen time (Giorgi et al., 2021).

Organizations are recognizing the need to provide their employees with resources and tools to maintain their mental health and well-being, such as access to mental health professionals, mindfulness and wellness programs, and flexible work arrangements (Sasaki et al., 2020). This shift towards prioritizing employee wellbeing is expected to continue in the post-pandemic era, and will likely shape the way that smart working is implemented and managed in the future.

Studies have indicated that individuals engaged in remote work are tending to experience emotions such as isolation, loneliness, and burnout, which may be more prevalent compared to those working in traditional office settings (Kossek, Lautsch & Eaton, 2006). This highlights the need for employers to implement strategies that promote social connection, work-life balance, and self-care among remote workers (Keith, Harms, & Long, 2020).

Another important social and cultural trend is the rise of the "gig economy" and independent workers. The gig economy refers to a dynamic marketplace that operates on a global scale, enabling companies and independent contractors to engage in short-term, flexible, and skill-based professional relationships. Platforms like Upwork or Fiverr have played a significant role in facilitating this ecosystem by providing a space where a multitude of freelancers, including individuals with full-time jobs seeking additional income, can showcase their unique skill sets. Simultaneously, businesses can access a diverse talent pool from around the world, allowing them to tap into specialized expertise for specific projects or tasks without the need for long-term commitments or incurring extensive recruitment and selection costs. This arrangement grants businesses the opportunity to leverage costly skills for shorter durations while offering a wide array of candidates to choose from. In recent years, there has been a shift away from traditional employment arrangements towards more flexible and independent work models (Gig Economy Data Hub, 2021). The growth of the "gig economy" has significant implications for smart working, as independent workers often rely on technology to connect with clients and manage their work.

Researchers are likely to explore the challenges and opportunities associated with the gig economy and smart working, including issues related to job security, income stability, and the role of technology in supporting independent workers (Dwivedi et al., 2022). For example, some studies have shown that gig workers experience higher levels of income volatility and financial stress than traditional employees (Keith, Harms & Long, 2020). Therefore, understanding the impact of smart working on the gig economy and independent workers is crucial for policymakers and employers.

Digital Technologies

The integration of digital technologies has become a key factor in enabling organizations to embrace smart working. Digital technologies refer to a range of tools and systems that facilitate communication, collaboration, and the exchange of information, data, and knowledge among remote teams. The growing importance of digital technologies in smart working has sparked interest in exploring their impact on innovation and entrepreneurship (Shim et al., 2002).

Research has shown that digital technologies play a crucial role in facilitating "collaboration and knowledge sharing" among geographically dispersed teams. For example, virtual communication platforms, such as "video conferencing, instant messaging, and online document sharing," allow remote teams to communicate and share ideas in real-time, regardless of their location (Daim et al., 2012). In addition, digital technologies like "cloud computing and artificial intelligence" can provide teams with access to "large amounts of data and information," which can be used to develop innovative solutions and products (Bughin et al., 2017).

Furthermore, the integration of digital technologies offers organizations the opportunity to streamline operations and enhance cost-effectiveness. By leveraging digital tools, organizations can automate mundane and repetitive tasks, such as data entry and analysis, which in turn allows employees to dedicate their time and energy to more innovative and strategic endeavours (van Astyne, Parker & Choudary, 2016). This increased efficiency not only boosts productivity but also facilitates quicker decision-making processes, empowering organizations to promptly adapt to evolving market dynamics.

However, the integration of digital technologies in smart working also presents several challenges, such as the risk of information overload, data security, and privacy concerns (Gibson et al., 2014). Moreover, the overreliance on technology can lead to a lack of face-to-face interaction, which may negatively impact employee well-being and social connectedness (Griffiths, 2003).

Social Networks

Social networks are emerging as a promising area of research in the field of smart working. Social networks refer to the connections between people in an organization, both formal and informal, that influence how knowledge and information are shared within the organization. Studies have shown that social networks play a significant role in facilitating "innovation and entrepreneurship" (Battilana & Casciaro, 2013).

Researchers are exploring how social networks can be used to enhance collaboration and knowledge sharing among remote workers in smart working environments. For example, one study found that employees who had more connections within their social network were more likely to engage in knowledge-sharing behaviours, like providing feedback and advice to colleagues (Cao et al., 2021). Another study found that employees who had a stronger social network were more likely to report "higher levels of job satisfaction and work engagement" (Caesens, Stinglhamber & Luypaert, 2014).

Furthermore, social network analysis is being used to identify key individuals who are central to innovation and entrepreneurship in smart working contexts. Social network analysis is a method that uses mathematical models to map and analyse social networks. By analysing the connections between individuals within an organization, social network analysis can identify individuals who are influential in shaping the organization's culture and driving innovation and entrepreneurship (Gupta & Govindarajan, 2020).

Focusing on social networks aims to provide organizations with valuable insights on harnessing the power of social networks to boost their innovation capabilities and entrepreneurial prospects. By comprehending the significance of social networks in the context of smart working environments, organizations can uncover strategies to promote effective collaboration and knowledge exchange among remote workers. Additionally, this research facilitates the identification of influential individuals who can serve as catalysts for innovation and entrepreneurship within the organization (Chen & Wang, 2008).

Sharing Economy

The sharing economy refers to a socio-economic system in which individuals and organizations share resources, goods, and services through online platforms and networks. This system has been rapidly growing over the past few years, disrupting traditional business models and transforming the way people live, work, and interact. The rise of the sharing economy has significant implications for smart working, as it enables individuals to work independently and flexibly, and facilitates the creation of new types of jobs and business opportunities (Pouri & Hilty, 2021).

The gig economy revolves around individuals offering their skills to companies of all sizes on a part-time basis, typically for short-term assignments, and receiving payment per task or project. On the other hand, the sharing economy encompasses a broader concept that includes the gig economy but extends beyond it. In the sharing economy, people not only share their skills but also their assets, facilitated by large-scale digital technology and data collection. This concept enables individuals to participate in collaborative consumption, where they can share resources such as vehicles, accommodation, or other goods and services with others, often through online platforms. The sharing economy harnesses the power of technology to connect people and optimize the utilization of resources, promoting a more efficient and sustainable way of living and doing business (Görög, G. 2018).

In recent studies, there has been a growing interest in examining how the sharing economy influences innovation and entrepreneurship within the realm of smart working. Sundararajan (2017) conducted a notable study in this area, revealing that the sharing economy plays a significant role in fostering innovation. By providing individuals and small businesses with access to untapped markets, resources, and opportunities for collaboration, the sharing economy facilitates the exploration of novel ideas and business models. Furthermore, the study emphasized the crucial role of trust, reputation, and social capital in the sharing economy, as they contribute to the development of relationships and networks that support innovative and entrepreneurial endeavours.

Another study by Schor and Attwood-Charles, (2016) examined the role of digital platforms in facilitating smart working practices in the sharing economy. The study found that digital platforms such as Uber, Airbnb, and TaskRabbit have created new opportunities for individuals to work flexibly and earn income on their own terms. However, the study also highlighted the challenges associated with platform-mediated work, such as the lack of job security, benefits, and legal protections, as well as the potential for exploitation and social inequality.

Emerging Research Trends

The concept of smart working has gained significant popularity in recent times, particularly due to the widespread impact of the COVID-19 pandemic, which has triggered a significant transformation in work practices (Amankwah-Amoah et al., 2021). As a result, researchers have been exploring new and innovative ways to improve smart working practices, and several promising new research trends are emerging. Here are a few of the most notable:

AI and Machine Learning for Smart Working

Smart working has become increasingly popular in recent years as a means to enhance productivity, improve work-life balance, and mitigate the negative environmental impact of commuting. A particularly intriguing area of research within smart working is the utilization of "artificial intelligence (AI) and machine learning (ML)" to optimize productivity and streamline work processes. AI involves computer systems simulating human intelligence, while ML allows computers to learn from data without explicit programming (Lazar, Osoian, & Ratiu, 2010).

Researchers are actively exploring various applications of AI and ML in the context of smart working. One such application involves using ML algorithms to optimize work schedules. Studies have demonstrated that personalized schedules can significantly boost productivity and job satisfaction (Spector, 1997). By considering individual work patterns, preferences, and deadlines, ML algorithms can generate optimal schedules tailored to each worker. This not only enhances productivity but also helps reduce work-related stress and burnout (Guenard, 2021).

Another application of AI and ML in smart work is the automation of repetitive tasks. Repetitive tasks such as data entry, invoicing, and reporting can be time-consuming and can take away from more important tasks. AI and ML algorithms can automate these tasks, freeing up time for more creative and strategic work (Sobczak & Ziora, 2021). This can also reduce errors and increase efficiency in work processes.

Finally, AI and ML can also improve collaboration between remote workers. Virtual collaboration tools such as Zoom, Slack, and Microsoft Teams have become essential for remote teams. However, these tools can sometimes lead to information overload and can be difficult to navigate. AI and ML algorithms can help to manage this overload by filtering and prioritizing information, providing relevant recommendations, and identifying knowledge gaps (Wang et al., 2020). This can lead to more efficient and effective communication and collaboration among remote workers.

The Impact of Smart Working on Employee Well-Being

The surge in smart working has experienced rapid development in recent years, with the COVID-19 pandemic acting as a catalyst for many companies to adopt remote work practices to ensure business continuity. Smart working leverages technology to empower employees to work from any location, freeing them from the constraints of physical office space (Abulibdeh, 2020).

An important focus of research in the field of smart working revolves around its impact on employee well-being. Numerous studies have highlighted the positive effects of remote work on job satisfaction. For instance, a comprehensive meta-analysis of 39 studies revealed a positive correlation between telecommuting and job satisfaction, as well as organizational commitment (Gajendran & Harrison, 2007). Additionally, another study found that "remote workers reported higher levels of job satisfaction, improved work-life balance, and increased autonomy" (Golden & Veiga, 2005).

However, remote work can also have negative effects on employee well-being.

One major challenge of remote work is the risk of "social isolation and loneliness," which can negatively influence mental health (Hill, Ferris & Märtinson, 2003; Golden & Veiga, 2005). In addition, remote work can make it difficult to separate "work and personal life," leading to longer working hours and a greater risk of burnout (Hill, Ferris & Märtinson, 2003).

To address these challenges, researchers are exploring new ways to support remote workers and promote their mental health. One area of research focuses on developing strategies to promote work-life balance in remote settings. This includes establishing clear boundaries, encouraging regular breaks, and advocating for flexible work schedules that accommodate personal responsibilities. Studies are examining the effectiveness of interventions such as time management techniques, setting realistic goals, and implementing structured downtime to help remote workers create a healthier work-life integration.

Another important aspect of supporting remote workers' mental health is fostering social connections and reducing feelings of isolation. Researchers are exploring ways to facilitate virtual social interactions, team-building activities, and opportunities for informal communication to enhance remote workers' sense of belonging and connection with their colleagues. Virtual platforms and tools are being evaluated to identify effective approaches for promoting social cohesion and combating the potential negative impact of social isolation.

Furthermore, studies are examining the role of organizational support in remote work environments. This includes exploring how managers can provide remote employees with the necessary resources, feedback, and support to help them navigate challenges and maintain their well-being. Research is also investigating the impact of leadership styles, communication practices, and organizational policies on remote workers' mental health and job satisfaction.

In addition to organizational interventions, researchers are investigating individual-level strategies for remote workers to cope with stress and prevent burnout. This includes exploring mindfulness techniques, stress management strategies, and promoting self-care practices (Efthymiou, I. P., 2017). Studies aim to identify effective approaches that individuals can implement to enhance their well-being and resilience in a remote work context.

For example, a recent study found that virtual social support from coworkers can help to reduce feelings of isolation and loneliness among remote workers (Hager, 2018). Other studies have explored the use of mindfulness interventions and flexible work arrangements to promote well-being among remote workers (Hill, Ferris & Märtinson, 2003).

Smart Working and Sustainability

In recent years, researchers have been investigating the intersection between smart working and sustainability, recognizing the potential of this work model to contribute to environmental and social goals (Cascio & Montealegre, 2016; Iapichino, De Rosa & Liberace, 2018).

One of the main environmental advantages of smart working is the reduction of greenhouse gas emissions, which are responsible for climate change. A study by the International Labour Organization (ILO) found that remote work could reduce CO2 emissions by up to 8.3 billion tons per year by 2030, which is equivalent to the annual emissions of India (ILO, 2019).

The reduction in emissions is mainly due to the decrease in commuting, which is one of the largest sources of carbon emissions in many countries (Iapichino, De Rosa & Liberace, 2018). For example, a study conducted in the USA found that if 10% of the workforce switched to telecommuting, it would save "5.8 million metric tons of CO_2 emissions per year, the equivalent of taking 1.2 million cars off the road" (RMI, 2017).

In addition to reducing greenhouse gas emissions, smart working can also promote energy efficiency by reducing the use of office spaces and equipment. A study by the Crow and Millot (2020) found that remote work could reduce energy consumption in the European Union by up to 1.5%, equivalent to the annual energy consumption of Greece. The reduction in energy consumption is because smart workers use their own devices and work from home, which reduces the need for office spaces, lighting, heating, and cooling.

Finally, smart working can contribute to a more sustainable future by reducing pressure on urban infrastructure and improving the quality of life of workers. By reducing commuting, smart working can alleviate traffic congestion, which is a major problem in many cities (Iapichino, De Rosa & Liberace, 2018). In addition, smart working can reduce stress and burnout, improve the work-life balance of employees, and increase job satisfaction (Tamunomiebi & Oyibo, 2020). By promoting sustainable lifestyles and well-being, smart working can contribute to the "achievement of the United Nations Sustainable Development Goals (SDGs)."

Implications for Innovation and Entrepreneurship

The implications of these emerging research trends are significant for innovation and entrepreneurship. Here are some potential implications:

- Greater use of digital technologies: With the rapid adoption of digital technologies, organizations can now access vast amounts of data and leverage powerful tools to analyze and interpret that data. This can lead to new opportunities for innovation and entrepreneurship, such as "the development of new products and services, the creation of new business models, and the optimization of existing processes" (Vassakis, Petrakis & Kopanakis, 2018).
- Increased collaboration and networking: The rise of social networks and the sharing economy has made it easier for individuals and organizations to connect and collaborate. This can lead to greater innovation and entrepreneurship, as organizations can tap into a wider range of resources and expertise (Hamari, Sjöklint & Ukkonen, 2016).
- Enhanced agility and adaptability: In today's rapidly changing business landscape, organizations must agile and respond quickly. By staying up-to-date with the latest research trends, organizations can stay ahead of the curve and position themselves to take advantage of emerging opportunities (Sharifi et al., 2001).

- Greater emphasis on customer needs: With the increasing focus on customer experience and satisfaction, organizations need to be able to understand and anticipate customer needs. By leveraging the latest research trends, organizations can gain valuable insights into "customer behaviour and preferences," and use this knowledge to create "new products and services" that better meet customer needs (Berman, 2012; Spiess et al., 2014).

Challenges and Opportunities

The field of smart working research has grown significantly in recent years, driven by technological advancements and the increasing demand for work-life balance. As with any rapidly evolving field, smart working research faces several challenges and opportunities including the need to keep up with technological change, balancing benefits and drawbacks, and the potential for enhancing innovation and reducing environmental impact (Chung & Van der Lippe, 2020).

CHALLENGES

Keeping Up With Technological Change

Staying abreast of the ever-evolving technological landscape is a paramount challenge in smart working research. The rapid pace of technological change and innovation necessitates a continuous effort to remain "up to date" with the latest advancements, ensuring the relevance of insights for informing policy and practice. However, this dynamic environment can be overwhelming, requiring researchers to navigate the influx of emerging tools and technologies. It is crucial to develop effective strategies for identifying and evaluating these advancements, such as "artificial intelligence and the Internet of Things," to harness their potential for enhancing smart working practices (Lake, 2016; Brunetti et al., 2020). Strategies like stay informed about the latest developments in AI and IoT technologies and their applications in the workplace. Invest in research to understand how these advancements can specifically benefit remote work and smart working practices . Implement pilot projects or proof of concepts to test the feasibility and effectiveness of AI and IoT solutions in remote work scenarios. Identify specific use cases where these technologies can add value, such as automated task management, data analysis, or remote monitoring and control. Collaborate with technology providers, researchers, and industry experts to leverage their expertise in AI and IoT. Partnering with specialists can help in evaluating different solutions, identifying best practices, and implementing effective strategies tailored to your organization's unique needs. Consider the data privacy and security implications associated with the use of AI and IoT technologies. Ensure that adequate measures are in place to protect sensitive information and comply with relevant regulations. Conduct thorough risk assessments and implement robust cybersecurity protocols. Be mindful of ethical considerations associated with the use of AI and IoT technologies, such as bias in algorithms or potential job displacement. Ensure that these technologies are implemented and used responsibly, with a focus on promoting fairness, equity, and inclusivity.

Balancing Benefits and Drawbacks

Striking a balance between the advantages and disadvantages is another pressing challenge in smart working research. On one hand, the flexibility and independence offered by smart working empower employees to work from diverse locations, fostering enhanced work-life balance and diminishing commuting burdens. Conversely, there are concerns about potential social isolation and reduced collaboration as remote workers may miss out on valuable interactions and relationship-building opportunities with colleagues. Furthermore, maintaining a healthy work-life balance becomes challenging, as remote workers may struggle to disconnect from work and establish boundaries between their personal and professional lives (Weideman & Hofmeyr, 2020; Ren & Xu, 2023).

OPPORTUNITIES

Enhancing Innovation and Entrepreneurial Opportunities

Smart working research presents the substantial potential for bolstering innovation capabilities and fostering entrepreneurial opportunities. The adoption of remote work enables seamless collaboration across geographical barriers, granting organizations access to a diverse talent pool and untapped markets. Moreover, smart working enhances employee efficiency and effectiveness, resulting in streamlined task completion and resource utilization. This optimization of resources creates room for innovation and experimentation, empowering organizations with a distinct competitive edge (Podgorski et al., 2017).

Improving Work-Life Balance

Another opportunity associated with smart working research is the potential to improve work-life balance. Remote work can enable employees to manage their time more effectively, enabling them to prioritize personal commitments and hobbies alongside work. This can lead to improved mental health and well-being, reducing stress and burnout (Chung & Van der Lippe, 2020).

Reducing Environmental Impact

Smart working research plays a vital role in mitigating environmental impact. It offers organizations the opportunity to reduce commuting time and costs, leading to a decrease in greenhouse gas emissions and alleviating road congestion. Moreover, the adoption of smart working allows organizations to minimize their physical footprint by enabling employees to work remotely, thereby reducing the need for a centralized office location (Hopkins & McKay, 2019).

CONCLUSION

In conclusion, organizations must recognize the importance of staying up-to-date on new research trends in smart working to grasp innovation and entrepreneurial opportunities. The field has seen substantial growth, driven by technology advancements and the increasing demand for work-life balance. While smart working offers numerous advantages, such as productivity and flexibility, it also poses challenges related to employee well-being and remote team collaboration.

Technological trends, particularly the integration of artificial intelligence and machine learning, are shaping the future of smart working, empowering enhanced productivity, work-life balance, and environmental sustainability. Social and cultural trends, including a heightened focus on mental health and well-being, are also influencing smart working research.

Digital technologies and social networks play pivotal roles in enabling and facilitating effective smart working practices. Organizations need to invest in appropriate tools and infrastructure to support seamless communication and collaboration among remote teams. Leveraging social networks within organizations fosters knowledge sharing, innovation, and entrepreneurship.

Furthermore, emerging research trends in smart working, such as the intersection with sustainability, hold significant implications for innovation and entrepreneurship. Smart working research provides opportunities to strengthen innovation capabilities, improve work-life balance, and mitigate environmental impact.

However, smart working research faces challenges, including keeping pace with rapid technological advancements, striking a balance between the benefits and drawbacks, and effectively managing the transition to remote work models. By addressing these challenges and embracing the opportunities presented by smart working research, organizations can position themselves for success in the ever-evolving landscape of work.

REFERENCES

Abulibdeh, A. (2020). Can COVID-19 mitigation measures promote telework practices? *Journal of Labor and Society*, *23*(4), 551–576. doi:10.1111/wusa.12498

Afonso, P., Fonseca, M., & Teodoro, T. (2022). Evaluation of anxiety, depression and sleep quality in full-time teleworkers. *Journal of Public Health (Oxford, England)*, *44*(4), 797–804. doi:10.1093/pubmed/fdab164 PMID:34036369

Amankwah-Amoah, J., Khan, Z., Wood, G., & Knight, G. (2021). COVID-19 and digitalization: The great acceleration. *Journal of Business Research*, *136*, 602–611. doi:10.1016/j.jbusres.2021.08.011 PMID:34538980

Autor, D. H. (2015). Why are there still so many jobs? The history and future of workplace automation. *The Journal of Economic Perspectives*, *29*(3), 3–30. doi:10.1257/jep.29.3.3

Battilana, J., & Casciaro, T. (2013). The network secrets of great change agents. *Harvard Business Review*, *91*(7), 62–68. PMID:24730170

Berman, S. J. (2012). Digital transformation: Opportunities to create new business models. *Strategy and Leadership*, *40*(2), 16–24. doi:10.1108/10878571211209314

Betti, N., & Sarens, G. (2021). Understanding the internal audit function in a digitalised business environment. *Journal of Accounting & Organizational Change*, *17*(2), 197–216. doi:10.1108/JAOC-11-2019-0114

Brunetti, F., Matt, D. T., Bonfanti, A., De Longhi, A., Pedrini, G., & Orzes, G. (2020). Digital transformation challenges: Strategies emerging from a multi-stakeholder approach. *The TQM Journal*, *32*(4), 697–724. doi:10.1108/TQM-12-2019-0309

Buffer. (2021). *State of Remote Work 2021*. Buffer. https://buffer.com/state-of-remote-work/2021

Bughin, J., Hazan, E., Ramaswamy, S., Chui, M., Allas, T., Dahlstrom, P., & Trench, M. (2017). *Artificial intelligence: The next digital frontier?* McKinsey Global Institute.

Caesens, G., Stinglhamber, F., & Luypaert, G. (2014). The impact of work engagement and workaholism on well-being: The role of work-related social support. *Career Development International*, *19*(7), 813–835. doi:10.1108/CDI-09-2013-0114

Cao, X., Ali, A., Pitafi, A. H., Khan, A. N., & Waqas, M. (2021). A socio-technical system approach to knowledge creation and team performance: Evidence from China. *Information Technology & People*, *34*(7), 1976–1996. doi:10.1108/ITP-10-2019-0536

Cascio, W. F., & Montealegre, R. (2016). How technology is changing work and organizations. *Annual Review of Organizational Psychology and Organizational Behavior*, *3*(1), 349–375. doi:10.1146/annurev-orgpsych-041015-062352

Chen, M. H., & Wang, M. C. (2008). Social networks and a new venture's innovative capability: The role of trust within entrepreneurial teams. *R & D Management*, *38*(3), 253–264. doi:10.1111/j.1467-9310.2008.00515.x

Chung, H., & Van der Lippe, T. (2020). Flexible working, work–life balance, and gender equality: Introduction. *Social Indicators Research*, *151*(2), 365–381. doi:10.100711205-018-2025-x PMID:33029036

Cioffi, R., Travaglioni, M., Piscitelli, G., Petrillo, A., & De Felice, F. (2020). Artificial intelligence and machine learning applications in smart production: Progress, trends, and directions. *Sustainability (Basel)*, *12*(2), 492–515. doi:10.3390u12020492

Coombs, C., Hislop, D., Taneva, S. K., & Barnard, S. (2020). The strategic impacts of Intelligent Automation for knowledge and service work: An interdisciplinary review. *The Journal of Strategic Information Systems*, *29*(4), 101600. doi:10.1016/j.jsis.2020.101600

Crow, D., & Millot, A. (2020, June 12). *Working from home can save energy and reduce emissions. But how much?* [Commentary]. International Energy Agency. https://www.iea.org/commentaries/working-from-home-can-save-energy-and-reduce-emissions-but-how-much

Daim, T. U., Ha, A., Reutiman, S., Hughes, B., Pathak, U., Bynum, W., & Bhatla, A. (2012). Exploring the communication breakdown in global virtual teams. *International Journal of Project Management*, *30*(2), 199–212. doi:10.1016/j.ijproman.2011.06.004

Dwivedi, Y. K., Hughes, L., Baabdullah, A. M., Ribeiro-Navarrete, S., Giannakis, M., Al-Debei, M. M., Dennehy, D., Metri, B., Buhalis, D., Cheung, C. M. K., Conboy, K., Doyle, R., Dubey, R., Dutot, V., Felix, R., Goyal, D. P., Gustafsson, A., Hinsch, C., Jebabli, I., & Wamba, S. F. (2022). Metaverse beyond the hype: Multidisciplinary perspectives on emerging challenges, opportunities, and agenda for research, practice and policy. *International Journal of Information Management*, *66*, 102542. doi:10.1016/j.ijinfomgt.2022.102542

Efthymiou, I. P. (2017). *Wellness: A new word for Ancient Ideas.* Xlibris UK, Efthymiou, I. P., (2020). Non-Cognitive Skills and AI: A New Era of Learning and Development. *International Case Studies Journal, 9*(10), 42–46.

Gajendran, R. S., & Harrison, D. A. (2007). The good, the bad, and the unknown about telecommuting: Meta-analysis of psychological mediators and individual consequences. *The Journal of Applied Psychology, 92*(6), 1524–1541. doi:10.1037/0021-9010.92.6.1524 PMID:18020794

Gibson, C. B., Huang, L., Kirkman, B. L., & Shapiro, D. L. (2014). Where global and virtual meet: The value of examining the intersection of these elements in twenty-first-century teams. *Annual Review of Organizational Psychology and Organizational Behavior, 1*(1), 217–244. doi:10.1146/annurev-orgpsych-031413-091240

Gig Economy Data Hub. (2021). *What is the gig economy*? Gig Economy Data Shop. https://www.gigeconomydata.org/

Giorgi, G., Lecca, L. I., Alessio, F., Finstad, G. L., Bondanini, G., Lulli, L. G., Arcangeli, G., & Mucci, N. (2020). COVID-19-related mental health effects in the workplace: A narrative review. *International Journal of Environmental Research and Public Health, 17*(21), 7857. doi:10.3390/ijerph17217857 PMID:33120930

Golden, T. D., & Veiga, J. F. (2005). The impact of extent of telecommuting on job satisfaction: Resolving inconsistent findings. *Journal of Management, 31*(2), 301–318. doi:10.1177/0149206304271768

Görög, G. (2018). The Definitions of Sharing Economy: A Systematic Literature Review. *Management (18544223), 13*(2).

Griffiths, R. F. (2003). *Time management in telework and other autonomous work environments*. Kansas State University.

Guenard, R. (2021). The COVID-19 pandemic, one year later. *Inform (Champaign, Ill.)*, 6–11.

Hager, F. W. (2018). Links between telecommuting, social support and mental well-being among teleworkers. In *Links between telecommuting, social support and mental well-being among teleworkers*. Hager, Frank W. doi:10.20472/BM.2018.6.2.003

Hamari, J., Sjöklint, M., & Ukkonen, A. (2016). The sharing economy: Why people participate in collaborative consumption. *Journal of the Association for Information Science and Technology, 67*(9), 2047–2059. doi:10.1002/asi.23552

Hill, E. J., Ferris, M., & Märtinson, V. (2003). Does it matter where you work? A comparison of how three work venues (traditional office, virtual office, and home office) influence aspects of work and personal/family life. *Journal of Vocational Behavior*, *63*(2), 220–241. doi:10.1016/S0001-8791(03)00042-3

Himanen, L., Geurts, A., Foster, A. S., & Rinke, P. (2019). Data-driven materials science: Status, challenges, and perspectives. *Advancement of Science*, *6*(21), 1900808. doi:10.1002/advs.201900808 PMID:31728276

Hopkins, J. L., & McKay, J. (2019). Investigating 'anywhere working' as a mechanism for alleviating traffic congestion in smart cities. *Technological Forecasting and Social Change*, *142*, 258–272. doi:10.1016/j.techfore.2018.07.032

Iapichino, A., De Rosa, A., & Liberace, P. (2018). Smart organizations, new skills, and smart working to manage companies' digital transformation. *Digitized Labor: The Impact of the Internet on Employment*, 215-227. doi:10.1007/978-3-319-78420-5_13

International Labour Organization. (2019). *Working anytime, anywhere: The effects on the world of work*. ILO. https://www.ilo.org/global/publications/books/WCMS_544138/lang--en/index.htm

Keith, M. G., Harms, P. D., & Long, A. C. (2020). Worker health and well-being in the gig economy: A proposed framework and research agenda. *Entrepreneurial and small business stressors, experienced stress, and well-being, 18*(1), 1-33. doi:10.1108/S1479-355520200000018002

Kelliher, C., & Anderson, D. (2010). Doing more with less? Flexible working practices and the intensification of work. *Human Relations*, *63*(1), 83–106. doi:10.1177/0018726709349199

Kossek, E. E., Lautsch, B. A., & Eaton, S. C. (2006). Telecommuting, control, and boundary management: Correlates of policy use and practice, job control, and work–family effectiveness. *Journal of Vocational Behavior*, *68*(2), 347–367. doi:10.1016/j.jvb.2005.07.002

Lake, A. (2016). *Smart flexibility: Moving smart and flexible working from theory to practice*. CRC Press. doi:10.4324/9781315609379

Lazar, I., Osoian, C., & Ratiu, P. I. (2010). The role of work-life balance practices in order to improve organizational performance. *European Research Studies*, *13*(1), 202–214. doi:10.35808/ersj/267

Lukosch, S., Billinghurst, M., Alem, L., & Kiyokawa, K. (2015). Collaboration in augmented reality. [CSCW]. *Computer Supported Cooperative Work*, *24*(6), 515–525. doi:10.100710606-015-9239-0

Malhotra, A., Majchrzak, A., & Rosen, B. (2007). Leading virtual teams. *The Academy of Management Perspectives*, *21*(1), 60–70. doi:10.5465/amp.2007.24286164

Malik, A. A., Masood, T., & Bilberg, A. (2020). Virtual reality in manufacturing: Immersive and collaborative artificial-reality in design of human-robot workspace. *International Journal of Computer Integrated Manufacturing*, *33*(1), 22–37. doi:10.1080/0951192X.2019.1690685

Mishra, A., Agarwal A., & Agarwal V. (2020). Work from Home: The Modus Operandi During COVID-19. *Horizon, 2*(s), 67-74.

Moore, H. F., & Gheisari, M. (2019). A review of virtual and mixed reality applications in construction safety literature. *Safety (Basel, Switzerland)*, *5*(3), 51–70. doi:10.3390afety5030051

Moss, J. (2021). Beyond burned out. *Harvard Business Review*. https://hbr.org/2021/02/beyond-burned-out

Oztemel, E., & Gursev, S. (2020). Literature review of Industry 4.0 and related technologies. *Journal of Intelligent Manufacturing*, *31*(1), 127–182. doi:10.100710845-018-1433-8

Podgorski, D., Majchrzycka, K., Dąbrowska, A., Gralewicz, G., & Okrasa, M. (2017). Towards a conceptual framework of OSH risk management in smart working environments based on smart PPE, ambient intelligence and the Internet of Things technologies. *International Journal of Occupational Safety and Ergonomics*, *23*(1), 1–20. doi:10.1080/10803548.2016.1214431 PMID:27441587

Pouri, M. J., & Hilty, L. M. (2021). The digital sharing economy: A confluence of technical and social sharing. *Environmental Innovation and Societal Transitions*, *38*(1), 127–139. doi:10.1016/j.eist.2020.12.003

Ren, X., & Xu, H. (2023). Flexible working during the COVID-19 pandemic: Gains and strains in a Chinese state-owned organisation. *Journal of Asia Business Studies*, *17*(1), 75–96. doi:10.1108/JABS-03-2022-0109

Roberto, R., Penna, M., Felici, B., & Rao, M. (2023). Smart working and flexible work arrangements: opportunities and risks for sustainable communities. In *Intelligent Environments* (pp. 243–283). North-Holland. doi:10.1016/B978-0-12-820247-0.00001-1

Sasaki, N., Kuroda, R., Tsuno, K., & Kawakami, N. (2020). Workplace responses to COVID-19 associated with mental health and work performance of employees in Japan. *Journal of Occupational Health, 62*(1), e12134. doi:10.1002/1348-9585.12134 PMID:32529654

Savić, D. (2020). COVID-19 and work from home: Digital transformation of the workforce. [TGJ]. *Grey Journal, 16*(2), 101–104.

Schor, J. B., & Attwood-Charles, W. (2017). The "sharing" economy: Labor, inequality, and social connection on for-profit platforms. *Sociology Compass, 11*(8), e12493. doi:10.1111oc4.12493

Sharifi, H., Colquhoun, G., Barclay, I., & Dann, Z. (2001). Agile manufacturing: A management and operational framework. *Proceedings of the Institution of Mechanical Engineers. Part B, Journal of Engineering Manufacture, 215*(6), 857–869. doi:10.1243/0954405011518647

Shim, J. P., Warkentin, M., Courtney, J. F., Power, D. J., Sharda, R., & Carlsson, C. (2002). Past, present, and future of decision support technology. *Decision Support Systems, 33*(2), 111–126. doi:10.1016/S0167-9236(01)00139-7

Sobczak, A., & Ziora, L. (2021). The use of robotic process automation (RPA) as an element of smart city implementation: A case study of electricity billing document management at Bydgoszcz city Hall. *Energies, 14*(16), 5191. doi:10.3390/en14165191

Soga, L. R., Bolade-Ogunfodun, Y., Mariani, M., Nasr, R., & Laker, B. (2022). Unmasking the other face of flexible working practices: A systematic literature review. *Journal of Business Research, 142*, 648–662. doi:10.1016/j.jbusres.2022.01.024

Sorensen, C. (2004). The future role of trust in work–the key success factor for mobile productivity. *Tomorrow's Work Research Paper.*

Spector, P. E. (1997). *Job satisfaction: Application, assessment, causes, and consequences* (Vol. 3). Sage. doi:10.4135/9781452231549

Spiess, J., T'Joens, Y., Dragnea, R., Spencer, P., & Philippart, L. (2014). Using big data to improve customer experience and business performance. *Bell Labs Technical Journal, 18*(4), 3–17. doi:10.1002/bltj.21642

Sundararajan, A. (2017). *The sharing economy: The end of employment and the rise of crowd-based capitalism.* MIT press.

Tamunomiebi, M. D., & Oyibo, C. (2020). Work-life balance and employee performance: A literature review. *European Journal of Business and Management Research, 5*(2), 196–204. doi:10.24018/ejbmr.2020.5.2.196

van Astyne, M. W., Parker, G. G., & Choudary, S. P. (2016). Pipelines, platforms, and the new rules of strategy. *Harvard Business Review*, *94*(4), 16.

Vassakis, K., Petrakis, E., & Kopanakis, I. (2018). Big data analytics: applications, prospects and challenges. *Mobile big data: A roadmap from models to technologies*, 10(1), 3-20. https://doi.org/ doi:10.1007/978-3-319-67925-9_1

Wang, L., Liu, S., Liu, H., & Wang, X. V. (2020). Overview of human-robot collaboration in manufacturing. In *Proceedings of 5th International Conference on the Industry 4.0 Model for Advanced Manufacturing: AMP 2020* (pp. 15-58). Springer International Publishing. 10.1007/978-3-030-46212-3_2

Weideman, M., & Hofmeyr, K. B. (2020). The influence of flexible work arrangements on employee engagement: An exploratory study. *SA Journal of Human Resource Management*, *18*(1), 1–18. doi:10.4102ajhrm.v18i0.1209

Woods, M. (2021). Technology Impacts on Employee Engagement During Covid-19. In *Research and Innovation Forum 2021: Managing Continuity, Innovation, and Change in the Post-Covid World: Technology, Politics and Society* (pp. 45-58). Springer International Publishing. https://doi.org/10.1007/978-3-030-84311-3_5

Chapter 4
Harnessing Parasocial Interaction in Entrepreneurial Education:
Virtual Mentoring for Distance Learning

Thanuja Rathakrishnan
https://orcid.org/0000-0002-5470-8931
School of Management and Marketing, Taylor's University, Lakeside, Malaysia

Feranita Feranita
https://orcid.org/0000-0002-2228-1953
School of Management and Marketing, Taylor's University, Lakeside, Malaysia

Thivashini B. Jaya Kumar
https://orcid.org/0000-0002-3265-3191
School of Management and Marketing, Taylor's University, Lakeside, Malaysia

Woon Leong Lin
https://orcid.org/0000-0002-6568-412X
School of Management and Marketing, Taylor's University, Lakeside, Malaysia

ABSTRACT

This chapter examines the use of virtual mentors in distance learning for entrepreneurship education. Virtual mentors establish a strong connection with students via sharing personal stories, overcoming the challenges of physical interaction in distance learning. The benefits of learning from global experts are discussed, along with the importance of parasocial interaction for meaningful engagement in the context of distance learning. Virtual mentors provide personalized guidance, industry-specific insights, and networking opportunities, contributing to entrepreneurial knowledge. The chapter contributes to the theoretical understanding of entrepreneurship education and expands the application of parasocial interaction

DOI: 10.4018/978-1-7998-8797-3.ch004

beyond media and entertainment. It provides practical strategies for educators to enhance the distance learning experiences, leveraging virtual mentors to provide real-world insights and facilitate networking. Overall, this chapter highlights that integration between parasocial interaction and virtual mentors facilitate entrepreneurial education in distance learning.

1.0 INTRODUCTION

Parasocial interaction is a term that refers to a one-sided psychological relationship that individuals form with media figures or celebrities. Despite having no direct personal interaction with that individual, people tend to develop a strong fondness, bond or emotional attachment with someone they perceive as a media or social media persona (Brestovanský & Sekerešová, 2022). This phenomenon has gained significant relevance in the education context, in particularly in distance learning. This book chapter then dive into the scope of entrepreneurial education, as entrepreneurship has been gaining a lot of traction in the past due to their significance and beneficial to themselves, society and to the country.

In the social media and interactive online content era, individuals have the opportunity to establish themselves as media figures, in particularly entrepreneurs in showcasing their expertise, sharing opinions, advices, experiences, memories, "bringing" the students along with their journey – thereby receiving likes and gaining more followers (Aw et al., 2022; Rudeloff & Damms, 2022; Scherer et al., 2022). Parasocial interaction also refers to students building a one-sided relationship and connection with a virtual mentor, often through video content, podcasts, or blogs (Jarzyna, 2021). These virtual mentors can be industry experts, celebrity entrepreneurs, successful entrepreneurs, or social media influencers who are entrepreneurs themselves. This enables the virtual mentors in cultivating a bond - parasocial relationship, where the students feel connected and warm with them; albeit unrequited. Generally, in this type of relationship, the individual will feel emotionally connected to the media figure or character, despite the absence of a pre-existing acquaintance, familiarity, or established relationship between the individuals involved. By capitalizing on parasocial interaction, the virtual mentors can capture the attention and interest of aspiring entrepreneurs (students) making the educational content more engaging and memorable.

One aspect of parasocial interaction relevant to entrepreneurial education is on the legitimacy of the persona themselves. Entrepreneurs who are successful or influencer entrepreneurs often share and upload contents such as personal stories, experiences, and values to engage with their students. By sharing their journey, successes, challenges, and even failures, entrepreneurs establish the closeness, connectivity, and portray a more "friend-like" and authentic persona that relates with their followers (Aw et al., 2022). This aspect fosters a sense of trust, credibility, attractiveness and closeness, thereby influencing their audiences' perceptions and inspire them to take action (Taillon et al., 2020).

In the aspect of parasocial interaction, past research has put in more effort in the relationship to social media usage and its antecedents (Kowert & Daniel, 2021; Liebers & Schramm, 2019; Stein, Linda & Anders, 2022). The findings from extent literature also provided an opportunity to education (Frentzel-Beyme, Holtze, Szczuka, & Krämer, 2022; John, Walford, & Purayidathil, 2022; Soriani & Bonafede, 2023). Additionally, literature also found that mentoring plays an important role in entrepreneurial education (Babatunde & El-Gohary, 2019; Badwan, Tamvada & Rentocchini, 2022). However, Hu et al. (2019) found that mentorship was not a significant factor to entrepreneurship. This leads to a connotation that when the mentor-mentee connection or bond was not formed, mentorship might not translate to entrepreneurship. Due to this, this chapter strives to look into the underexplored linkage between parasocial interaction with entrepreneurial education (Ratten & Rashid, 2021).

The construction of parasocial interaction that influences individuals' entrepreneurial behaviour and attitudes were formed due to a pattern of thoughts in the past. For instance, when individuals observe successful entrepreneurs as media figures, they often identify with their aspirations and desires for achievement (Abbasianchavari & Moritz, 2021; Dwivedi et al., 2021). The parasocial relationship enables the individuals to experience the entrepreneur's journey, motivating them to embodying the traits and values that students desire to develop. By optimizing this connection, entrepreneurs can provide a learning experience with their audiences to develop an entrepreneurial mindset, take calculated risks, and inspire them to pursue their own entrepreneurial ventures.

Moreover, parasocial interaction is essential towards its formation of networks and communities. Expert entrepreneurs along with their audiences can create a sense of belonging, community and pride among the like-minded students that contributes to the entrepreneurial ecosystems (Pocek, Politis & Gabrielsson, 2021). By having a circle of connections, this would facilitate knowledge sharing, collaboration, exchange of ideas, and reducing the sense of loneliness which ultimately enhances the entrepreneurial education experience. To add, having this network is crucial for connection, collaboration, and potentially find partners, mentors, or investors.

Based on the discussion above, parasocial interaction needs to be cultivated especially in entrepreneurial education as an innovative method of learning experiences in the scope of distance learning. More discussions and insights are provided below on distance learning.

1.1 The Growing Trend of Distance Learning in the Education Industry

Distance learning is defined as a mode of education where both educators and students are geographically separated but connected through digital platforms (Gurcan & Cagiltay, 2023). They are also commonly known as online learning or e-learning. Although distance learning has been introduced in the past, its existence has gained more attention during the pandemic due to the widespread closure of schools and educational institutions, necessitating a shift towards remote learning methods.

Distance learning offers students the opportunity to gain knowledge and skills at their own pace and schedule. Regardless of their physical location, students can have the accessibility to their courses from anywhere in the world, as long as they have a reasonable internet connection (Ng, 2021). The flexibility of such arrangements is particularly useful for working professionals who may not have the time to commit and attend traditional classes. Through online courses, virtual discussions, forums, and group projects, educators could tailor a wide range of educational resources to the students' needs (Gerard, Bradford & Linn, 2022). This provides convenience which traditional educational institutions could not provide.

With distance learning, students have the advantage to learn from a wide range of global experts and industry practitioners (Lock & Redmond, 2021). The ease and convenience of the online platforms often bring instructors and guest speakers from different countries and backgrounds to provide a wide range of learning experience to students (Ratten & Jones, 2021; Schou, Bucher & Waldkirch, 2022). Instructors from different countries usually bring in new experience, challenges and ways of problem solving, that creates higher engagements with the students. This broadens students' perspectives and give them a competitive edge in the global business environment.

Online courses and programs are designed to be agile and adaptable, incorporating real-world case studies, current industry examples, and practical tools that reflect the dynamic nature of entrepreneurship. This ensures that entrepreneurs receive relevant and up-to-date knowledge that can be directly applied to their ventures. Lastly, distance learning cultivates learning independence, self-reliance, initiative taking and entrepreneurial mindset development as students take ownership of their learning journey (Sörensen et al., 2022). These traits illustrate an important role towards the growth and nurturing of an entrepreneur.

However, one of the highly mentioned challenges of distance learning is the lack of face-to-face interactions between the mentors and students, which can be a critical aspect of fostering entrepreneurial success (Abdellatif et al., 2023; Al-Mawee, Kwayu & Gharaibeh, 2021; Heidari, Mehrvarz, Marzooghi & Stoyanov, 2021). When there is a limitation of physical engagement with the other person, it is difficult to keep the learning momentum as there would be distractions or feeling uninspired to maintain focus (Abdellatif et al., 2023). One solution to this problem could be to create virtual mentors through parasocial interaction.

1.2 Virtual Mentor as a Form of Learning Delivery for Distance Learning

By definition, virtual mentors are individuals – usually an expert or business founders who provide knowledge, guidance, and support to aspiring entrepreneurs via online platforms (e.g., Webinar, mentorship program, online courses, virtual communities and such). They bring practical and updated knowledge of the entrepreneurial landscape. Students are able to gain access to mentorship from experts and experienced individuals from other parts of the world. The concept of virtual mentors reduced the gap between mentor-mentee and address the limitations of a physical mentor, thus getting recognition and favour in the scope of entrepreneurship education due to its advantage in nurturing entrepreneurial skills and knowledge (Lall, Chen & Mason, 2022).

The great thing about implementing virtual mentors into the curriculum is on their ability to share experiences, provide personalised guidance according to the students' industry of interest, and support (Andersen & West, 2021). These virtual mentors are experts or have vast experiences in sharing challenges, past mistakes, share best practices, recommend resources that saves aspiring entrepreneurs time and effort and how they overcome those challenges as well as facilitate networking opportunities. Accessibility to virtual mentors across the globe, enables connection from international perspectives and backgrounds. This would widen the students' knowledge base thereby exposing them to different decision making, problem solving and approaches which foster innovative thinking and exploration of new possibilities for their own ventures.

As experienced professionals or successful entrepreneurs themselves, they possess first-hand insights into the challenges, trends, and opportunities within the industry. By doing so, this would portray a more human-like persona; rather than how one would only read about them on news, media - where those platforms typically share the rosy part of their lives as an established entrepreneur. By following the journeys of successful entrepreneurs, students can learn valuable lessons about resilience, persistence, creativity and innovation (Fernández-Díaz et al., 2021). Virtual mentors do not only offer customised advice but also play a role in guiding the students in thinking the bigger picture, providing job-realistic as an entrepreneur, and industry-specific challenges which would prepare the students better on what they can expect (Iqbal, 2020; Nabi, Walmsley & Akhtar, 2021). This would enable them in making informed and educated decisions and avoiding common pitfalls.

Table 1 below summarizes the three important key terms in this chapter for clarity and better comprehension.

2.0 UNDERSTANDING PARASOCIAL INTERACTION IN THE RELATIONSHIP BETWEEN VIRTUAL MENTORS AND DISTANCE LEARNING

Parasocial interaction holds a great psychological significant, particularly in the realm of virtual mentorship in distance learning. Understanding the relevance of these relationships will help to shed light on their implications for effective mentorship. To spark inspirations among aspiring entrepreneurs, the virtual mentor assumes the role of a media figure or persona. Through online platforms and digital interactions such as video lectures, online discussions, webinars, or personalized mentorship sessions, mentors have the opportunity to establish a genuine parasocial relationship with their mentees.

Referring to the definition of parasocial interaction, the mentees may develop a strong emotional, sense of intimacy and connection and perceive a sense of closeness to their mentors despite of its one-way personal interaction (Andersen & West, 2021; Jarzyna, 2021; Larose et al., 2019). Past studies have also explained on the importance of social support in virtual mentorship (Kaufman et al., 2022; McReynolds et al., 2020). Since virtual mentors are looked upon as sources of emotional support, encouragement, and validation, parasocial interaction creates a safe space where students are not worried about being misunderstood and judged by their mentors (Dutton, Bullen & Deane, 2019). This provides a significant impact on students' confidence, motivation, and overall learning experience. In return,

Table 1. Definition of key terms

Key Terms	Definition	Sources
Distance Learning	A way of learning that happens online, using digital tools, materials, and technology. It offers a wide variety of ways for learners to interact and work together with their instructors or classmates outside of a traditional classroom setting according to the learners' own pace and convenience.	Bashir and Warraich (2023); Gurcan & Cagiltay (2023); Tibingana-Ahimbisibwe et al., (2022).
Virtual Mentor	Individuals who offer knowledge, guidance, and support to the audience via virtual, asynchronous, technology-based approach such as webinar, virtual communities, YouTube and as such.	Briscoe (2019); Tinoco-Giraldo, Torrecilla Sanchez and García-Peñalvo (2020).
Parasocial Interaction	Unreciprocated emotional connections that people form with media personalities, influencers or celebrities without any personal interaction.	Aw and Labrecque (2020); Brestovanský and Sekerešová (2022); Jarzyna (2021).

this would lead the aspiring entrepreneurs to emulate the behaviour and thinking process of the virtual mentor.

Parasocial interaction based on virtual mentorship can have several implications. Firstly, there is a sense of familiarity and trust towards the mentor by the mentee (Sarabipour et al., 2019). When mentors share experiences, insights, and expertise through digital platforms, the mentees would perceive them to be credible and knowledgeable figures; whom they could relate. This would also contribute to the mentees' motivation and engagement along with the trusts that was built. With the parasocial interaction, mentees will develop closeness with their mentors where they would be more interested and invested in the mentorship process leading to participation, commitment and dedication to the mentorship journey (Sarabipour et al., 2019); making the learning process dynamic and enriching (Kim, Kim & Yang, 2019).

On another note, social media has become an essential tool for entrepreneurs, providing them with a platform to build brand awareness, interact with customers, and reach out to potential investors. Influencers, who have significant followers on social media platforms, can help entrepreneurs reach a broader audience and gain valuable insights into consumer behavior (Ye et al., 2021). To bridge this idea, bringing virtual mentors specifically those who are also a social digital influencer could provide motivation, inspiration, and similarity as students today relate more to their favourite or local influencers (Kim & Kim, 2022; Myers, 2021). By doing so, this would diversify innovation and creativity in teaching for distance learning.

While distance learning offers the convenience of studying from any location, it may pose certain challenges such as distractions and limited social interaction (Sadeghi, 2019). Thus, incorporating parasocial interaction into the syllabus would expand possibilities for everyone involved (Virtual mentors, students, education industry, government) which could be a win-win. This is because virtual mentors are willing to share their entrepreneurial journey as well as their successes and failures which, in return could garner more likes and followers. As for the students, they would be more involved in their studies and inclined to stay focused and engaged under such arrangements in the syllabus, since they have developed a sense of connection with the virtual mentors. Additionally, when students engage in parasocial interaction, their behaviour and cognitive skills would emulate the virtual mentor (Lim, Choe, Zhang & Noh, 2020). Subsequently, this could lead them to portraying seriousness, discipline, perspiration, innovation, and decision-making skills. With the success of parasocial interaction as a syllabus, this would provide positive impact into the education industry.

On that note, parasocial interaction, which refers to the relationship between an individual and a media personality or a role model, can play a vital role in enhancing entrepreneurial success (Nowiński & Haddoud, 2019; Rudeloff & Damms, 2022).

Parasocial interaction involves learning from media personalities such as influencers, and social media platforms (Balaban, Szambolics & Chirică, 2022) can facilitate this interaction by providing students with access to influencers and virtual mentors. Incorporating parasocial interaction for entrepreneurship in distance learning can provide students with practical insights and inspiration from successful entrepreneurs/influencers. By using a combination of virtual lecture or sharing session, recorded interviews, case studies, virtual conferences and events, mentorship programs, and entrepreneurship competitions, students can learn from the experiences of successful entrepreneurs and apply these insights to their own entrepreneurial ventures.

Therefore, in this book chapter, the authors will explore how virtual mentors can inspire and motivate students in the scope of distance learning in entrepreneurship education, the challenges faced, and offer suggestions on how entrepreneurship education can facilitate distance learning with a focus on parasocial interaction and virtual mentors. With these suggestions, the authors aim to provide insights to the education industry, policy-makers, virtual mentors and trainers to incorporate parasocial syllabus into their curriculum for distance learning.

2.1 The Impact of Virtual Mentors in Inspiring and Motivating Students for Entrepreneurship

The advantages of virtual mentors have been established and explained in the beginning of the chapter. However, the question remains on how virtual mentors can inspire and motivate students, fostering their entrepreneurial mindset and confidence? To answer this question, we explored past literature and discuss as below.

One of the ways for virtual mentors to inspire students is by sharing first-hand stories on their entrepreneurial journey. By highlighting their successes and achievements, virtual mentors provide confidence and inspiration that entrepreneurship is attainable and that students can also achieve success if they have the right discipline and mind-set. On the flipside, sharing failure stories can be highly inspiring and valuable for entrepreneur students (Alvarado Valenzuela et al., 2020). In fact, it is found that failure stories have more long-lasting impact than successful stories (Lattacher & Wdowiak, 2020; Zhou Mao & Tang, 2020). This is because sharing failed experiences instils the emotions and fear to the students which translates to learning from virtual mentors past mistakes. By understanding what went wrong and the resulting consequences, students can navigate from making a similar occurrence in their venture. Such stories also provide realization to students on the reality of being an entrepreneur and the resilience and determination required to overcome obstacles and continue pursuing their goals (Liu, Ma & Li, 2019). Additionally, failures or stories on challenges create a sense of bond and support system among aspiring and young entrepreneurs by sharing mistakes and bad experiences (Gibbs et al., 2018). This allows students in finding comfort and support in knowing that they are not alone in facing failures and setbacks. Having this safe space and environment help in motivating and encouraging them not to give up and to look at those obstacles as opportunities. As such, both successful and failure stories serve as powerful motivators, inspiring students to pursue their entrepreneurial endeavors and providing them with a roadmap for their paths to success.

Moreover, the emergence of virtual mentors has been identified to serve as a strong role model for students (Ouvrein et al., 2021). Typically, individuals would portray a similar characteristics, traits, values and culture when they are inspired and have a deep sentiment and intimacy with their role model (Abbasianchavari & Moritz, 2021). By observing the mentors' behavior, decision-making processes, and approaches to challenges, students gain valuable insights into what it takes to succeed as an entrepreneur – which subsequently translate into students actual thinking or entrepreneurial behavior.

Furthermore, by having virtual mentors from a specific industry, they could offer guidance and advice customized to the precise needs of students (Li, 2019). The relevant strategies, resources, and tools will facilitate students in overcoming the challenges and uncertainties of entrepreneurship. This guidance and mentorship instil a sense of preparedness and confidence in students, empowering them to tackle entrepreneurial challenges with resilience and determination (Badwan, Tamvada & Rentocchini, 2022). To introduce such concept, virtual mentors that present real-world challenges could develop the students problem-solving skills by getting the students to think critically and creatively to generate potential solutions. Mentors may ask probing questions, offer alternative perspectives, and encourage mentees to consider different approaches. Students will be trained in becoming more adept at finding innovative solutions to challenges they may encounter in their entrepreneurial endeavors.

When it comes to entrepreneurial education, the ability to network has always been emphasised in the past (Klyver & Arenius, 2022; Turkina, 2018). However, networking involves costs and it can be nerve-wrecking for those who are a novice (Brand, Croonen & Leenders, 2018; Casale et al., 2022). Most networking platforms are mainly those established business owners, which many aspiring or new entrepreneurs would have the fear, lack of self-esteem or feel demotivated to partake (Ahmadi & Soga, 2022). Therefore, virtual mentors could facilitate the development of networking skills, which are crucial to boost aspiring entrepreneurs' confidence and success. One way is to establish network opportunities catering specifically to aspiring entrepreneurs. Mentors could leverage their own networks and connections to introduce mentees to industry professionals, potential collaborators, or mentors in specific domains. By providing networking opportunities, mentors help mentees expand their professional contacts, build relationships, and access resources that can support their entrepreneurial journey. This would ease the fear among new and potential entrepreneurs since the network event is tailored to a specific group. Mentors may also offer guidance on effective networking strategies, such as attending events, leveraging online platforms, and nurturing meaningful connections. Through these experiences and mentorship, mentees develop networking skills that are essential for business growth, partnership opportunities, and accessing valuable resources.

This chapter highlights the role of virtual mentors in fostering students' entrepreneurial mindset and confidence in the context of distance learning entrepreneurship education. In brief, virtual mentors serve as catalysts for the development of critical entrepreneurial skills. They serve an important role in inspiring, motivating, and fostering students' entrepreneurial mindset and confidence (Memon et al., 2015). Guided by their vast experiences, stories, and guidance lead to contribution to the holistic development of aspiring entrepreneurs. This creates a supportive and empowering environment for their growth and success in entrepreneurship. Integrating these skills are integral to a successful and confident entrepreneur, as the students learn about handling challenges, making informed choices, and have a platform to make new connections for business sustainability and development (Nabi, Walmsley & Akhtar, 2021). The mentor's guidance and support play a pivotal role in nurturing these skills, equipping mentees with the tools they need to thrive in the entrepreneurial landscape.

2.2 Implementing Virtual Mentorship as a Co-Curriculum for Entrepreneurship Distance Learning

Past studies have shown that individuals with aspirations to become entrepreneurs are more likely to engage in parasocial behavior (Abbasianchavari & Moritz, 2021; Guinez-Cabrera & Aqueveque, 2021; Rudeloff & Damms, 2022). Entrepreneurship often involves taking risks, making tough decisions, and dealing with high levels of stress and uncertainty where these factors often lead to feelings of loneliness and a need for emotional support (Zhu et al., 2023). Due to that, aspiring entrepreneurs would turn to their role models for inspiration, usually with those they have established a parasocial relationship. Integrating virtual mentors into distance learning programs for entrepreneurial education requires several practical and considerations in ensuring a seamless and effective mentorship experience. The authors developed a few key practices as below:

2.2.1 Mentor Selection

Selection of mentors is not as easy as it sounds. Mentor selection is the first and crucial step in ensuring effective distance learning. Schools need to carefully select virtual mentors who possess relevant expertise and experience in entrepreneurship for the program (Brodie, Van Saane & Osowska, 2017; Gulbahar & Kalelioglu, 2015). Additionally, engaging with their contents will help the school to have an idea the industries the mentors are in and what kind of knowledge and sharing they can provide to the students. Generally, these mentors should have a successful track record in starting and scaling businesses. Having a deep understanding of the entrepreneurial process as well as the ability to explain on those processes in with clarity and comprehension would provide an effective delivery of the learning objective. Within the parasocial theory, since this relationship is not double-sided, the mentors are completely unaware of the students. This means they could not reciprocate with the students at the same time. However, to make distance learning effective, the institution could consider reaching out to the virtual mentors to provide an hour or two online lectures or podcasts for the program where students can listen or view the recording on their own pace and convenience (Johnston, Rockhill & Pastore, 2021). It is also important to consider that the mentors have the passion for virtual mentorship and possess effective communication and coaching skills.

2.2.2 Matching Mentors With Mentees

Upon the selection of suitable and interested mentors, the process of matching them with mentees begins. To ensure the right mentor-mentee fit, there are a few considerations that should be addressed. Those are the specific needs, goals, and interests of the mentees. Mentors with expertise in the students' areas of interest or industries as well as backgrounds, experiences, or entrepreneurial aspirations can also contribute to a stronger mentorship connection (Kern, Harrison, Custer & Mehta, 2019). As such, a well-aligned mentorship can foster effective learning, support and guidance.

2.2.3 Clear Communication Channels

Technology has advanced in many different forms. To ensure effective virtual mentoring via parasocial relationship, clear guidelines should be provided regarding the preferred communication channel (Kowert & Daniel, 2021; McLaughlin & Wohn, 2021) (e.g., Podcast, livestreaming, interview sessions, online lecture, webinar etc). Additionally, the virtual mentors could provide a summative or formative activities that can enhance the learning experience. For instance, the mentors could provide the mentees with relevant readings, case studies, or assignments to deepen their understanding of entrepreneurship. Depending on the module, this activity can be done in a group to encourage collaboration, knowledge sharing, and peer-to-peer learning. These activities foster engagement, provide practical insights, and stimulate critical thinking among mentees of a similar interest.

2.2.4 Goal Setting and Action Plans

While virtual mentors can only be present to a certain extent, the school needs to shift the paradigm of their teaching and students learning by setting meaningful goals and developing actionable plans. Upon the virtual mentor sessions, the program can be designed in to help mentees identify their strengths, weaknesses, and goal-setting and milestones they wish to achieve (Tinoco-Giraldo et al., 2020). Together, they can develop action plans with clear steps, timelines, and measurable outcomes. Regular check-ins and progress reviews from the instructors can help students stay focused and track their development throughout the learning journey.

2.2.5 Support and Guidance

Despite on the mentor unawareness of the specific individual, the mentors can still provide support and guidance to their students. For instance, sharing personal experiences, stories, or provide empathetic responses to their students's challenges and emotions via replying to their comments in the social platforms that they use to disseminate their content. Reaching out to the individuals will make them feel understood and less alone in their struggles. Another form of support is through inspiring the students. By sharing their journey, achievements, and lessons learned, virtual mentors can inspire their students and provide guidance on overcoming obstacles, pursuing goals, and embracing personal development (Prastyaningtyas et al., 2023; Secundo et al., 2021). Virtual mentors can provide educational resources, tips, and recommendations to empower their students for related content such as online presence, effective marketing, green behaviour, finances and as such (Carpenter, Shelton & Schroeder, 2022; Chwialkowska, 2019; Gil-Quintana & Vida de León, 2021; Secundo et al., 2021). Another take is on virtual mentors fostering a sense of community among their students by utilizing social media platforms like Twitter, Facebook groups, or Twitch communities to create spaces where their students can engage with one another (Blight, Ruppel & Schoenbauer, 2017; Sherrick et al., 2023). They can encourage discussions, ask questions, and facilitate connections between individuals who share common interests or goals. For instance, they could create an online community where students with different skills and expertise come together to share their knowledge. This allows the students to offer tutorials, workshops, or webinars on various topics, allowing others to learn new skills or enhance existing ones which create a sense of togetherness.

Virtual mentors can also consider organizing live events or webinars where their students can come together virtually. These events can include Q&A sessions, panel discussions, or workshops, allowing participants to interact with both the mentor and fellow students. It provides an opportunity for individuals to network, share experiences, and learn from each other. For example, an industry expert can host a live webinar on entrepreneurship, featuring guest speakers and interactive sessions to encourage students' engagement. Virtual mentors can initiate collaborative projects that involve the students. This could be a community-driven charity campaign, a crowd-sourced project, or business idea competitions. By involving their students in these activities, mentors encourage collaboration and provide a platform for students to connect and support one another.

2.2.6 Evaluation and Feedback

To measure the effectiveness of such learning delivery, it is important to listen to the students' opinion and views. End of the virtual mentor session, students need to provide evaluation and feedback to understand the effectiveness of virtual mentorship adoption in entrepreneurial education. Prior to that, students need to understand the concept of virtual mentorship and its potential benefits in their entrepreneurial journey. By explaining how virtual mentorship can provide unique learning opportunities, students would be able to see its relevance and the long-term benefits. Additionally, emphasizing the value of student feedback is crucial as they need to be made aware that their perspectives and insights are essential in shaping and improving the educational experience (Yukawa et al., 2020). By highlighting how their feedback helps in contributing to the program's development and refinement – specifically in the implementation of virtual mentorship, students will be motivated to participate actively and communicate transparently in the surveys or interviews (Hoel & Dahl, 2019). A well-designed survey with targeted questions (Hoel & Dahl, 2019) or conducting one-on-one interviews enable students to express their opinions, experiences, expectations, and concerns related to virtual mentorship. Open-ended questions are able to capture detailed feedback, ask follow-up questions for clarification and elaboration. Focus groups can also be an effective way to gather student input collectively pertaining to the advantages, limitations, and potential areas of improvement of virtual mentorship. Ultimately, ensuring that the evaluation is done in a safe, respectful and inclusive environment where all voices are heard ensures that students feel comfortable expressing their opinions and provides a platform for collaborative brainstorming and idea-sharing. By involving students in the evaluation and feedback process for the adoption of virtual mentorship in entrepreneurial education, their insights and perspectives can facilitate in shaping the program to better meet their needs. This collaborative approach not only empowers students but also fosters a sense of ownership and investment in their own educational journey, leading to a more effective and impactful entrepreneurial education experience.

2.27 Outcome Assessments on Virtual Mentoring

After the evaluation and feedback phase, it is also important to identify the differences in the outcomes. The differences in the outcomes lie on the students' behaviour, problem-solving, decision-making, networking, leadership skill and as such. The assessment criteria need to reflect the desired learning outcomes. Additionally, the criteria should be measurable and observable, allowing for objective evaluation (Chatterjee & Corral, 2017). To have a clearer picture, the school can conduct pre- and post-assessments to measure students' progress and growth throughout the entrepreneurial education program (Tiven et al., 2018). The pre-assessment establishes a reference point of students' skills and knowledge prior to the virtual mentorship, while the post-assessment evaluates the outcomes after exposure to virtual mentorship. In return, the comparison provides valuable insights and judgements into the impact of virtual mentorship on students' development. In addition to surveys, observations on the changes in the entrepreneurial behaviour could be another form of outcome assessment.

3.0 ADDRESSING CHALLENGES IN VIRTUAL MENTORSHIP

Although the benefits of virtual mentorship have been discussed, the downfalls and ethical considerations on this style of learning delivery in distance learning need to be considered. The challenges in virtual mentorship are discussed below, followed by how institutions can overcome and address these challenges.

3.1 Lack of Personal Connection and Building Trust

It is always a challenge when it comes to establishing a deep personal connection with the students in virtual platforms. The absence of physical proximity and face-to-face interactions makes it harder to build trust and rapport (Lall, Chen & Mason, 2022). Establishing trust is crucial for a productive parasocial and virtual mentor-mentee relationship. Gaining the credibility and confidence of the students may require additional efforts since there the relationship between mentor and mentee is parasocial (Lou & Kim, 2019). To do so, the mentor needs to ensure authenticity by being genuine in their interactions. Additionally, by showing vulnerability and sharing weaknesses, the mentor creates a sense of authenticity that resonates with the students. The mentor should also come with a good background and expertise pertaining to the entrepreneurial field. People tend to believe people with a set of experience rather than a person with no prior experience. This can be done by sharing practical tips, market trends, and showcasing their venture would demonstrate the mentor's competence and authority. This helps build trust in the mentor's abilities. Additionally, if the mentors choose to upload their contents on social media or other online platforms, being responsive and practicing active listening to the students' queries, thoughts, feelings and experiences would show that the mentor genuinely care about their progress and success (Niu et al., 2023; Penttinen, Ciuchita & Čaić, 2022)

3.2 Ensuring Mentor Availability

Ensuring and setting the mentor's time availability is a common challenge in virtual mentorship programs. In general, mentors may have busy schedules, as they could be an entrepreneurs' themselves or influencers which make it difficult for them to allocate sufficient time for mentoring activities. To address this, mentor selection should consider the availability and commitment of mentors. To encourage the mentors participation, the school can establish a mentoring schedule with dedicated time slots for mentor-mentee interactions. Furthermore, mentors can be encouraged to suggest individuals from their network to serve as virtual mentors. Additionally, alumni who have become successful entrepreneurs could be given the opportunity to contribute as mentors as well (Kurian & Nair, 2023).

3.3 Difficulty Tailoring Advice to Individual Situations

As mentioned as one of the advantages, having a specific virtual mentor helps in customizing advices and exposures to students. However, with diverse group of students with varying entrepreneurial goals and challenges, providing personalized advice and guidance can be challenging especially when there is no direct interaction or in-depth understanding of each individual's circumstances. The struggle here is on finding an equilibrium between general advice and addressing specific situations.

3.4 Ethical Considerations and Maintaining Professional Boundaries

In a parasocial relationship, the students might develop a connection with mentors especially when the mentors are perceived to be a role model. It is therefore, important to maintain appropriate professional boundaries to maintain the integrity of the relationship, avoid exploiting or taking advantage of the parasocial relationship for personal gain (Aravind, Krishnaram & Thasneem, 2012; Burns, 2019). Expert entrepreneurs and mentors must be mindful of the potential for manipulation or exploitation of their students' emotional connections, vulnerabilities, financial resources, or intellectual property. To maintain an ethical and healthy relationship with the mentees, it is essential to demonstrate transparency and authenticity of the mentors' background (Jiang & Luo, 2018). The mentors selected should have the passion in giving back to the society, offer guidance and support without seeking personal gain at their expense. By implementing these solutions and best practices, the challenges associated with virtual mentorship in distance learning can be effectively addressed. With a well-structured and supportive mentorship framework, students can receive the guidance and support they need to develop their entrepreneurial skills and succeed in their entrepreneurial endeavors (Burns, 2019).

4.0 SIGNIFICANCE OF THE CHAPTER

The theoretical and practical significance of the chapter exploring the integration of parasocial interaction and virtual mentors into distance learning for entrepreneurship education is as discussed below.

4.1 Theoretical Significance

The chapter contributes to the theoretical understanding of entrepreneurship education in the context of distance learning. The study of parasocial interaction and virtual mentoring on its own, have been done in the past. However, the integration of parasocial interaction and virtual mentors have been under-studied or discussed. Past studies have looked into a similar concept (e.g., e-mentoring, online mentoring, mentorship) towards education. However, when it comes to distance learning, a different approach to mentoring needs to be conducted. This is because distance learning in itself poses challenges such as lack of physical interaction, trust, distractions and such. Thus, by leveraging on parasocial interaction in distance learning, students will form a strong connections and respect to the virtual mentors; whom they see as a role model. By proposing this integration, these elements could enhance the learning experience and provide practical insights to students. This contributes to enriching the theoretical foundations of entrepreneurship education. To add, this will open up to more nuances towards the theoretical understanding of this phenomenon beyond its traditional applications in media and entertainment. Additionally, the exploration of virtual mentoring within the scope of parasocial interaction can be leveraged to foster entrepreneurial success and provides insights into the potential benefits and challenges of incorporating parasocial interaction into distance learning. This chapter also contributes to the theory of parasocial by looking it in the lens of distance learning and virtual mentorship. By incorporating virtual mentors who are experienced entrepreneurs and industry experts, it provides students with real-world insights and practical knowledge. This integration enhances the theoretical foundations of entrepreneurship education by connecting academic concepts with practical applications.

4.2 Practical Significance

This chapter aims to contribute to practical significance in the education industry – in particularly on entrepreneurship which has been gaining a lot of attention due to its contribution towards the individual, society and country. However, lack of recommendations has been discussed in the scope of distance learning. To reduce this gap, this chapter endeavours to enhance distance learning in entrepreneurship education by offering practical suggestions via integrating parasocial interaction and virtual mentors. It provides educators, mentors and institutions with actionable strategies to create engaging and interactive online learning experiences for students, enabling them to develop the skills and mindset necessary for entrepreneurial success.

By diving into how expertise and entrepreneurs from other parts of the world can inspire students, this chapter provides suggestion on leveraging the diverse expertise using online platforms. The incorporation of virtual mentors through parasocial interaction expands students' access to diverse expertise from successful entrepreneurs and industry professionals. This exposure to different perspectives and experiences can broaden students' understanding of entrepreneurship and provide them with valuable insights into various industries and markets.

Subsequently, having a myriad of expertise as a virtual mentor in place, this would enable networking opportunities for students. Virtual mentors can connect students with other entrepreneurs, industry professionals, and like-minded peers, facilitating the exchange of ideas, collaborations, and potential partnerships. This networking aspect could contribute to students' future entrepreneurial endeavors.

Ultimately, the chapter's insights aim to bring positive changes into the educational practices in entrepreneurship programs, curriculum development, and instructional design for distance learning. Educators and institutions can deliberate from the proposed strategies and considerations to design and deliver effective online entrepreneurship courses that leverage the power of parasocial interaction and virtual mentors.

5.0 LIMITATIONS AND FUTURE SUGGESTIONS

This chapter has limitations which future studies can aim to address. Firstly, is on the generalizability. The chapter focuses generally on distance learning in the context of entrepreneurship education and the integration of parasocial interaction and virtual mentors. Hence, the suggestions may not be directly applicable to specific countries or educational settings. Further research is needed to explore the effectiveness of parasocial interaction and virtual mentors in different cultural and educational contexts.

While the chapter discusses the potential benefits of parasocial interaction and virtual mentors in entrepreneurship education, it relies heavily on theoretical perspectives and evidence from past literatures. To encourage new insights in enhancing entrepreneurial success in a distance learning environment, future studies can consider collecting quantitative (survey) or qualitative data (interviews, focus group discussions etc.).

Another limitation is on technical and internet access in certain areas. Distance learning relies heavily on technology infrastructure and internet connectivity. As such, without understanding the technical situation of certain areas, the suggestions might not be suitable. Future studies could extensively examine and discuss the technical challenges and limitations that students and institutions may face in implementing distance learning and incorporating parasocial interaction as well as identifying the strategies to overcome potential barriers.

Additionally, future studies could consider comparing different countries effectiveness to parasocial interaction and virtual mentoring in entrepreneurship education. Subsequently, the study could explore on the best practices of the countries which provide insights into the most effective methods for integrating parasocial interaction and virtual mentors into distance learning programs.

By addressing these limitations and pursuing these future suggestions, researchers and educators can further enhance the understanding and implementation of parasocial interaction and virtual mentors in entrepreneurship education within the distance learning context.

6.0 CONCLUSION

This chapter reviews the potential of leveraging parasocial interaction through virtual mentors in entrepreneurial education. It highlights how distance learning facilitate by virtual mentorship, can provide students with valuable guidance, support, and real-world insights from experienced mentors. By establishing a sense of connection and rapport with virtual mentors, students can benefit from the mentor's expertise, industry background, and mentoring skills.

Distance learning is receiving more importance due to its significant role in expanding access to entrepreneurial education. This learning delivery provides flexible learning opportunities and enables individuals to acquire entrepreneurial knowledge and skills at their own pace. It breaks down geographical barriers and allows students from diverse backgrounds to participate in entrepreneurship programs. This accessibility fosters innovation and economic growth by nurturing a diverse pool of aspiring entrepreneurs who can contribute to the development of new ideas, products, and services with the guidance of respective mentors.

Additionally, the engagement of virtual mentorship in distance learning programs offers several advantages. By incorporating various strategies such as online discussions, collaborative projects, virtual workshops, and gamification elements, this creates engaging and interactive learning experiences for students. In response, students would actively participate, exchange ideas, and develop critical entrepreneurial skills such as decision-making, problem-solving, and networking.

The chapter also touched on the psychological aspects of parasocial interaction between students and virtual mentors on how connections can be built in a virtual setting. leading to meaningful and impactful mentorship relationships. Furthermore, it has been discussed on the role of technological advancements in enhancing the effectiveness and convenience of virtual mentorship, enabling seamless communication and collaboration between mentors and students.

All in all, the potential of leveraging parasocial interaction through virtual mentors in entrepreneurial education is immense. Distance learning has expanded access to entrepreneurial education, fostering innovation and economic growth. Therefore, it is encouraged for the education industry to explore and embrace virtual mentorship as a valuable approach in distance learning programs. By leveraging technology, meaningful connections can be nurtured between students and virtual mentors, as well as the best practices can be implemented. By doing so, this will cultivate engaging environment, interactive, and impactful learning experiences that empower aspiring entrepreneurs to thrive in the distance learning setting.

REFERENCES

Abbasianchavari, A., & Moritz, A. (2021). The impact of role models on entrepreneurial intentions and behavior: A review of the literature. *Management Review Quarterly*, *71*(1), 1–40. doi:10.100711301-019-00179-0

Abdellatif, S., Shomotova, A., Trabelsi, S., Husain, S., Alsalhi, N., & Eltahir, M. (2023). Transition to Distance Learning: Student Experience and Communication during the COVID-19 Pandemic in the United Arab Emirates. *Sustainability (Basel)*, *15*(8), 6456. doi:10.3390u15086456

Ahmadi, A., & Soga, L. R. (2022). To be or not to be: Latent entrepreneurship, the networked agent, and the fear factor. *Technological Forecasting and Social Change*, *174*, 121281. doi:10.1016/j.techfore.2021.121281

Al-Mawee, W., Kwayu, K. M., & Gharaibeh, T. (2021). Student's perspective on DL during COVID-19 pandemic: A case study of Western Michigan University, United States. *International Journal of Educational Research Open*, *2*, 100080. doi:10.1016/j.ijedro.2021.100080 PMID:35059670

Alvarado Valenzuela, J. F., Wakkee, I., Martens, J., & Grijsbach, P. (2020). Lessons from entrepreneurial failure through vicarious learning. *Journal of Small Business and Entrepreneurship*, 1–25.

Andersen, C. L., & West, R. E. (2021). We Overwhelm Them with Hope": How Online Mentors Can Support Online Learners. *Online Learning : the Official Journal of the Online Learning Consortium*, *25*(4), 388–415. doi:10.24059/olj.v25i4.2440

Aravind, V. K., Krishnaram, V. D., & Thasneem, Z. (2012). Boundary crossings and violations in clinical settings. *Indian Journal of Psychological Medicine*, *34*(1), 21–24. doi:10.4103/0253-7176.96151 PMID:22661802

Aw, E. C. X., & Labrecque, L. I. (2020). Celebrity endorsement in social media contexts: Understanding the role of parasocial interactions and the need to belong. *Journal of Consumer Marketing*, *37*(7), 895–908. doi:10.1108/JCM-10-2019-3474

Aw, E. C. X., Tan, G. W. H., Chuah, S. H. W., Ooi, K. B., & Hajli, N. (2022). Be my friend! Cultivating parasocial relationships with social media influencers: Findings from PLS-SEM and fsQCA. *Information Technology & People*.

Babatunde, S., & El-Gohary, H. (2019). Necessity of mentoring in entrepreneurship education: Reflection by practitioners. *Journal of Professional Issues in Engineering Education and Practice*, *145*(1), 02518007. doi:10.1061/(ASCE)EI.1943-5541.0000399

Badwan, A. R., Tamvada, J. P., & Rentocchini, F. (2022). Evaluating mentorship-based learning in entrepreneurship education. *International Review of Entrepreneurship*, *20*, 69–86.

Balaban, D. C., Szambolics, J., & Chirică, M. (2022). Parasocial relations and social media influencers' persuasive power. Exploring the moderating role of product involvement. *Acta Psychologica, 230*, 103731. doi:10.1016/j.actpsy.2022.103731 PMID:36057200

Bashir, F., & Warraich, N. F. (2023). Systematic literature review of Semantic Web for distance learning. *Interactive Learning Environments, 31*(1), 527–543. doi:10.1080/10494820.2020.1799023

Blight, M. G., Ruppel, E. K., & Schoenbauer, K. V. (2017). Sense of community on Twitter and Instagram: Exploring the roles of motives and parasocial relationships. *Cyberpsychology, Behavior, and Social Networking, 20*(5), 314–319. doi:10.1089/cyber.2016.0505 PMID:28498041

Brand, M. J., Croonen, E. P., & Leenders, R. T. (2018). Entrepreneurial networking: A blessing or a curse? Differential effects for low, medium and high performing franchisees. *Small Business Economics, 50*(4), 783–805. doi:10.100711187-017-9895-1

Brestovanský, M., & Sekerešová, D. (2022). Parasocial Interaction Does Not Function as a Relationship Mediator between the Influencer's Online Content and the Adolescent's Prosocial Moral Reasoning and Behaviour. *Communication Today, 13*(1).

Briscoe, P. (2019). Virtual mentor partnerships between practising and preservice teachers: Helping to enhance professional growth and well-being. *International Journal of Mentoring and Coaching in Education, 8*(4), 235–254. doi:10.1108/IJMCE-02-2019-0023

Brodie, J., Van Saane, S. H., & Osowska, R. (2017). Help wanted: Exploring the value of entrepreneurial mentoring at start-up. *Industry and Higher Education, 31*(2), 122–131. doi:10.1177/0950422217691666

Burns, S. T. (2019). Students' ethical decision-making when considering boundary crossings with counselor educators. *Counseling and Values, 64*(1), 53–71. doi:10.1002/cvj.12094

Carpenter, J. P., Shelton, C. C., & Schroeder, S. E. (2022). The education influencer: A new player in the educator professional landscape. *Journal of Research on Technology in Education*, 1–16. doi:10.1080/15391523.2022.2119452

Casale, S., Akbari, M., Bocci Benucci, S., Seydavi, M., & Fioravanti, G. (2022). Interpersonally-Based Fears and Problematic Social Networking Site Use: The Moderating Role of Online Social Support. *International Journal of Mental Health and Addiction*, 1–13. doi:10.100711469-022-00908-9

Chatterjee, D., & Corral, J. (2017). How to write well-defined learning objectives. *The Journal of Education in Perioperative Medicine : JEPM*, *19*(4). PMID:29766034

Chwialkowska, A. (2019). How sustainability influencers drive green lifestyle adoption on social media: The process of green lifestyle adoption explained through the lenses of the minority influence model and social learning theory. *Management of Sustainable Development*, *11*(1), 33–42.

Dutton, H., Bullen, P., & Deane, K. L. (2019). "It is OK to let them know you are human too": Mentor self-disclosure in formal youth mentoring relationships. *Journal of Community Psychology*, *47*(4), 943–963. doi:10.1002/jcop.22165 PMID:30714171

Dwivedi, Y. K., Ismagilova, E., Hughes, D. L., Carlson, J., Filieri, R., Jacobson, J., Jain, V., Karjaluoto, H., Kefi, H., Krishen, A. S., Kumar, V., Rahman, M. M., Raman, R., Rauschnabel, P. A., Rowley, J., Salo, J., Tran, G. A., & Wang, Y. (2021). Setting the future of digital and social media marketing research: Perspectives and research propositions. *International Journal of Information Management*, *59*, 102168. doi:10.1016/j.ijinfomgt.2020.102168

Fernández-Díaz, J. R., Gutiérrez-Ortega, M., Llamas-Salguero, F., & Cantón-Mayo, I. (2021). Creativity and resilience as predictors of career success. *Sustainability (Basel)*, *13*(8), 4489. doi:10.3390u13084489

Frentzel-Beyme, L., Holtze, M., Szczuka, J. M., & Krämer, N. C. (2022). Posting from the Past-A Longitudinal Study of the Potentials of Parasocial Interaction with a Historical Figure for History Education.

Gerard, L., Bradford, A., & Linn, M. C. (2022). Supporting Teachers to Customize Curriculum for Self-Directed Learning. *Journal of Science Education and Technology*, *31*(5), 660–679. doi:10.100710956-022-09985-w

Gibbs, S., Singh, R. P., Butler, J. S., & Scott, C. (2018). *The role of networking, entrepreneurial environments, and support systems in the creation, survival and success of ventures founded by minority, women, and immigrant entrepreneurs*. New England Journal of Entrepreneurship. doi:10.1108/NEJE-10-2018-018

Gil-Quintana, J., & Vida de León, E. (2021). Educational influencers on instagram: Analysis of educational channels, audiences, and economic performance. *Publications / MDPI*, *9*(4), 43. doi:10.3390/publications9040043

Guinez-Cabrera, N., & Aqueveque, C. (2021). Entrepreneurial influencers and influential entrepreneurs: Two sides of the same coin. *International Journal of Entrepreneurial Behaviour & Research, 28*(1), 231–254. doi:10.1108/IJEBR-08-2020-0563

Gulbahar, Y., & Kalelioglu, F. (2015). Competencies for e-Instructors: How to qualify and guarantee sustainability. *Contemporary Educational Technology, 6*(2), 140–154.

Gurcan, F., & Cagiltay, N. E. (2023). Research trends on distance learning: A text mining-based literature review from 2008 to 2018. *Interactive Learning Environments, 31*(2), 1007–1028. doi:10.1080/10494820.2020.1815795

Heidari, E., Mehrvarz, M., Marzooghi, R., & Stoyanov, S. (2021). The role of digital informal learning in the relationship between students' digital competence and academic engagement during the COVID-19 pandemic. *Journal of Computer Assisted Learning, 37*(4), 1154–1166. doi:10.1111/jcal.12553 PMID:34230741

Hoel, A., & Dahl, T. I. (2019). Why bother? Student motivation to participate in student evaluations of teaching. *Assessment & Evaluation in Higher Education, 44*(3), 361–378. https://books.google.com.my/books?hl=en&lr=&id=r7UwEAAAQBAJ&oi=fnd&pg=PA87&ots=64I7nkx6U9&sig=IykWo_0CLJRq6QUih_jjv2GZCHs&redir_esc=y#v=onepage&q=para&f=false. doi:10.1080/02602938.2018.1511969

Hu, B., Zheng, Q., Wu, J., Tang, Z., Zhu, J., Wu, S., & Ling, Y. (2021). Role of Education and Mentorship in Entrepreneurial Behavior: Mediating Role of Self-Efficacy. *Frontiers in Psychology, 12*, 5042. doi:10.3389/fpsyg.2021.775227 PMID:34917001

Iqbal, H. (2020). E-mentoring: an effective platform for distance learning. *e-mentor. Czasopismo naukowe Szkoły Głównej Handlowej w Warszawie, 84*(2), 54-61.

Jarzyna, C. L. (2021). Parasocial interaction, the COVID-19 quarantine, and digital age media. *Human Arenas, 4*(3), 413–429. doi:10.100742087-020-00156-0

Jiang, H., & Luo, Y. (2018). Crafting employee trust: From authenticity, transparency to engagement. *Journal of Communication Management (London), 22*(2), 138–160. doi:10.1108/JCOM-07-2016-0055

John, S. P., Walford, R., & Purayidathil, J. (2022). Factors affecting the adoption of social media in marketing of higher education: An empirical analysis. *FIIB Business Review, 11*(4), 422–437. doi:10.1177/23197145211072198

Johnston, D., Rockhill, C., & Pastore, D. (2021). The effectiveness of podcasts in sport management education part two: A qualitative analysis. *Journal of Hospitality, Leisure, Sport and Tourism Education*, *29*, 100338. doi:10.1016/j.jhlste.2021.100338

Kaufman, M. R., Wright, K., Simon, J., Edwards, G., Thrul, J., & DuBois, D. L. (2022). Mentoring in the time of COVID-19: An analysis of online focus groups with mentors to youth. *American Journal of Community Psychology*, *69*(1-2), 33–45. doi:10.1002/ajcp.12543 PMID:34318506

Kern, L., Harrison, J. R., Custer, B. E., & Mehta, P. D. (2019). Factors that enhance the quality of relationships between mentors and mentees during Check & Connect. *Behavioral Disorders*, *44*(3), 148–161. doi:10.1177/0198742918779791

Kim, J., Kim, J., & Yang, H. (2019). Loneliness and the use of social media to follow celebrities: A moderating role of social presence. *The Social Science Journal*, *56*(1), 21–29. doi:10.1016/j.soscij.2018.12.007

Kim, J., & Kim, M. (2022). Rise of Social Media Influencers as a New Marketing Channel: Focusing on the Roles of Psychological Well-Being and Perceived Social Responsibility among Consumers. *International Journal of Environmental Research and Public Health*, *19*(4), 2362. doi:10.3390/ijerph19042362 PMID:35206553

Klyver, K., & Arenius, P. (2022). Networking, social skills and launching a new business: A 3-year study of nascent entrepreneurs. *Entrepreneurship Theory and Practice*, *46*(5), 1256–1283. doi:10.1177/1042258720967063

Kowert, R., & Daniel, E. Jr. (2021). The one-and-a-half sided parasocial relationship: The curious case of live streaming. *Computers in Human Behavior Reports*, *4*, 100150. doi:10.1016/j.chbr.2021.100150

Kowert, R., & Daniel, E. Jr. (2021). The one-and-a-half sided parasocial relationship: The curious case of live streaming. *Computers in Human Behavior Reports*, *4*, 100150. doi:10.1016/j.chbr.2021.100150

Kurian, P. S., & Nair, S. S. K. (2023). Alumni mentoring: An approach to build community of learners. In *SHS Web of Conferences* (*Vol. 156*, p. 08003). EDP Sciences.

Lall, S. A., Chen, L. W., & Mason, D. P. (2022). Digital platforms and entrepreneurial support: A field experiment in online mentoring. *Small Business Economics*, 1–24.

Larose, S., Tarabulsy, G. M., Boisclair-Châteauvert, G., & Karcher, M. (2019). When insecure attachment dispositions affect mentoring relationship quality: An exploration of interactive mentoring contexts. *Journal of Relationships Research*, *10*, e6. doi:10.1017/jrr.2019.1

Lattacher, W., & Wdowiak, M. A. (2020). Entrepreneurial learning from failure. A systematic review. *International Journal of Entrepreneurial Behaviour & Research*, *26*(5), 1093–1131. doi:10.1108/IJEBR-02-2019-0085

Li, C. T. (2019). Mentor-spotting: Recommending expert mentors to mentees for live trouble-shooting in Codementor. *Knowledge and Information Systems*, *61*(2), 799–820. doi:10.100710115-018-1298-3

Liebers, N., & Schramm, H. (2019). Parasocial interactions and relationships with media characters–an inventory of 60 years of research. *Communication Research Trends*, *38*(2), 4–31.

Lim, J. S., Choe, M. J., Zhang, J., & Noh, G. Y. (2020). The role of wishful identification, emotional engagement, and parasocial relationships in repeated viewing of live-streaming games: A social cognitive theory perspective. *Computers in Human Behavior*, *108*, 106327. doi:10.1016/j.chb.2020.106327

Liu, F., Ma, J., & Li, R. (2019). Which role model is more effective in entrepreneurship education? An investigation of storytelling on individual's entrepreneurial intention. *Frontiers in Psychology*, *10*, 837. doi:10.3389/fpsyg.2019.00837 PMID:31068853

Lock, J., & Redmond, P. (2021). Embedded experts in online collaborative learning: A case study. *The Internet and Higher Education*, *48*, 100773. doi:10.1016/j.iheduc.2020.100773

Lou, C., & Kim, H. K. (2019). Fancying the new rich and famous? Explicating the roles of influencer content, credibility, and parental mediation in adolescents' parasocial relationship, materialism, and purchase intentions. *Frontiers in Psychology*, *10*, 2567. doi:10.3389/fpsyg.2019.02567 PMID:31803110

McLaughlin, C., & Wohn, D. Y. (2021). Predictors of parasocial interaction and relationships in live streaming. *Convergence (London)*, *27*(6), 1714–1734. doi:10.1177/13548565211027807

McReynolds, M. R., Termini, C. M., Hinton, A. O. Jr, Taylor, B. L., Vue, Z., Huang, S. C., Roby, R. A. S., Shuler, H., & Carter, C. S. (2020). The art of virtual mentoring in the twenty-first century for STEM majors and beyond. *Nature Biotechnology*, *38*(12), 1477–1482. doi:10.103841587-020-00758-7 PMID:33273732

Memon, J., Rozan, M. Z. A., Ismail, K., Uddin, M., & Daud, D. (2015). Mentoring an entrepreneur: Guide for a mentor. *SAGE Open*, *5*(1), 2158244015569666. doi:10.1177/2158244015569666

Myers, S. (2021). Instagram source effects: The impact of familiarity and likeability on influencer outcomes. *Journal of Marketing Development and Competitiveness*, *15*(3), 50–55.

Nabi, G., Walmsley, A., & Akhtar, I. (2021). Mentoring functions and entrepreneur development in the early years of university. *Studies in Higher Education*, *46*(6), 1159–1174. doi:10.1080/03075079.2019.1665009

Ng, C. F. (2021). The Physical Learning Environment of Online Distance Learners in Higher Education – A Conceptual Model. *Frontiers in Psychology*, *12*, 635117. doi:10.3389/fpsyg.2021.635117 PMID:34650464

Niu, S., Lu, Z., Zhang, A. X., Cai, J., Griggio, C. F., & Heuer, H. (2023, April). Building Credibility, Trust, and Safety on Video-Sharing Platforms. In *Extended Abstracts of the 2023 CHI Conference on Human Factors in Computing Systems* (pp. 1-7).

Nowiński, W., & Haddoud, M. Y. (2019). The role of inspiring role models in enhancing entrepreneurial intention. *Journal of Business Research*, *96*, 183–193. doi:10.1016/j.jbusres.2018.11.005

Ouvrein, G., Pabian, S., Giles, D., Hudders, L., & De Backer, C. (2021). The web of influencers. A marketing-audience classification of (potential) social media influencers. *Journal of Marketing Management*, *37*(13-14), 1313–1342. doi:10.1080/0267257X.2021.1912142

Penttinen, V., Ciuchita, R., & Čaić, M. (2022). YouTube it before you buy it: The role of parasocial interaction in consumer-to-consumer video reviews. *Journal of Interactive Marketing*, *57*(4), 561–582. doi:10.1177/10949968221102825

Pocek, J., Politis, D., & Gabrielsson, J. (2021). Entrepreneurial learning in extra-curricular start-up programs for students. *International Journal of Entrepreneurial Behaviour & Research*, *28*(2), 325–345. doi:10.1108/IJEBR-04-2020-0206

Prastyaningtyas, E. W., Sutrisno, S., Soeprajitno, E. D., Ausat, A. M. A., & Suherlan, S. (2023). Analysing the Role of Mentors in Entrepreneurship Education: Effective Support and Assistance. *Journal of Education*, *5*(4), 14571–14577.

Ratten, V., & Jones, P. (2021). Covid-19 and entrepreneurship education: Implications for advancing research and practice. *International Journal of Management Education, 19*(1), 100432. doi:10.1016/j.ijme.2020.100432

Ratten, V., & Rashid, S. (2021). Entrepreneurship Education and digital marketing: What does the future hold? In *Developing Digital Marketing* (pp. 87–101). Emerald Publishing Limited. doi:10.1108/978-1-80071-348-220211006

Rudeloff, C., & Damms, J. (2023). Entrepreneurs as influencers: The impact of parasocial interactions on communication outcomes. *Journal of Research in Marketing and Entrepreneurship, 25*(2), 328–346. doi:10.1108/JRME-04-2022-0052

Sadeghi, M. (2019). A shift from classroom to distance learning: Advantages and limitations. *International Journal of Research in English Education, 4*(1), 80–88. doi:10.29252/ijree.4.1.80

Sarabipour, S., Hainer, S. J., Arslan, F. N., De Winde, C. M., Furlong, E., Bielczyk, N., Jadavji, N. M., Shah, A. P., & Davla, S. (2022). Building and sustaining mentor interactions as a mentee. *The FEBS Journal, 289*(6), 1374–1384. doi:10.1111/febs.15823 PMID:33818917

Scherer, H., Diaz, S., Iannone, N., McCarty, M., Branch, S., & Kelly, J. (2022). "Leave Britney alone!": Parasocial relationships and empathy. *The Journal of Social Psychology, 162*(1), 128–142. doi:10.1080/00224545.2021.1997889 PMID:34850669

Schou, P. K., Bucher, E., & Waldkirch, M. (2022). Entrepreneurial learning in online communities. *Small Business Economics, 58*(4), 2087–2108. doi:10.100711187-021-00502-8

Secundo, G., Gioconda, M. E. L. E., Del Vecchio, P., Gianluca, E. L. I. A., Margherita, A., & Valentina, N. D. O. U. (2021). Threat or opportunity? A case study of digital-enabled redesign of entrepreneurship education in the COVID-19 emergency. *Technological Forecasting and Social Change, 166*, 120565. doi:10.1016/j.techfore.2020.120565 PMID:33518821

Sherrick, B., Smith, C., Jia, Y., Thomas, B., & Franklin, S. B. (2023). How Parasocial Phenomena Contribute to Sense of Community on Twitch. *Journal of Broadcasting & Electronic Media, 67*(1), 47–67. doi:10.1080/08838151.2022.2151599

Sörensen, A., Mitra, R., Hulthén, E., Hartmann, T., & Clausen, E. (2022). Bringing the entrepreneurial mindset into mining engineering education. *Mining, Metallurgy & Exploration, 39*(4), 1333–1344. doi:10.100742461-022-00620-1

Soriani, A., & Bonafede, P. (2023). Metaverse and education: Which pedagogical perspectives for the school of tomorrow? *Journal of Inclusive Methodology and Technology in Learning and Teaching*, *3*(1).

Stein, J. P., Linda Breves, P., & Anders, N. (2022). Parasocial interactions with real and virtual influencers: The role of perceived similarity and human-likeness. *New Media & Society*, 14614448221102900. doi:10.1177/14614448221102900

Taillon, B. J., Mueller, S. M., Kowalczyk, C. M., & Jones, D. N. (2020). Understanding the relationships between social media influencers and their followers: The moderating role of closeness. *Journal of Product and Brand Management*, *29*(6), 767–782. doi:10.1108/JPBM-03-2019-2292

Tibingana-Ahimbisibwe, B., Willis, S., Catherall, S., Butler, F., & Harrison, R. (2022). A systematic review of peer-assisted learning in fully online higher education distance learning programmes. *Open Learning*, *37*(3), 251–272. doi:10.1080/02680513.2020.1758651

Tinoco-Giraldo, H., Torrecilla Sanchez, E. M., & García-Peñalvo, F. J. (2020). E-mentoring in higher education: A structured literature review and implications for future research. *Sustainability (Basel)*, *12*(11), 4344. doi:10.3390u12114344

Tinoco-Giraldo, H., Torrecilla Sanchez, E. M., & García-Peñalvo, F. J. (2020). E-mentoring in higher education: A structured literature review and implications for future research. *Sustainability (Basel)*, *12*(11), 4344. doi:10.3390u12114344

Tiven, M. B., Fuchs, E. R., Bazari, A., & MacQuarrie, A. (2018). Evaluating global digital education: Student outcomes framework. New York, NY: Bloomberg Philanthropies and the Organisation for Economic Co-operation and Development, 114.

Turkina, E. (2018). The importance of networking to entrepreneurship: Montreal's artificial intelligence cluster and its born-global firm element AI. *Journal of Small Business and Entrepreneurship*, *30*(1), 1–8. doi:10.1080/08276331.2017.1402154

Ye, G., Hudders, L., De Jans, S., & De Veirman, M. (2021). The value of influencer marketing for business: A bibliometric analysis and managerial implications. *Journal of Advertising*, *50*(2), 160–178. doi:10.1080/00913367.2020.1857888

Yukawa, M., Gansky, S. A., O'Sullivan, P., Teherani, A., & Feldman, M. D. (2020). A new mentor evaluation tool: Evidence of validity. *PLoS One*, *15*(6), e0234345. doi:10.1371/journal.pone.0234345 PMID:32544185

Zhou, Q., Mao, J. Y., & Tang, F. (2020). Don't be afraid to fail because you can learn from it! How intrinsic motivation leads to enhanced self-development and benevolent leadership as a boundary condition. *Frontiers in Psychology*, *11*, 699. doi:10.3389/fpsyg.2020.00699 PMID:32425847

Zhu, F., Yu, W., Fan, S. X., & Jonathan, J. G. (2023). Should I stay or should I go? The impact of entrepreneurs' loneliness on business exit intentions through entrepreneurial passion. *Journal of Business Venturing Insights*, *19*, e00368. doi:10.1016/j.jbvi.2022.e00368

Chapter 5
Enhancing Creative Performance:
The Role of Knowledge Management System Usage, Absorptive Capacity, and Motivation

Tobias D. Herbst
https://orcid.org/0000-0001-7922-053X
Avacon Netz GmbH, Germany

J. Piet Hausberg
Osnabrück University, Germany

ABSTRACT

The COVID-19 pandemic has disrupted firms' prior working modes. As more employees are required to work from home, firms need to successfully implement remote working and distance learning conditions. In this context, knowledge management systems (KMSs) are helpful in sharing knowledge and enhancing employee creativity, regardless of their place of work. This study elucidates the antecedents that moderate the impact of KMS usage on employees' creative performance. It explores how absorptive capacity (AC), as well as extrinsic and intrinsic motivation, directly influences employees' creative performance and their moderating effects. Results from an online survey of 415 employees indicate that KMS usage increases employees' creative performance. Moreover, AC as well as extrinsic and intrinsic motivation have a positive direct effect on employees' creative performance. However, the authors find no positive moderating effect of AC or extrinsic and intrinsic motivation on the relationship between KMS usage and employees' creative performance.

DOI: 10.4018/978-1-7998-8797-3.ch005

INTRODUCTION

In today's competitive and dynamic environments, firms need to find ways to operate successfully, and thus achieve competitive advantage. In most sectors, to sustain competitive advantage and survive in the long run, firms also need to innovate continuously, at least to some degree. Extant research highlights the importance of knowledge as a resource that enables innovation, and thus, sustainable competitive advantage. However, the mere existence of knowledge in a portion of a firm is not sufficient. To develop new products and services, knowledge must be transferred within and across firm boundaries. In the past, remote work was viewed mainly as a change in the spatiality of work; for example, it improved the lives of long-distance commuters (Hardill & Green, 2003). However, the COVID-19 pandemic has revealed both the challenges as well as the vital importance of effective, continued remote collaboration (Wang et al., 2021). Some studies show ways to improve knowledge sharing under such peculiar circumstances (Lee et al., 2020). However, knowledge sharing by itself is not sufficient to generate creative outputs. Firms need to facilitate the creative usage of available knowledge.

Therefore, how to manage internal and external knowledge effectively is highly relevant for strategic innovation management, particularly with the increasing diffusion of remote and smart work practices. Due to advancements in information technology (IT), knowledge management systems (KMSs) are effective and used extensively in corporate settings. Prior studies highlight the positive direct effect of KMS usage on firm performance, which helps to create knowledge by linking individuals and organizations. Specifically, employees provide the creative output. Up to 70 percent of initiatives fail because they do not integrate and link human resources, processes, and technology (Petter et al., 2008). Hence, investing in KMSs alone is not sufficient. Despite their relevance and the evident difficulty in implementing them effectively, the contingency factors that render KMS usage effective have been scarcely studied. Therefore, the authors investigate the effect of KMS usage on employees' creative performance and help clarify relevant contingencies that positively affect this relationship.

The authors noted a lack of research on the moderating role of intrinsic and extrinsic motivation, as well as absorptive capacity (AC), on the relationship between KMS usage and employees' creative performance. Despite employee creativity being an essential factor in firm innovation performance, research examining the effects of AC, KMS usage, and motivation on creative performance at the employee level is scarce. In rare exceptions, employees' motivation and ability are investigated jointly to understand the effect of AC on some form of innovative output; however, this does not consider KMS usage and returns to firm-level of analysis in the dependent variable (Liao et al., 2007).

Against these backdrops, the authors endeavor to contribute to the understanding of KMS usage and the impact on creative performance, at the individual (employee) level. Further, the authors analyze the direct and moderating effects of employee motivation and AC that affect the impact of KMS usage on employee creative performance. The specific research question is as follows: How does KMS usage influence employees' creative performance, and what roles do AC and motivation play? Based on the research question, a theoretical model that links KMS usage at the individual (employee) level to creative performance and incorporates relevant contingencies, namely motivation and AC, will be developed.

This study makes several contributions. First, it provides an interdisciplinary model connecting the research on knowledge management, motivation, and creativity. Second, the authors intend to demonstrate that KMS usage supports employees' creative performance and motivation, and that AC supports this effect. Finally, the study aims to elucidate the direct effects of intrinsic and extrinsic motivation, as well as AC on employees' creative performance.

BACKGROUND

Scholars have explored many vital factors that may positively influence innovation capability. In particular, knowledge is viewed as an essential resource for driving innovation and gaining competitive advantages (Grant, 1996; Penrose, 1959). Moreover, knowledge is pivotal in fostering employees' creative performance, defined as generating novel and useful ideas at the individual level. This creative output by employees is the first step toward innovation (Anderson et al., 2014). Prior exploratory (Cao et al., 2013) and empirical (Wu & Wang, 2006) studies highlight the crucial impact of KMS usage on facilitating competitive advantage. However, they focus on the firm level, while disregarding the employee level, which drives a system's success. Building on the Motivation-Opportunity-Ability framework (MacInnis & Jaworski, 1989), the authors suggest a similar concept, but on an individual level. Further, behavioral output, in terms of creative performance, depends on more than just the opportunities available, such as the presence of KMSs. Instead, motivation and ability must reach a certain threshold to allow for the effective generation of creative outputs.

First, motivation is pivotal in increasing employee creativity (Amabile & Pratt, 2016). Most relevant studies distinguish between intrinsic and extrinsic motivation (Deci et al., 1982). Intrinsically motivated employees perform tasks based on pure interest or pleasure. Extrinsically motivated employees are driven and engaged by personal benefit (e.g., material or social rewards; Amabile, 1993; Vallerand, 2000). Of these two, prior research mainly focuses on the positive influence of intrinsic motivation on innovation and creativity (Anderson et al., 2014). The influence of extrinsic motivation on creativity is debatable (Anderson et al., 2014). After investigating the positive effect of extrinsic motivation on more complex (creative) tasks, researchers find added value in tasks that are easy to perform and measure (Bareket-Bojmel et al., 2017).

Second, if knowledge is key for creativity and innovation, the ability to absorb knowledge should be among the most important abilities in this context. AC was first defined as the ability to "identify, assimilate, and exploit knowledge from the environment" (Cohen & Levinthal, 1989, p. 589). Existing studies highlight the link between AC and firm learning, innovation, and performance (Volberda et al., 2010) and, ultimately, firms' competitive advantage (Lane et al., 2006). However, recent studies have investigated AC on more profound analysis levels, such as departmental (Hausberg & Leeflang, 2019) and individual (Beck et al., 2020) levels. In fact, individual-level AC has been found to affect—jointly with knowledge sharing—the innovative behavior of R&D employees (Kang & Lee, 2017).

Knowledge Management Systems

Knowledge is generated when an individual processes information(Alavi & Leidner, 2001). In this context, firms should identify and exploit their knowledge, defined as knowledge management (von Krogh, 1998, 2009), as knowledge enables innovation (Collins & Smith, 2006; Penrose, 1959). Firms increasingly leverage IT to manage internal and external knowledge (Lin & Huang, 2008). More specifically, they use knowledge management techniques based on IT, defined as KMSs, to manage their corporate knowledge across their boundaries (Alavi & Leidner, 2001).

Furthermore, according to Alavi and Leidner, (2001), firms may benefit from corporate knowledge directories, knowledge networks, and coding and sharing best practices. Prior studies (e.g., Cao et al., 2013; Wu & Wang, 2006), highlight the crucial impact of KMSs' usage on facilitating competitive advantage. However, they focus on the firm level, while disregarding the employee level, which drives a system's success. Cao et al., (2013) analyze the role of KMSs on individual and business performance. They find that KMS utilization positively influences business performance and, more importantly, leads to improved firm and individual (employee) performance. One of the scarce empirical studies on KMSs, at the individual level, analyzes the effect of KMSs on innovation (Elmorshidy, 2018). The study finds that KMS usage improves multiple aspects of employees' work, for instance, facilitates new ideas to solve problems and accomplish complex tasks faster (Elmorshidy, 2018). Thus, in contrast to the existing research on KMSs at a firm level and its impact on (innovation) performance (Petter et al., 2008), the authors attempt to elucidate the effects of KMS usage at the individual level.

Employee Creative Performance

Employees' creative performance refers to the development of novel and useful ideas that address the firm level and are related to products (including services), procedures, and practices (Amabile, 1988; Oldham & Cummings, 1996; Shalley et al., 2004). Novel ideas contribute to the firm's existing ideas (Oldham & Cummings, 1996). Ideas are useful when (directly or indirectly) they contribute to a firm's success (Shalley et al., 2004). Further Anderson et al. (2014) and Shalley et al. (2004) highlight employee creativity as the first step toward innovation and as vital for firms' competitiveness (Oldham & Cummings, 1996).

The importance of employee creativity in terms of innovation is widely recognized (e.g., Madjar et al., 2002; Oldham & Cummings, 1996; Shalley et al., 2004). Thus, prior research has found extensive contextual factors and personal drivers fostering employee creativity (Anderson et al., 2014; Oldham & Cummings, 1996; Shalley et al., 2004). Importantly, in their study, Mumford and Hunter (2005) found that knowledge supports new and useful ideas.

Absorptive Capacity

In their seminal work, Cohen and Levinthal (1990) built the AC concept, based on three dimensions: identification (recognize the value of, and acquire, new knowledge), assimilation (processing of new knowledge), and utilization (effective use of new knowledge). Furthermore, Jansen et al. (2005) highlight AC as being resident at both firm and unit levels (Cohen & Levinthal, 1990). AC has been studied extensively (Lane et al., 2006; Zahra & George, 2002) on both firm and unit levels (e.g., Hausberg & Leeflang, 2018; Hotho et al., 2012; Jansen et al., 2005; Kostopoulos et al., 2011; Liao et al., 2007).

Although firms AC depends on their employees' AC (Cohen & Levinthal, 1990), AC has been scarcely studied at the individual level (Enkel et al., 2016). In line with Cohen & Levinthal's (1990) definition, Enkel et al. (2016) refer to individual AC, comprising "three dimensions: individuals' ability to identify valuable knowledge external to the existing firm environment, individuals' ability to assimilate the external knowledge to existing organizational identity, and individuals' ability to advocate for the utilization of the external knowledge within an organization" (Enkel et al., 2016, p. 1). Davis and Da Silva (2011) investigate AC in academia at the individual level and demonstrate the positive effect of AC on creativity and innovation. Some rare studies investigate AC and IT (Deng et al., 2008) or information systems link (IS) (Wang et al., 2014). Deng et al. (2008) highlight the positive effect of AC on IT enabled engineer work and further highlight its impact on task innovation. Wang et al. (2014) emphasize that individual AC positively mediates the relationship between innovations and IS usage. Based on these findings, this study aims to investigate the direct and moderating effect of individual AC on employee creative performance.

Motivation

According to the self-determination theory (Deci & Ryan, 1987) (employees') behavior may be intrinsically or extrinsically motivated. Further, Amabile (1993) split motivation, as a multidimensional construct, into intrinsic and extrinsic motivation. Intrinsic motivation stems from the task itself; hence, employees process tasks out of enjoyment or interest in the topic (Amabile, 1993; Deci & Ryan, 1987). In contrast, extrinsically motivated employees are driven by personal benefits, such as external incentives (e.g., material rewards; Amabile (1993)). Prior research highlights motivation as a key factor fostering IT acceptance (Davis et al., 1992; Teo et al., 1999; Venkatesh et al., 2003) and the greater effectiveness of intrinsic motivation (Cho & Perry, 2012).

HYPOTHESES AND CONCEPTUAL MODEL

Direct effects

The Use of Knowledge Management Systems

Proper KMSs, accompanied by advanced IT infrastructure (e.g., platforms, communication technology), support the effective sharing of internal and external knowledge (Chen et al., 2017; Soto-Acosta & Cegarra-Navarro, 2016). Further, IT infrastructure may help employees to communicate and share internal and external information within knowledge networks (Alavi & Leidner, 2001; Lu & Ramamurthy, 2011) and thus develop new knowledge for novel ideas. In addition, KMSs help in setting up a well-diverse and transparent information sharing structure that is available throughout the firm, thus help in acquiring new information (Alavi & Leidner, 2001). Therefore, the authors hypothesize the following:

Hypothesis One: The higher the knowledge management system (KMS) usage, the higher the employee creativity (MCRE).

Individual Level Absorptive Capacity

Some studies have revealed a positive effect of individual AC on individual creativity (Seo et al., 2015), innovative behavior (Kang & Lee, 2017), and innovation capability (Liao et al., 2007). Moreover, prior studies highlight that AC causes more willingness to share knowledge (Ko et al., 2005) and thus may increase the use of new knowledge for innovative ideas. Following this reasoning, the authors hypothesize the following:

Hypothesis Two: The higher the employee absorptive capacity (AC), the higher the employee creativity (MCRE).

Extrinsic and Intrinsic Motivation

Montag et al. (2012) demonstrated that extrinsic motivation raises creativity when creative performance is part of the job requirements. As such, the authors expect the same results and hypothesize the following:

Hypothesis Three: The higher the extrinsic motivation (EXMO), the higher the employee creativity (MCRE).

Ryan and Deci (2020) found that intrinsic motivation fosters individual engagement. Moreover, existing studies highlight the positive impact of intrinsic motivation on creative performance (Cerasoli et al., 2014; Liu et al., 2016). Hence, the authors hypothesize the following:

Hypothesis Four: The higher the intrinsic motivation (INMO), the higher the employee creativity (MCRE).

Moderating Effects

The Moderating Role of Individual Level Absorptive Capacity

Minbaeva et al. (2003) revealed that, in prior research, the combined effect of motivation and AC at a firm level is not examined; the same is true for the individual level. At the individual level, Yildiz et al. (2019) reveal that employees' intrinsic motivation is an important antecedent of AC, while their extrinsic motivation fails to perform as a predictor. Further, the authors follow Liao et al.'s (2007) argument that only motivated employees are willing to share their knowledge, and through motivation, employees are willing to learn. In addition, the authors conclude that Minbaeva et al.'s (2003) findings, at a firm level, that motivation is a key dimension for firms' AC, may also be true at the individual level. Moreover, the greater the AC, the more employees use IT to solve problems, resulting in an improved task innovation performance (Deng et al., 2008). Further, Wang et al. (2014) found this positive correlation tin the IS environment by showing the moderating effect of AC on innovation with IT usage. Based on the previous discussion, the authors conclude that AC leads to greater IT usage and improved creative performance. Combining these aspects, the authors may assume:

Hypothesis Five: The higher the employee absorptive capacity (AC), the higher the effect of knowledge management system (KMS) usage on employee creativity (MCRE).

The Moderating Roles of Extrinsic and Intrinsic Motivation

Hansen & Levin (2016) highlight a strong effect of employees' extrinsic motivation on their intention to use (social media) technology for work tasks. More specifically, extrinsic motivation incentivizes employees to use and contribute to KMSs, which may positively influence the generation of new ideas (Eisenberger & Shanock, 2003; Montag et al., 2012). Hence, the authors hypothesize the following:

Hypothesis Six: The higher the extrinsic motivation (EXMO), the higher the effect of knowledge management systems (KMS) usage on employee creativity (MCRE).

Motivation drives IT acceptance (Teo et al., 1999; Venkatesh et al., 2003) and intrinsic motivation is a prerequisite for great achievements (Meyer et al., 2004). Kuvaas & Dysvik (2009) demonstrate that intrinsically motivated employees exhibit great creative performance and are self-motivated to use KMSs while facing new tasks. Therefore, the authors hypothesize the following:

Hypothesis Seven: The higher the intrinsic motivation (INMO), the higher the effect of the use of knowledge management systems (KMS) on employee creativity (MCRE).

Figure 1 shows the research model used and summarizes the hypotheses formulated in this study.

Figure 1. Overview of results in the structural model

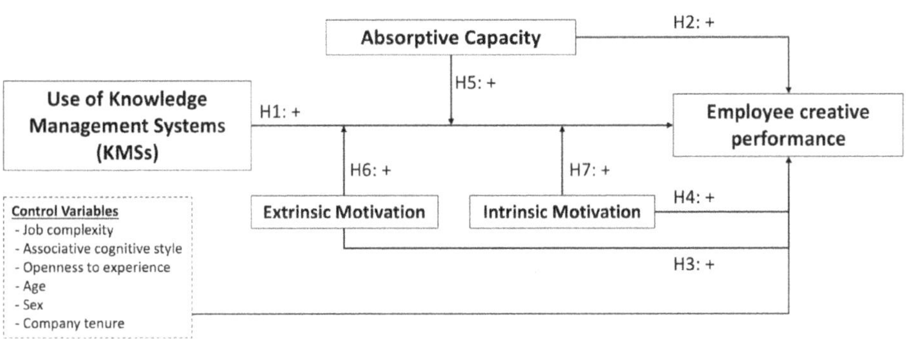

METHODOLOGY

Operationalization

The multi-items scales employed in this study are mainly based on existing studies. Respondents answered questions based on adapted items and scales to fit this study's individual research level (self-rated items).

The use of Knowledge Management Systems: This study adapted eight items from Lin & Huang (2008) that measure KMS usage and support. As this study explores KMS usage at the individual (employee) level, the authors adjusted the items accordingly. For instance, a statement read, "I use the KMSs of our organization to collaborate with other persons inside the organization." Participants rated the eight items based on a five-point scale, ranging from "never" (0) to "very frequently" (4).

Employee creative performance: The authors adapted three items from Shalley et al. (2009) that are based on Oldham & Cummings (1996). The participants rated their creative performance individually, based on a seven-point Likert-type scale, ranging from "disagree very strongly" (3) to "agree very strongly" (+3) and with a midpoint labeled "neither agree nor disagree" (0).

Absorptive Capacity: The researchers adapted Enkel et al.'s (2017) operationalization at the individual level, based on three dimensions (identification, assimilation, and utilization of knowledge). A statement read, "I systematically analyze advantages and weaknesses of existing products and services on the market." Participants were required to answer an overall of 23 items based on a seven-point Likert-type scale, ranging from "disagree very strongly" (3) to "agree very strongly" (+3) and with a midpoint labeled "neither agree nor disagree" (0).

Extrinsic motivation: The authors adapted four items from Zhu et al. (2016) that are based on Manolopoulos (2006). Participants rated the four items based on seven-point Likert scales, ranging from "disagree very strongly" (-3) to "agree very strongly" (+3) and with a midpoint labeled "neither agree nor disagree" (0).

Intrinsic motivation: This study adapted four items from Wilkesmann et al. (2009). Participants rated the four items based on seven-point Likert scales, ranging from "disagree very strongly" (-3) to "agree very strongly" (+3) and with a midpoint labeled "neither agree nor disagree" (0).

Control variables: Multiple control variables control effects that may significantly influence employees' creativity (X. Zhang & Bartol, 2010; Xiaomeng Zhang & Bartol, 2010). This study controls for age, sex (female, male, diverse), and company tenure (Gong et al., 2012; X. Zhang & Bartol, 2010; Xiaomeng Zhang & Bartol, 2010). In addition, the authors control for job complexity, adapted from Zacher and Frese (2011) and based on Semmer (1982), using four items that participants need to rate, which are based on a five-point scale ranging from "never" (0) to "very frequently"

(4). Moreover, the study controls for associative cognitive style, adapted from Shalley et al. (2009) and, based on Jabri (1991), using three items. Participants rated the three items based on seven-point Likert scales ranging from "disagree very strongly" (-3) to "agree very strongly" (+3) and with a midpoint labeled "neither agree nor disagree" (0). Finally, the authors control for openness to experience, adapted from Schweisfurth & Raasch (2018) and based on Rammstedt and John (2007), using two items that participants need to answer, which are based on seven-point Likert-type scales ranging from "disagree very strongly" (-3) to "agree very strongly" (+3) and with a midpoint labeled "neither agree nor disagree" (0).

Satisfaction (marker variable): For quality purposes, the authors included a theoretically distinct marker variable (Simmering et al., 2015). They adapted three items from Seiders et al. (2005) to measure the participants' satisfaction with Amazon MTurk, based on Voss et al. (1998). A statement read, "I am pleased with the overall service at MTurk." Participants rated the three items based on a scale varying from "disagree very strongly" (-3) to "agree very strongly" (+3), with a midpoint labeled "neither agree nor disagree" (0).

Sample and Data

The authors used an (online) survey design to empirically test the study's hypotheses. To achieve a high and useable feedback rate, the authors used Amazon Mechanical Turk (MTurk) as a crowdsourcing platform. Prior research highlights that MTurk provides reliable and construct validity, compared to conventional online research approaches (Kees et al., 2017; Smith et al., 2016), if certain specifications are complied with (Cheung et al., 2017). This study implemented various quality checks suggested by Cheung et al. (2017). First, the authors employed two filter requirements, which possible participants were required to meet before taking the survey. (1) MTurk users were required to have a full-time job (at least 35 hours per week) to avoid potential interference with mediating constructs (e.g., motivation or job complexity). (2) MTurk users were required to have a prior task approval rate of at least 96%. Second, the authors set various conditions for participation, which were required for the MTurk user's task to be accepted. These conditions included a maximum survey duration of 25 minutes to ensure a concentrated process without interruptions and sufficient understanding of items, by providing definitions and examples upfront and during the survey. The authors also highlighted rigorous quality checks (e.g., checking the same answers). If the quality checks were not met, participants could only repeat the survey once. To track non-repeated participation, the authors used the participants' MTurk worker IDs.

The survey was hosted on a private and secure university server, using an official university domain. The authors designed the survey as user-friendly and efficient to avoid interference and increase the response rate. Moreover, to ensure anonymous execution of the survey, the authors did not track any participants' data. The questionnaire was made available in English and German, and all items were presented randomly. A pre-test was conducted to check for clarity and average duration of completion, and the authors assumed good construct validity as all items and scales were well understood.

RESULTS

Data Screening and Sample Size

Thereafter, the survey was released for completion on MTurk. Overall, the authors received 515 complete questionnaires. First, the data were checked for plausibility, after which two cases had to be dropped because of invalid data. After controlling for the correct responses to the authors' filter variable, 444 cases remained. In 30 cases, age had to be recoded, because the year of birth had been entered. Next, data were inspected for unusual fast responses, while deleting cases in which the entire questionnaire had been completed in less than two minutes; overall, 415 cases remained, which is an acceptable sample size.

Factor Analysis and Item Bundling

First, Harman's single factor test was performed, showing that 37% of variance could be explained by a single factor, which is well below the 50% threshold. Hence, this test did not provide any indication of an issue with common method bias. Next, inter-item correlations were checked and a principal component analysis was performed, which clearly showed the predicted number of latent variables. However, some items were dropped due to low factor loadings. The final items were bundled by dividing the sum of all latent variable items by the number of items. Table 1 shows the correlations of the thus created item-bundles.

Regression Model

The variables were included stepwise in a sequence of multivariate ordinary least squares (OLS) regression models. The results of all six models are presented in Table 2. All models exhibited significant F-values and an adjusted R2 of up to 0.448. Given the sample size of 415 cases and 10 predictors, a statistical power of 0.8 was achieved for effects as small as 0.2. Given that the correlations between independent variables were high, particular care was taken to identify potential multicollinearity.

Table 1. Pearson correlations with two-tailed significance levels; abbreviations used in this table: use of knowledge management systems (KMSs), absorptive capacity (AC), extrinsic motivation (EXMO), intrinsic motivation (INMO), employee creativity (MCRE), job complexity (JCX), associative cognitive style (ACS), and openness to experience (OTE)

		AC	EXMO	INMO	MCRE	JCX	ACS	OTE
KMS	Correlation	,585**	,382**	0,069	,481**	,449**	,264**	,303**
	p-value	0,000	0,000	0,158	0,000	0,000	0,000	0,000
AC	Correlation	1	,444**	,341**	,591**	,482**	,400**	,454**
	p-value		0,000	0,000	0,000	0,000	0,000	0,000
EXMO	Correlation	,444**	1	,147**	,406**	,297**	,311**	,303**
	p-value	0,000		0,003	0,000	0,000	0,000	0,000
INMO	Correlation	,341**	,147**	1	,298**	,197**	,298**	,211**
	p-value	0,000	0,003		0,000	0,000	0,000	0,000
MCRE	Correlation	,591**	,406**	,298**	1	,481**	,294**	,424**
	p-value	0,000	0,000	0,000		0,000	0,000	0,000
JCX	Correlation	,482**	,297**	,197**	,481**	1	,238**	,265**
	p-value	0,000	0,000	0,000	0,000		0,000	0,000
ACS	Correlation	,400**	,311**	,298**	,294**	,238**	1	,269**
	p-value	0,000	0,000	0,000	0,000	0,000		0,000

However, all variance inflation factors (VIF) in models 1 to 5 were below 2.5, the highest being that of AC with 2.222. Only the interaction terms exhibited VIFs of 8.5, 12.1, and 7.8, which is, however, a necessary side effect of interaction terms. Finally, the residuals were also normally distributed.

In model 1, only control variables were included. Model 1 results indicate that four of the six control variables are significant predictors of employee creative performance. As predicted, higher openness to experience, associated cognitive style, and job complexity all lead to higher employee creative performance. Furthermore, as predicted, employee creative performance decreases with increasing age. In contrast, sex and tenure do not significantly influence employee creative performance.

In models 2 and 3, KMS and AC were also included, respectively. The inclusion of AC in model 3 did not affect the significance of KMS in model 2. Both KMS and AC exhibited highly significant effects on MCRE, with standardized regression coefficients of 0.259 and 0.314, respectively. However, the coefficient for KMS dropped to 0.140 once AC was included. Hence, KMS usage and individual AC both raise employee creative performance. Therefore, hypotheses One and Two were confirmed.

Table 2. Multivariate OLS regression results of models 1 to 6; abbreviations used in this table: see Table 1

N = 415	Model 1		Model 2		Model 3		Model 4		Model 5		Model 6	
	Beta	**Sig.**	**Beta**	**Sig.**	**Beta**	**Sig.**	**Beta**	**Sig.**	**Beta**	**Sig.**	**Beta**	**Sig.**
(Constant)		0.042		0.000		0.011		0.008		0.001		0.007
AGE	-0.053	0.261	-0.001	0.978	-0.003	0.941	0.018	0.682	-0.006	0.899	-0.005	0.910
SEX	0.013	0.748	0.027	0.488	0.021	0.577	0.019	0.614	0.029	0.433	0.029	0.428
TENURE	0.017	0.712	0.011	0.805	-0.008	0.856	-0.007	0.877	-0.009	0.833	-0.007	0.864
JCX	0.370	0.000	0.279	0.000	0.214	0.000	0.208	0.000	0.198	0.000	0.205	0.000
ACS	0.126	0.003	0.096	0.021	0.035	0.393	0.019	0.645	-0.003	0.937	-0.006	0.895
OTE	0.292	0.000	0.247	0.000	0.172	0.000	0.159	0.000	0.153	0.000	0.150	0.000
KMS			0.259	0.000	0.140	0.004	0.127	0.009	0.149	0.002	0.171	0.089
AC					0.314	0.000	0.287	0.000	0.248	0.000	0.190	0.021
EXMO							0.119	0.007	0.115	0.008	0.226	0.016
INMO									0.121	0.004	0.143	0.091
ACxKMS											0.091	0.393
KMSxINMO											-0.043	0.737
KMSxEXMO											-0.136	0.183
Adj. R^2	0.333		0.380		0.428		0.437		0.448		0.446	
Change in F	35.456	0.000	31.807	0.000	35.510	0.000	7.478	0.000	8.474	0.783	0.654	0.391

In models 4 and 5, the two types of motivations (EXMO and INMO) were included, which did not affect the significance of the previous two predictors. Both, EXMO and INMO, were highly significant, with standardized regression coefficients of 0.119 and 0.121, respectively. Thus, models 4 and 5 results indicate that extrinsic and intrinsic motivation significantly relate to employee creative performance. Hence, hypotheses Three and Four were confirmed, as well.

Finally, in model 6, the interaction terms of AC, INMO and EXMO with KMS were included into the model. However, in these cases, neither the interaction terms nor the changes in the two models' F-values were significant. The results did not change when the terms were included one by one. Thus, higher extrinsic motivation, intrinsic motivation, and, individual AC do not raise the effect of KMSs on employee creativity. Therefore, Hypotheses Five to Seven were rejected. This could mean that in the work environment the knowledge on how to perform a task was enough to utilize and exploit the available KMSs and its information. Thus, the employees may be aware that using KMSs would help them to perform tasks more efficiently themselves and ultimately cause their engagement.

Figure 2 gives an overview of the findings of this study.

Figure 2. Overview of results in the structural model

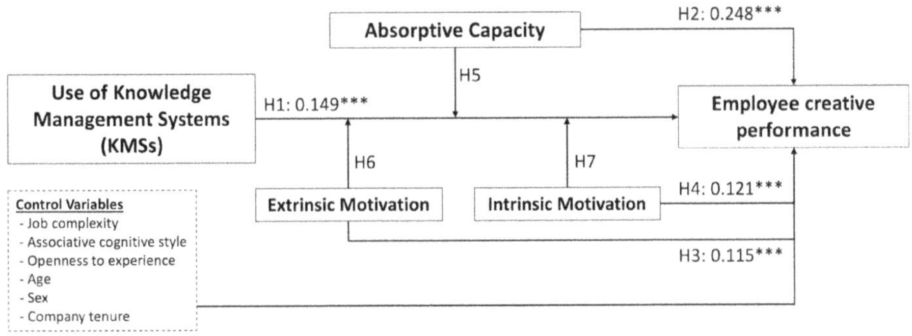

SOLUTIONS AND RECOMMENDATIONS

Based on the existing literature on KMS usage and employee creative performance, the authors developed a research model to investigate the effect of using KMSs on employee creative performance. Moreover, this study investigates the direct and moderating effect of individual AC, extrinsic motivation, and intrinsic motivation. Specifically, the research question was: Do individual AC and extrinsic and intrinsic motivations positively moderate the effect of KMS usage on employee creative performance?

Based on prior research, which states that the actual use of a system positively affects firm performance (Petter et al., 2008; Wu & Wang, 2006), the authors argued that KMS usage increases employees' creative performance; thereby, the authors contribute to the scarce research on KMS usage at the individual level (e.g., Khalifa et al., 2008). This study's results support the view that employee creative performance increases with higher KMS usage, which is in line with prior research that highlights the positive effect of information systems (e.g., Aldholay et al., 2018; Nguyen et al., 2015; Xinli, 2015).

The authors further revealed that both extrinsic and intrinsic motivations positively and directly affect employees' creative performance. For intrinsic motivation, this is in line with the existing research on creative performance (Cerasoli et al., 2014; Liu et al., 2016) and qualitative tasks (Zhu et al., 2016). For extrinsic motivation, however, prior studies found mixed results (Shalley et al., 2004), meaning, extrinsic motivation has positive and negative correlations, depending on the level of task complexity (e.g., Gagné & Deci, 2005; Kuvaas et al., 2016; Montag et al., 2012; Zhu et al., 2016).Following the call by Cerasoli et al. (2014), the authors explicitly contribute to the literature on extrinsic motivation, revealing its positive impact on employee creative performance. In contrast to the developed hypotheses, the authors could not find any evidence supporting the positive moderating effect of intrinsic and extrinsic motivation. This may be because employees execute creative tasks while valuing the benefit of KMS usage nevertheless. In other words, employees know that the task needs to be done anyway and perform it, while utilizing KMSs, hoping for quicker and better quality results (Aldholay et al., 2018).

Moreover, the authors analyzed the direct and moderating effects of individual AC on employees' creative performance, which further contributes to the understanding of AC at the individual level (Minbaeva et al., 2007). This study found a significant direct effect of individual AC, which is in line with prior studies that highlight the positive effect of individual AC on several innovation-relevant dimensions (e.g., individual creativity, innovative behavior, innovation capability; Kang & Lee, 2017; Liao et al., 2007; Seo et al., 2015). Thus, this study suggests that a higher individual AC leads to higher employee creative performance. However, the study findings did not support the hypothesis that individual AC positively moderates the effect of KMS usage on employee creative performance. This may be because, absorbed knowledge that is transformed into innovative ideas using KMSs needs to be processed by employees that have relevant knowledge capabilities (Liao et al., 2007). This could also be explained by the fact that AC is only significant in certain fields of work (e.g., engineering work), where it has a stronger effect on the use of KMSs and a stronger impact on employee creative performance (Deng et al., 2008). Therefore, the creative engagement of employees may define the effect of the individual AC. Thus, individual AC may have a more significant impact on the effect of KMS usage on employee creativity, in the case of little creative engagement. Moreover, as Enkel et al., (2017) suggest, at an employee level, employee characteristics (e.g., independent thinking, alertness to new opportunities, ambition) may lead to the ability to further identify internal and external knowledge in the work environment. Ultimately, the findings suggest that companies should aim to increase KMS usage in general to improve employees' creative performance. Hence, firms may focus on the efficient and easy use of KMSs (Aldholay et al., 2018), leading to general satisfaction with the KMSs (Al-Kofahi et al., 2020; Stefanovic et al., 2016).

FUTURE RESEARCH DIRECTIONS

During the COVID-19 pandemic, studies are increasingly focusing on remote working as an increasing number of companies need their employees to work from home, to keep up the daily operation and innovation tasks for future products and services. For remote working and distance learning, multiple factors exist, which may influence employees' perceived (creative) performance. For instance, Van Der Voordt (2004) revealed that frequent changes in the work environment (e.g., constant changes of workplace) and lack of privacy reduce perceived productivity. Professionals working from home may not have a dedicated room for work or may need to alternate shifts, when both partners are working. Moreover, when working in a noisy and busy open room, employees ability to solve and work on complex (creative) tasks may reduce, as these tasks require more privacy (Van Der Voordt, 2004). Hence, the benefits of remote working may alter and, instead, working from home may have a varying impact on multiple performance related dimensions (e.g., knowledge sharing, innovation; Allen et al. (2015)). Furthermore, although remote working may increase work efficiency (Allen et al., 2015), the increasing use of technology while working remotely may also reduce employees' wellbeing (Molino et al., 2020). Thus, remote working can be perceived as a double-sided sword, and future studies need to examine the advantages or disadvantages in conjunction with the enabling factors (e.g., technologies).

In this context, the authors analyzed an important factor that enables remote working, that is, KMSs, and its impact on employee creative performance. However, there are several limitations of this study to be considered. First, it may be beneficial to empirically test this study's model after the COVID-19 pandemic and in a more settled work environment. However, using a more structured workweek (e.g., hybrid working in the work office and from home) may lead to different results. Second, it may be interesting to test the model in different countries, as technology usage varies between countries (Oliveira & Martins, 2012). In this context, it may be useful to use a variation in the methodology, as MTurk users are mainly from North America and India (Cheung et al., 2017). Third, while different KMSs (e.g., platforms, person to person) may have varying effects on creative performance, different antecedents may influence this effect. Finally, future studies may apply this study's model in different industries (e.g., automotive, railway, energy) and compare large firms and small and medium enterprises.

CONCLUSION

The authors make several theoretical contributions based on this study's results. They apply the Motivation–Opportunity–Ability framework to the individual (employee) level and reveal that employees' creative performance depends on KMS usage and, more importantly, motivation and ability to exhibit a certain correlation level. The study empirically demonstrates the importance of utilizing KMSs in corporate innovation settings and at the individual (employee) level to foster creative performance. Furthermore, the authors highlight the relevance of exploring the contingency perspective of KMSs to specify further on what drives KMSs' success. The study contributes to the motivation literature through the analysis of extrinsic and intrinsic motivation in the research model. Moreover, by empirically exploring extrinsic motivation, the study contributes to the broader understanding of extrinsic motivation. Thus, the authors answer the call by Cerasoli et al. (2014) to investigate the impact of extrinsic motivation further. Furthermore, by empirically analyzing the direct and moderating effects of AC, this study adds to the understanding of AC at the employee level (e.g., Deng et al., 2008; Enkel et al., 2017; Minbaeva et al., 2007). Finally, the authors contribute to the understanding of which technologies are required for, and drive, efficient remote collaboration (e.g., Baker et al., 2006; Wang et al., 2021).

From a managerial perspective, this study provides various significant implications for decision-makers. It underlines the significance of KMSs and, specifically, their usage for employees' creative performance. Further, the authors provide practitioners with a better understanding on how to improve employee creative performance, and thus they intend to demonstrate the relevance of KMSs in corporate settings, by analyzing contingencies.

In conclusion, the increased focus, especially on remote work due to the COVID-19 pandemic, reveals that enabling effective, continued remote collaboration (B. Wang et al., 2021) is greatly important. Thus, for firms to not only remain competitive but also survive, they essentially rely on innovation, whether through, for example, offering new products or services. Enabling the transfer of internal and external knowledge within and across firms' boundaries is key, not only to facilitate commuters work, but also to enable the remote work of innovation-oriented tasks. KMSs may be a key driver to enable and foster innovation in a remote work environment.

ACKNOWLEDGMENT

The authors are grateful to the editors and anonymous reviewers for their valuable feedback.

This research received no specific grant from any funding agency in the public, commercial, or not-for-profit sectors.

REFERENCES

Al-Kofahi, M. K., Hassan, H., & Mohamad, R. (2020). Information systems success model: A review of literature. *International Journal of Innovation. Creativity and Change*, *12*(10), 104–128.

Alavi, M., & Leidner, D. E. (2001). Review: Knowledge management and knowledge management systems: Conceptual foundations and research issues. *Management Information Systems Quarterly*, *25*(1), 107–136. doi:10.2307/3250961

Aldholay, A. H., Isaac, O., Abdullah, Z., & Ramayah, T. (2018). The role of transformational leadership as a mediating variable in DeLone and McLean information system success model: The context of online learning usage in Yemen. *Telematics and Informatics*, *35*(5), 1421–1437. doi:10.1016/j.tele.2018.03.012

Allen, T. D., Golden, T. D., & Shockley, K. M. (2015). How effective is telecommuting? Assessing the status of our scientific findings. *Psychological Science in the Public Interest*, *16*(2), 40–68. doi:10.1177/1529100615593273 PMID:26403188

Amabile, T. M. (1988). A model of creativity and innovation in organizations. *Research in Organizational Behavior*, *10*, 123–167.

Amabile, T. M. (1993). Motivational synergy: Toward new conceptualizations of intrinsic and extrinsic motivation in the workplace. *Human Resource Management Review*, *3*(3), 185–201. doi:10.1016/1053-4822(93)90012-S

Amabile, T. M., & Pratt, M. G. (2016). The dynamic componential model of creativity and innovation in organizations: Making progress, making meaning. *Research in Organizational Behavior*, *36*, 157–183. doi:10.1016/j.riob.2016.10.001

Anderson, N., Potočnik, K., & Zhou, J. (2014). Innovation and creativity in organizations: A state-of-the-science review, prospective commentary, and guiding framework. *Journal of Management*, *40*(5), 1297–1333. doi:10.1177/0149206314527128

Baker, E., Avery, G. C., & Crawford, J. (2006). Home alone: The role of technology in telecommuting. *Information Resources Management Journal*, *19*(4), 1–22. doi:10.4018/irmj.2006100101

Bareket-Bojmel, L., Hochman, G., & Ariely, D. (2017). It's (not) all about the Jacksons: Testing different types of short-term bonuses in the field. *Journal of Management*, *43*(2), 534–554. doi:10.1177/0149206314535441

Beck, S., Bergenholtz, C., Bogers, M., Brasseur, T. M., Conradsen, M. L., Di Marco, D., Distel, A. P., Dobusch, L., Dörler, D., Effert, A., Fecher, B., Filiou, D., Frederiksen, L., Gillier, T., Grimpe, C., Gruber, M., Haeussler, C., Heigl, F., Hoisl, K., & Xu, S. M. (2020). The open innovation in science research field: A collaborative conceptualisation approach. *Industry and Innovation*, 1–50.

Cao, Q., Thompson, M. A., & Triche, J. (2013). Investigating the role of business processes and knowledge management systems on performance: A multi-case study approach. *International Journal of Production Research*, *51*(18), 5565–5575. doi: 10.1080/00207543.2013.789145

Cerasoli, C. P., Nicklin, J. M., & Ford, M. T. (2014). Intrinsic motivation and extrinsic incentives jointly predict performance: A 40-year meta-analysis. *Psychological Bulletin*, *140*(4), 980–1008. doi:10.1037/a0035661 PMID:24491020

Chen, L., Zhao, X., Tang, O., Price, L., Zhang, S., & Zhu, W. (2017). Supply chain collaboration for sustainability: A literature review and future research agenda. *International Journal of Production Economics*, *194*(April), 73–87. doi:10.1016/j.ijpe.2017.04.005

Cheung, J. H., Burns, D. K., Sinclair, R. R., & Sliter, M. (2017). Amazon Mechanical Turk in organizational psychology: An evaluation and practical recommendations. *Journal of Business and Psychology*, *32*(4), 347–361. doi:10.100710869-016-9458-5

Cho, Y. J., & Perry, J. L. (2012). Intrinsic motivation and employee attitudes: Role of managerial trustworthiness, goal directedness, and extrinsic reward expectancy. *Review of Public Personnel Administration*, *32*(4), 382–406. doi:10.1177/0734371X11421495

Cohen, W. M., & Levinthal, D. A. (1989). Innovation and learning: The two faces of R&D. *Economic Journal (London)*, *99*(397), 569–596. doi:10.2307/2233763

Cohen, W. M., & Levinthal, D. A. (1990). Absorptive capacity: A new perspective on learning and innovation. *Administrative Science Quarterly*, *35*(1), 128. doi:10.2307/2393553

Collins, C. J., & Smith, K. G. (2006). Knowledge exchange and combination: The role of human resource practices in the performance of high-technology firms. *Academy of Management Journal*, *49*(3), 544–560. doi:10.5465/amj.2006.21794671

Da Silva, N., & Davis, A. R. (2011). Absorptive capacity at the individual level: Linking creativity to innovation in academia. *Review of Higher Education*, *34*(3), 355–379. doi:10.1353/rhe.2011.0007

Davis, A. R., & Da Silva, N. (2011). Absorptive capacity at the individual level: Linking creativity to innovation in academia. *Review of Higher Education*, *34*(3), 355–379. doi:10.1353/rhe.2011.0007

Davis, F. D., Bagozzi, R. P., & Warshaw, P. R. (1992). Extrinsic and intrinsic motivation to use computers in the workplace. *Journal of Applied Social Psychology*, *22*(14), 1111–1132. doi:10.1111/j.1559-1816.1992.tb00945.x

Deci, E. L., & Ryan, R. M. (1987). The support of autonomy and the control of behavior. *Journal of Personality and Social Psychology*, *53*(6), 1024–1037. doi:10.1037/0022-3514.53.6.1024 PMID:3320334

Deci, E. L., Spiegel, N. H., Ryan, R. M., Koestner, R., & Kauffman, M. (1982). Effects of performance standards on teaching styles: Behavior of controlling teachers. *Journal of Educational Psychology*, *74*(6), 852–859. doi:10.1037/0022-0663.74.6.852

Deng, X., Doll, W. J., & Cao, M. (2008). Exploring the absorptive capacity to innovation / productivity link for individual engineers engaged in IT enabled work. *Information & Management*, *45*(2), 75–87. doi:10.1016/j.im.2007.12.001

Eisenberger, R., & Shanock, L. (2003). Rewards, intrinsic motivation, and creativity: A case study of conceptual and methodological isolation. *Creativity Research Journal*, *15*(2 & 3), 121–130. doi:10.1080/10400419.2003.9651404

Elmorshidy, A. (2018). The impact of knowledge management systems on innovation: An empirical investigation in Kuwait. *VINE Journal of Information and Knowledge Management Systems*, *48*(3), 388–403. doi:10.1108/VJIKMS-12-2017-0089

Enkel, E., Heil, S., Hengstler, M., & Wirth, H. (2017). Exploratory and exploitative innovation: To what extent do the dimensions of individual level absorptive capacity contribute? *Technovation*, *60–61*(August), 29–38. doi:10.1016/j.technovation.2016.08.002

Gagné, M., & Deci, E. L. (2005). Self-determination theory and work motivation. *Journal of Organizational Behavior*, *26*(4), 331–362. doi:10.1002/job.322

Gong, Y., Cheung, S. Y., Wang, M., & Huang, J. C. (2012). Unfolding the proactive process for creativity: Integration of the employee proactivity, information exchange, and psychological safety perspectives. *Journal of Management*, *38*(5), 1611–1633. doi:10.1177/0149206310380250

Grant, R. M. (1996). Toward a knowledge-based theory of the firm. *Strategic Management Journal*, *17*(S2), 109–122. doi:10.1002mj.4250171110

Hansen, J. M., & Levin, M. A. (2016). The effect of apathetic motivation on employees' intentions to use social media for businesses. *Journal of Business Research, 69*(12), 6058–6066. doi:10.1016/j.jbusres.2016.06.009

Hardill, I., & Green, A. (2003). Remote working – Altering the spatial contours of work and home in the new economy. *New Technology, Work and Employment, 18*(3), 212–222. doi:10.1111/1468-005X.00122

Hausberg, J. P., & Leeflang, P. S. H. (2019). Absorbing integration: Empirical evidence on the mediating role of absorptive capacity between functional-/cross-functional integration and innovation performance. *International Journal of Innovation Management, 23*(6), 1–37. doi:10.1142/S1363919619500567

Hotho, J. J., Becker-Ritterspach, F., & Saka-Helmhout, A. (2012). Enriching absorptive capacity through social interaction. *British Journal of Management, 23*(3), 383–401.

Jabri, M. M. (1991). The development of conceptually independent subscales in the measurement of modes of problem solving. *Educational and Psychological Measurement, 51*(4), 975–983. doi:10.1177/0013164491051004l7

Jansen, J. J. P., Van Den Bosch, F. A. J., & Volberda, H. W. (2005). Managing potential and realized absorptive capacity: How do organizational antecedents matter? *Academy of Management Journal, 48*(6), 999–1015. doi:10.5465/amj.2005.19573106

Kang, M., & Lee, M. J. (2017). Absorptive capacity, knowledge sharing, and innovative behaviour of R&D employees. *Technology Analysis and Strategic Management, 29*(2), 219–232. doi:10.1080/09537325.2016.1211265

Kees, J., Berry, C., Burton, S., & Sheehan, K. (2017). An analysis of data quality: Professional panels, student subject pools, and Amazon's Mechanical Turk. *Journal of Advertising, 46*(1), 141–155. doi:10.1080/00913367.2016.1269304

Khalifa, M., Yan, A. Y., & Ning, K. S. (2008). Knowledge management systems success: A contingency perspective. *Journal of Knowledge Management, 12*(1), 119–132. doi:10.1108/13673270810852430

Ko, D. G., Kirsch, L. J., & King, W. R. (2005). Antecedents of knowledge transfer from consultants to clients in enterprise system implementations. *Management Information Systems Quarterly, 29*(1), 59–85. doi:10.2307/25148668

Kostopoulos, K., Papalexandris, A., Papachroni, M., & Ioannou, G. (2011). Absorptive capacity, innovation, and financial performance. *Journal of Business Research, 64*(12), 1335–1343. doi:10.1016/j.jbusres.2010.12.005

Kuvaas, B., Buch, R., Gagné, M., Dysvik, A., & Forest, J. (2016). Do you get what you pay for? Sales incentives and implications for motivation and changes in turnover intention and work effort. *Motivation and Emotion*, *40*(5), 667–680. doi:10.100711031-016-9574-6

Kuvaas, B., & Dysvik, A. (2009). Perceived investment in employee development, intrinsic motivation and work performance. *Human Resource Management Journal*, *19*(3), 217–236. doi:10.1111/j.1748-8583.2009.00103.x

Lane, P. J., Koka, B. R., & Pathak, S. (2006). The reification of absorptive capacity: A critical review and rejuvenation of the construct. *Academy of Management Review*, *31*(4), 833–863. doi:10.5465/amr.2006.22527456

Lee, Y., Tao, W., Li, J. Y. Q., & Sun, R. (2020). Enhancing employees' knowledge sharing through diversity-oriented leadership and strategic internal communication during the COVID-19 outbreak. *Journal of Knowledge Management*.

Liao, S. H., Fei, W. C., & Chen, C. C. (2007). Knowledge sharing, absorptive capacity, and innovation capability: An empirical study of Taiwan's knowledge-intensive industries. *Journal of Information Science*, *33*(3), 340–359. doi:10.1177/0165551506070739

Lin, T. C., & Huang, C. C. (2008). Understanding knowledge management system usage antecedents: An integration of social cognitive theory and task technology fit. *Information & Management*, *45*(6), 410–417. doi:10.1016/j.im.2008.06.004

Liu, D., Jiang, K., Shalley, C. E., Keem, S., & Zhou, J. (2016). Motivational mechanisms of employee creativity: A meta-analytic examination and theoretical extension of the creativity literature. *Organizational Behavior and Human Decision Processes*, *137*, 236–263. doi:10.1016/j.obhdp.2016.08.001

Lu, Y., & Ramamurthy, K. (2011). Understanding the link between information technology capability and organizational agility: An empirical examination. *Management Information Systems Quarterly*, *35*(4), 931–954. doi:10.2307/41409967

MacInnis, D. J., & Jaworski, B. J. (1989). Information processing from advertisements: Toward an integrative framework. *Journal of Marketing*, *53*(4), 1–23. doi:10.1177/002224298905300401

Madjar, N., Oldham, G. R., & Pratt, M. G. (2002). There's no place like home? The contributions of work and nonwork creativity support to employees' creative performance. *Academy of Management Journal*, *45*(4), 757–767. doi:10.2307/3069309

Manolopoulos, D. (2006). What motivates R&D professionals? Evidence from decentralized laboratories in Greece. *International Journal of Human Resource Management, 17*(4), 616–647. doi:10.1080/09585190600581394

Meyer, J. P., Becker, T. E., & Vandenberghe, C. (2004). Employee commitment and motivation: A conceptual analysis and integrative model. *The Journal of Applied Psychology, 89*(6), 991–1007. doi:10.1037/0021-9010.89.6.991 PMID:15584837

Minbaeva, D. B., Makela, K., & Rabbiosi, L. (2007). *Individual absorptive capacity and knowledge transfer.* Unpublished Paper, Copenhagen Business School.

Minbaeva, D. B., Pedersen, T., Björkman, I., Fey, C. F., & Park, H. J. (2003). MNC knowledge transfer, subsidiary absorptive capacity, and HRM. *Journal of International Business Studies, 34*(6), 586–599. doi:10.1057/palgrave.jibs.8400056

Molino, M., Ingusci, E., Signore, F., Manuti, A., Giancaspro, M. L., Russo, V., Zito, M., & Cortese, C. G. (2020). Wellbeing costs of technology use during Covid-19 remote working: An investigation using the Italian translation of the technostress creators scale. *Sustainability (Basel), 12*(15), 1–20. doi:10.3390u12155911

Montag, T., Maertz, C. P. Jr, & Baer, M. (2012). A critical analysis of the workplace creativity criterion space. *Journal of Management, 38*(4), 1362–1386. doi:10.1177/0149206312441835

Mumford, M. D., & Hunter, S. T. (2005). Innovation in organizations: A multi-level perspective on creativity. *Research in Multi-Level Issues, 4*(05), 9–73. doi:10.1016/S1475-9144(05)04001-4

Nguyen, T. D., Nguyen, T. M., & Cao, T. H. (2015). Information systems success: A literature review. *Springer International Publishing Switzerland, 9446*, 242–256.

Oldham, G. R., & Cummings, A. (1996). Employee creativity: Personal and contextual factors at work. *Academy of Management Journal, 39*(3), 607–634. doi:10.2307/256657

Oliveira, T., & Martins, M. (2012). Literature review of information technology adoption models at firm level. *The Australasian Journal of Construction Economics and Building, 14*(1), 110–121.

Penrose, E. (1959). *The Theory of the Growth of the Firm.* Oxford University Press.

Petter, S., DeLone, W., & McLean, E. (2008). Measuring information systems success: Models, dimensions, measures, and interrelationships. *European Journal of Information Systems, 17*(3), 236–263. doi:10.1057/ejis.2008.15

Rammstedt, B., & John, O. P. (2007). Measuring personality in one minute or less: A 10-item short version of the Big Five Inventory in English and German. *Journal of Research in Personality*, *41*(1), 203–212. doi:10.1016/j.jrp.2006.02.001

Ryan, R. M., & Deci, E. L. (2020). Intrinsic and extrinsic motivation from a self-determination theory perspective: Definitions, theory, practices, and future directions. *Contemporary Educational Psychology*, *61*, 61. doi:10.1016/j.cedpsych.2020.101860

Schweisfurth, T. G., & Raasch, C. (2018). Absorptive capacity for need knowledge: Antecedents and effects for employee innovativeness. *Research Policy*, *47*(4), 687–699. doi:10.1016/j.respol.2018.01.017

Seiders, K., Voss, G. B., Grewal, D., & Godfrey, A. L. (2005). Do satisfied customers buy more? Examining moderating influences in a retailing context. *Journal of Marketing*, *69*(4), 26–43. doi:10.1509/jmkg.2005.69.4.26

Semmer, N. K. (1982). Stress at work, stress in private life and psychological well-being. In W. Bachmann, & I. Udris (Eds.), Mental load and stress in activity: European approaches (pp. 42–55). Elsevier.

Seo, Y. W., Chae, S. W., & Lee, K. C. (2015). The impact of absorptive capacity, exploration, and exploitation on individual creativity: Moderating effect of subjective well-being. *Computers in Human Behavior*, *42*, 68–82. doi:10.1016/j.chb.2014.03.031

Shalley, C., Gilson, L., & Blum, T. (2009). Interactive effects of growth need strength, work context, and job complexity on self-reported creative performance. *Academy of Management Journal*, *52*(3), 489–505. doi:10.5465/amj.2009.41330806

Shalley, C. E., Zhou, J., & Oldham, G. R. (2004). The effects of personal and contextual characteristics on creativity: Where should we go from here? *Journal of Management*, *30*(6), 933–958. doi:10.1016/j.jm.2004.06.007

Simmering, M. J., Fuller, C. M., Richardson, H. A., Ocal, Y., & Atinc, G. M. (2015). Marker variable choice, reporting, and interpretation in the detection of common method variance: A review and demonstration. *Organizational Research Methods*, *18*(3), 473–511. doi:10.1177/1094428114560023

Smith, S. M., Roster, C. A., Golden, L. L., & Albaum, G. S. (2016). A multi-group analysis of online survey respondent data quality: Comparing a regular USA consumer panel to MTurk samples. *Journal of Business Research*, *69*(8), 3139–3148. doi:10.1016/j.jbusres.2015.12.002

Soto-Acosta, P., & Cegarra-Navarro, J. G. (2016). New ICTs for knowledge management in organizations. *Journal of Knowledge Management*, *20*(3), 417–422. doi:10.1108/JKM-02-2016-0057

Stefanovic, D., Marjanovic, U., Delić, M., Culibrk, D., & Lalic, B. (2016). Assessing the success of e-government systems: An employee perspective. *Information & Management*, *53*(6), 717–726. doi:10.1016/j.im.2016.02.007

Teo, T. S. H., Lim, V. K. G., & Lai, R. Y. C. (1999). Intrinsic and extrinsic motivation in Internet usage. *Omega*, *27*(1), 25–37. doi:10.1016/S0305-0483(98)00028-0

Vallerand, R. J. (2000). Deci and Ryan's self-determination theory: A view from the hierarchical model of intrinsic and extrinsic motivation. *Psychological Inquiry*, *11*(4), 312–318.

Van Der Voordt, T. J. (2004). Productivity and employee satisfaction in flexible workplaces. *Journal of Corporate Real Estate*, *6*(2), 133–148. doi:10.1108/14630010410812306

Venkatesh, V., Morris, M. G., Davis, G. B., & Davis, F. D. (2003). User acceptance of information technology: Toward a unified view. *Management Information Systems Quarterly*, *27*(3), 425–478. doi:10.2307/30036540

Volberda, H. W., Foss, N. J., & Lyles, M. A. (2010). Absorbing the concept of absorptive capacity: How to realize its potential in the organization field. *Organization Science*, *21*(4), 931–951. doi:10.1287/orsc.1090.0503

von Krogh, G. (1998). Care in knowledge creation. *California Management Review*, *3*(3), 133–153. doi:10.2307/41165947

von Krogh, G. (2009). Individualist and collectivist perspectives on knowledge in organizations: Implications for information systems research. *The Journal of Strategic Information Systems*, *18*(3), 119–129. doi:10.1016/j.jsis.2009.08.001

Voss, G. B., Parasuraman, A., & Grewal, D. (1998). The roles of price, performance, and expectations in determining satisfaction in service exchanges. *Journal of Marketing*, *62*(4), 46–61. doi:10.1177/002224299806200404

Wang, B., Liu, Y., Qian, J., & Parker, S. K. (2021). Achieving Effective Remote Working During the COVID-19 Pandemic: A Work Design Perspective. *Applied Psychology*, *70*(1), 16–59. doi:10.1111/apps.12290 PMID:33230359

Wang, W., Liu, L., Feng, Y., & Wang, T. (2014). Innovation with IS usage: Individual absorptive capacity as a mediator. *Industrial Management & Data Systems*, *114*(8), 1110–1130. doi:10.1108/IMDS-05-2014-0160

Wilkesmann, U., Wilkesmann, M., & Virgillito, A. (2009). The absence of cooperation is not necessarily defection: Structural and motivational constraints of knowledge transfer in a social dilemma situation. *Organization Studies*, *30*(10), 1141–1164. doi:10.1177/0170840609344385

Wu, J. H., & Wang, Y. M. (2006). Measuring KMS success: A respecification of the DeLone and McLean's model. *Information & Management*, *43*(6), 728–739. doi:10.1016/j.im.2006.05.002

Xinli, H. (2015). Effectiveness of information technology in reducing corruption in China A validation of the DeLone and McLean information systems success model. *The Electronic Library*, *33*(1), 52–64. doi:10.1108/EL-11-2012-0148

Yildiz, H. E., Murtic, A., Zander, U., & Richtnér, A. (2019). What fosters individual-level absorptive capacity in MNCs? An extended motivation–ability–opportunity framework. [). Springer Berlin Heidelberg.]. *MIR. Management International Review*, *59*(1), 93–129. doi:10.100711575-018-0367-x

Zacher, H., & Frese, M. (2011). Maintaining a focus on opportunities at work: The interplay between age, job complexity, and the use of selection, optimization, and compensation strategies. *Journal of Organizational Behavior*, *32*(2), 291–318. doi:10.1002/job.683

Zahra, S. A., & George, G. (2002). Absorptive capacity: A review, reconceptualization, and extension. *Academy of Management Review*, *27*(2), 185–203. doi:10.2307/4134351

Zhang, X., & Bartol, K. M. (2010). Linking empowering leadership and employee creativity: The influence of psychological empowerment, intrinsic motivation, and creative process engagement. *Development and Learning in Organizations*, *24*(5), 4–9. doi:10.1108/dlo.2010.08124ead.007

Zhang, X., & Bartol, K. M. (2010). The influence of creative process engagement on employee creative performance and overall job performance: A curvilinear assessment. *The Journal of Applied Psychology*, *95*(5), 862–873. doi:10.1037/a0020173 PMID:20718512

Zhu, Y. Q., Gardner, D. G., & Chen, H. G. (2016). Relationships between work team climate, individual motivation, and creativity. *Journal of Management*, *44*(5), 2094–2115. doi:10.1177/0149206316638161

ADDITIONAL READING

Angelici, M., & Profeta, P. (2020). Smart-working: work flexibility without constraints. *CESifo Working Paper No. 8165.*

Becerra-Fernandez, I., & Sabherwal, R. (2014). *Knowledge management: Systems and processes*. Routledge.

Choi, J. N. (2004). Individual and contextual predictors of creative performance: The mediating role of psychollgical processes. *Creativity Research Journal, 16*(2-3), 187–199. doi:10.1080/10400419.2004.9651452

Dul, J., & Ceylan, C. (2011). Work environments for employee creativity. *Ergonomics, 54*(1), 12–20. doi:10.1080/00140139.2010.542833 PMID:21181585

Felstead, A., & Henseke, G. (2017). Assessing the growth of remote working and its consequences for effort, well-being and work-life balance. *New Technology, Work and Employment, 32*(3), 195–212. doi:10.1111/ntwe.12097

Nickson, D., & Siddons, S. (2012). *Remote Working*. Routledge. doi:10.4324/9780080474168

Ramlall, S. (2004). A review of employee motivation theories and their implications for employee retention with organizations. *The Journal of American Academy of Business, Cambridge, 5*(1/2), 52–63.

Shahzadi, I., Javed, A., Pirzada, S. S., Nasreen, S., & Khanam, F. (2014). Impact of employee motivation on employee performance. *European Journal of Business and Management, 6*(23), 159–166.

Thierauf, R. (1999). *Knowledge management systems for business*. Greenwood Publishing Group.

Von Hippel, E. (2007). The sources of innovation. In *Das Summa Summarum des Management* (pp. 111–120). Gabler. doi:10.1007/978-3-8349-9320-5_10

KEY TERMS AND DEFINITIONS

Employee Creativity: The development of novel and useful ideas within the corporate environment (e.g., solving problems, improving processes, developing products and processes).

Extrinsic Motivation: A human behavior driven by personal added value (e.g., rewards).

Individual Absorptive Capacity: An individual's ability to identify, assimilate, and advocate valuable knowledge within a firm.

Information System: A software or hardware related system that supports the, e.g., capturing, transferring, and transforming of data.

Information Technology: A term for electronic data processing and the hardware and software infrastructure used for this purpose.

Intrinsic Motivation: A human behavior driven by pure interest or pleasure.

Knowledge Management System: A type of information system that is applied to manage firms' internal and external knowledge.

Remote Working: A work setup in which employees work in sites or locations that are not their firms' offices, and they have no direct personal contact with colleagues but can communicate with them via enabling technology (e.g., computer or mobile phones and related software).

Chapter 6
Machine Learning Studies in Business During the COVID-19 Pandemic

Ozlem Erdas Cicek
Necmettin Erbakan University, Turkey

ABSTRACT

The accuracy of decision-makers in making managerial decisions and applying these decisions in uncertain environments will increase with the use of decision-making tools often and effectively. Machine learning, as one of these tools, provides a more effective definition of uncertainty conditions in the use of data in decision-making processes, on the basis of artificial intelligence. The rapid development of machine learning techniques enhances the Smart working models to help employees to execute functional jobs by processing information into each workflow. The change in business operations during and after the Covid-19 outbreak will enable machine learning techniques to be used more in predicting uncertainty. This attempt will be beneficial in pointing out new research trends of machine learning in the business context for the future.

1. INTRODUCTION

The effects of the COVID-19 pandemic have been seen all over the world since 2020. Countries have chosen different courses of action like online education and working, isolating the streets, restraining tourist activities, reducing the crowds in places and so on (Riswantini et. al., 2021). People's tendencies have changed from investing to saving money which causes a decrease in economic improvement. Since saving

DOI: 10.4018/978-1-7998-8797-3.ch006

money has affected the economy negatively, it's not sure that people will maintain their conservatism as in the previous period. Alterations in behaviour concerned to pandemic outbreaks appear to be linked to individual preservation (Funk, Gilad, Watkins, & Jansen,2009). The people of the current community have focused their lives around comfort rather than thinking about the annoying future (Donthu and Gustaffson, 2020).

Different areas of community have been affected by the COVID-19 outbreak in various directions. The business is one of the areas which have challenged difficulties during this period (Riswantini et al, 2021). Healthcare workers have faced extended work shifts and never-ending assignments. Moreover, percentage of unemployment is as high as the Great Depression of the 1930s. The areas with the huge increases in losing jobs are those that need the client's physical existence while interest for these services is decreasing (for example, accommodation, tourism and leisure) (Donthu and Gustaffson, 2020).

It is important for business owners to predict turnaround in client's actions since the actions and trading habits of the clients have been changed in this erratic pandemic outbreak. Business owners have turned to leveraging the online channel to maintain their business in the competition and have included product recommendation property to advance their services and client satisfaction. The pandemic has slowed down the investment rates and the finance environment is not stable because of the confused stakeholders. Although some investors detain their share, the other investors profit by this period.

The knowledge brought by the pandemic outbreak endorses this, as many companies fail to realize that their business functions were not suitable to deal with the crisis. Data science, which becomes crucial in this environment, presents huge conflicts for the business actions involving the ones based on data quality and integration. Data science is only an instrument which can be utilized for both constitution and demolition. Just like data science, artificial intelligence and machine learning have also been the focus of similar discussions.

Inevitable rise of artificial intelligence and machine learning leads companies to revise their hiring policies and employ data scientists. A breach for expertise in data science becomes an issue causing struggles in challenging new technical companies for a lot of empty positions and experts. On the other hand, this situation will not continue so long since machine learning will automatize the duties of data scientists. Apprehending difficulties in organizational processes, building mathematical models of those processes and utilizing the newly built models will stay pertinent in the age of automatization (McKinsey et. al., 2020). Eagerly naming this kind of magnification challenges will not only give business processes "street credit", but will enhance its organizational legitimacy and provide it with an opportunity to deal with the unexpected (Minbaeva, 2021).

In the organizational environment, where economic factors are intensely effective, strategic, tactical and technical decisions may not be taken correctly at the increasing uncertainty level due to the Covid-19 pandemic. In this context, it can be expected to benefit more from applications based on artificial intelligence, which allows to make accurate predictions, during the Covid-19 period.

Powerful machine learning (ML) algorithms have also been created in support of efficient data analysis and predictions. There are researches which aim to construct models for predicting upcoming events. One study (Chaves-Maza and Martel, 2020) proposes a model to estimate the chance of achievement and endurance of companies depending on peripheral factors and public assistance programs. In another study (Zhang et al., 2020), a model is constructed to collect users' data about the healthcare product shopping and usage in order to analyse the need for personalised health care recommendations.

Smart workers, referring to production systems that utilize assistive machine intelligence to create interactivity, collaboration, and workplace efficiency, have been widely used in different industries. Smart working significantly increased information utilization which integrates state-of-the-art machine learning techniques with the workplace scenarios of correct decision-making. Besides, IoT based smart system technologies and intelligent solutions utilize machine learning. Proactive knowledge-based analysis is used for operations through the framework of machine learning.

Due to various factors that can impact the effectiveness of machine learning models, it is crucial for researchers to conduct theoretical and practical studies based on field research in different business domains. These studies play a significant role in guiding researchers towards conducting new research. Understanding how the context differs across business functions is essential for maximizing the benefits of machine learning as a tool for smart work. Therefore, it is valuable to examine existing studies on this topic and present the findings using an inductive approach. It will be remarkable knowledge for business functional management areas in the strategy development processes.

2. DESIGN/METHOD

In this study, a qualitative research method is utilized. WoS database are searched using the keywords of "business", "Covid-19", "machine learning" from the starting date of Covid-19 outbreak till today. Theoretical, review or research types of articles included in the scope. The Price Rule can be utilized for categorizing of the academic studies. A literature review of the research was conducted via bibliometric analysis. The utilization of the Bradford technique was unfeasible due to the limited availability and diversity of journals exclusively dedicated to articles about remote work post the Covid-19 pandemic, preventing their classification within the 1/3 category. As outlined in Price's law, approximately fifty percent of scientific research papers are produced by a quantity of authors equivalent to the square root of the overall count of scientists. Similarly, half of the total article count is encompassed within the square root of the aggregate journal count. Given the focus on the topic of remote work following the Covid-19 pandemic, an anticipation of increased publications in this domain is reasonable. The information in the articles are summarized in terms of the published journal, theme, sampling, method, theory, industry, and contextual variables. SciMat software is also analysed for the articles themes. The information related to articles searched are listed Table 1.

Firstly, 51 articles are listed. But, 40 of the 51 published papers are taken into account for scope. The number of journals in the Wos database, which includes the relevant keywords in the scope of the publication, is 417. Square root (417) is almost equal to the half of the number of article, that is 20. Price rule is confirmed.

3. FINDINGS

All studies are examined in the light of reaching the desirable outcomes of the machine learning studies in business. All publications highlight the desirable outcome depending on the designed variables for the machine learning as a tool of smart working systems.

When the studies are examined, it is seen that machine learning studies include all business functions (production, marketing, strategic management, public relations, logistics, supply chain management) except accounting. It has been revealed that the analysis unit of the examined studies is the organization, followed by the studies at the individual analysis level.

The research questions addressed in the studies were generally changing roles during and after the covid-19 pandemic, system development, diagnosis of senior management trends, and the reactions of organizations to the covid-19 process. It is seen that the majority of the studies examined are published researches in the fields of information management systems and the service sector. It has been revealed that the focus is on the themes of Customer-Travel-Consumption and Hospitality.

Surveys, website data and information transfer from social media stand out as data collection methods. In some studies, it is seen that there are different techniques (social media analytics, web scraper) other than machine-learning. Highly utilized machine-learning methods in this concept are determined as Naïve Bayes, Linear regression, Logistic regression, Support Vector Machines (SVM), Random Forest, Neural Networks, and Deep Learning methods such as Convolutional Neural Networks (CNN) and Long Short-Term Memory (LSTM). Random Forest. Main techniques

Table 1. Machine learning studies in business during Covid-19 pandemic

No	Name of Journal	Problem definition	Sampling	Data Collection Method	Types of Machine Learning	Variables	Data Analysis Technique	Authors
1	Technovation	Disruptive digital innovations in healthcare	42 studies in healthcare domain	Review	-	-	Bibliographic analysis	Bamel et. al. (2023)
2	Technovation	Resource re-orchestration and firm survival	56 AI and Digital Driven-High Tech firms world wide	Bloomberg equity screening functionality with the "industry search criteria"	-	11 variables about business model drive in relation with firm performance	principal component analysis (PCA) and multicriteria decision analysis (PROMETHEE methods)	Attah-Boakye et. al. (2023)
3	Managerial and Decision Economics	Predicting firm resilience	15 sample groups of about 150,000 data points across North America, Europe, and APAC	Survey	artificial neural networks, decision tree, bagged trees, gradient boosting and random forest	35 variables for about a 4,100 firms	Logistic regression analysis, correlation analysis	Bughin, J. (2023)
4	International Journal of Forecasting	Real-time inflation forecasting	240 observations gathered from a rolling window of 20 years	FRED-MD database	time-varying parameter (TVP) regressions	105 variables about inflation	PCA, diffusion maps, Local linear embeddings (LLE), Isometric Feature Mapping (ISOMAP), Non-linear compression with Autoencoders	Hauzenberger et. al. (2023)
5	Journal of Business Research	user experience in mobile-health applications	40,852 user reviews of nine mHealth care applications from India from June to September 2021	Collected from health care applications	Logistic regression, Linear regression	15 variables corresponding utilitarian motivation, hedonic motivation, brand support and loyalty, perceived quality and moderating variables to predict user rating	pre-processing, text-cleaning, and stemming to create predictors. Sentiment analysis to create moderating variables.	Pal et. al. (2023)
6	Journal of Business Research	Vaccine suply chain management	215,063 online drug reviews for sentiment analysis and U.S. influenza vaccination volume (million doses) from 1980 to 2020 for the vaccine demand forecasting	Reviews from Drugs.com website	Convolutional neural networks (CNN) and Bidirectional Long short-term memory (BILSTM) for sentiment analysis. Recurrent neural networks (RNN), Long short-term memory (LSTM) networks, Gated recurrent unit (GRU) networks for forecasting	Words gathered from reviews for sentiment analysis and time-series data variables for forecasting	Data preprocessing techniques including tokenization, removing punctuation and numbers, lemmatization, padding, and truncation	Hu et. al.(2023)
7	Advanced Machine Learning Algorithms for Complex Financial Applications			Review				Pal, T. (2023)

continued on following page

Table 1. Continued

No	Name of Journal	Problem definition	Sampling	Data Collection Method	Types of Machine Learning	Variables	Data Analysis Technique	Authors
8	International Journal of Engineering Business Management	Flight demand forecasting	29,363 flight data for training and 2192 flight data for testing	Collected from an ailrine company in China	Support vector regression (SVR)	Time-series parameters	Regression analysis	Fan et. al. (2023)
9	Advances in Business Statistics, Methods and Data Collection			Book				
10	EuroMed Journal of Business	Predicting CAC 40 index of French stock market	513 rows of stock market observations belonging to 40 companies. Data is grouped	Yahoo Finance	K-nearest neighbors, LSTM, and ARIMA	41 groups of columns including the opening, low, and high values for each stock and the index	-	Lachaab and Omri (2023)
11	Logistics	Supply chain management	187 articles gathered from Google Scholar, Scopus, and Web of Science	Review	A variety of machine learning methods	-	-	Raja Santhi and Muthuswamy (2022)
12	International Journal of Information Management Data Insights	Stress management in workplaces and education	53 articles gathered from Scopus, Web of Science Database, ERIC, Google Scholar	Review	A variety of machine learning and deep learning methods	Personal, interpersonal, work-related, and pschological factors affecting stress	-	Mittal et. al. (2022)
13	Deep Learning for Healthcare Decision Making	Deep learning in healthcare systems	-	Review	CNN, RNN, Restricted Boltzmann machines (RBM), Deep belief networks (DBN), Generative Adversarial Networks (GAN)	-	-	Gnanasankaran et. al. (2022)
14	International Journal of Physical Distribution and Logistics Management	Predicting shipment times of therapeutic supplies in e-pharmacy supply chains	5.9 million records of therapeutic shipments collected before and after COVID lockdown	Gathered from one of the largest e-pharmacies in India	Random Forest (RF), Extra Trees (XRT), Decision Tree (DT), Multi-Layer Perceptron (MLP), Extreme Gradient Boosting (XGB), CatBoost (CB), Linear Stochastic Gradient Descent (SGD) and Naïve Bayes (NB)	A variety of variables including date time and cyclic variables, numerical variables, categorical variables, and several derived variables	-	Mariappan et. al. (2022)
15	Journal of Digital and Social Media Marketing	Marketing	-	-	Reiforcement learning	-	-	Murphy et. al. (2022)
16	Journal of Retailing and Consumer Services	Online food delivery (OFD)	Data from 4 OFD companies in India and USA. Number of samples are 11,134 for Zomato, 14,355 for Swiggy, 15,583 for Uber Eats, and 2030 for Grubhub	Twitter data	Ordinal least square (OLS) regressions	COVID-19 wave, brand, market size, country, and listed t predict customers' sentiments about OFD companies	Latent Dirichlet Allocation, Sentiment analysis	Meena and Kumar (2022)

continued on following page

Table 1. Continued

No	Name of Journal	Problem definition	Sampling	Data Collection Method	Types of Machine Learning	Variables	Data Analysis Technique	Authors
17	Quality - Access to Success	Online Teaching	-	Interviews	-	-	-	Moşteanu (2022)
18	Technological Forecasting and Social Change	Detecting cyber attacks for small entrepreneurs	100 seconds of DDos attack simulation	Simulation constructed using OMNET++.	Support vector machines (SVM), Logistic regression, Decision trees, Random forest, Gradient boosting, Multinominal Naïve Bayes	Network variables like received packets, entropy, nurmal data rate, and current data rate etc.	-	Gaurav et. al. (2022)
19	Journal of Enterprise Information Management	Sustainable development goals and entrepreneurial orientation of CEOs	User-generated data of CEOs who work for 75 Fortune companies and actively use social media	Gathered from Twitter	Multiple regression	social media reputation appreciation of the SDG, advocacy of the SDG	Automated content analysis, Inferential statistical analysis	Yadav et. al. (2022)
20	Handbook of e-Tourism	Accommodation in tourism sector	-	-	Recommendation systems	Text and image content	-	Krasnodebski, J. (2022)
21	2022 IEEE International Conference on Technology Management, Operations and Decisions	The effects of the COVID-19 pandemic on the Moroccan job market	Job advertisements from several sources between January 2019 and June 2021	Web scraping from job portals, Twitter and Facebook	Naive Bayes, SVM, Logistic Regression and Bert	The requirements and skills such as education level, type of contract, salary and soft skills	Removing duplicates, data filtering and normalization, feature extraction	Rahhal et. al. (2022)
22	2022 International Conference on Trends in Quantum Computing and Emerging Business Technologies	-	-	-	-	-	-	-
23	Benchmarking	The changes in the degree of scholars' attention to supply chain risk research after the outbreak of COVID-19	Supply chain publications between 2015 and 2022	Scopus, WoS, and Google Scholar	PCA	Number of publications and number of citations	-	Wang et. al. (2022)
24	Eurasian Studies in Business and Economics	the opinions regarding COVID-19 vaccination in education-related tweets	102,805 English tweets published in the month following the beginning of the vaccination process	Gathered from Twitter	Robustly Optimized BERT Pre-training Approach (ROBERTa) and deep learning meathods	Words collected from tweets	Latent Dirichlet Allocation and n-gram analysis	Kovacs et. al (2022)

continued on following page

Table 1. Continued

No	Name of Journal	Problem definition	Sampling	Data Collection Method	Types of Machine Learning	Variables	Data Analysis Technique	Authors
25	Journal of Financial Reporting and Accounting	Impact of prospectuses o initial public offering (IPO)	580 IPO prospectuses	Prospectuses were collected from the SEC Edgar database (US SEC, 2022), government policy indexes were gathered from OxCGRT (Blavatnik School of Government, 2020) and lastly, data for control variables were obtained from Thomson Reuters Eikon	Random Forest Regressor, Light Gradient Boosting Model, and Classical Linar Regression	Control variables like age, total assets, high technology company flag, market capitalisation, and research and development expenses etc.	Textual analysis, sentiment analysis	Fedorova et. al. (2022)
26	Technology Application in Tourism in Asia: Innovations, Theories and Practices	Technology applications in tourism	-	-	-	-	-	İştin et. al. (2022)
27	Lecture Notes in Information Systems and Organisation			Conference review				
28	International Series in Operations Research and Management Science	Detecting COVID-19 with deep learning	-	-	Differential evolution algorithm, CNN	-	-	Nagib et. al. (2022)
29	South African Journal of Economic and Management Sciences	Digital transformation projects in South Africa	1-hour interviews with 15 questions	-	-	-	-	Gertzen et. al. (2022)
30	Journal of Science and Technology Policy Management	The effects of COVID-19 on various industries such as health care, manufacturing, retail, food services, education,media and entertainment, banking and insurance, travel, and tourism	127 articles	Review	39 different smart technologies	-	-	Agarwal et. al. (2022)

continued on following page

Table 1. Continued

No	Name of Journal	Problem definition	Sampling	Data Collection Method	Types of Machine Learning	Variables	Data Analysis Technique	Authors
31	European Sport Management Quarterly	sport brand involvement	770 participants in China	Survey	recursive feature elimination (RFE) with a random forest classifier, Lasso regularization, fast correlation-based algorithm (FCBF)	sport brand involvement (SBI), crisis management performance, and perceived togetherness, fans' sense of hope and emptines	Bayesian structural mediation analysis	Su et al (2022)
32	Journal of Retailing and Consumer Services	Travel satisfaction	1538 web data and 369 questionnaire	Ratings and textual reviewers by TripAdvisor website Questionnaire	Fuzzy Rule-based system	Sleep, quality, value (cost-benefit), service, location, rooms, cleanliness	Lantent dirichlet allocation, K-meens, SEM, Higher order singular value decomposition	Nilashi et al (2022)
33	Human Resource Management Review	Disrupted changing role of Human Resources with Covid-19 outbreak	-	-	-	-	Literature Review.	Minbaeva et al (2021)
34	Big Data and Cognitive Computing	The use of big data analysis during Covid-19 outbreak	Journals, Proceedings from SCOPUS and IEEE	Qualitative, Literature review	Semantic network analysis	Hospitality and Tourism, Transportation, Finance	Word cloud	Riswantini et al.(2021)
35	Big Data Research	Big Data Analytics and IoT integration for predicting a novel disease	26000 records of male and female patients of different age groups	Obtained from different hospitals of Khyber-Pakhtunkhwa, Pakistan	Neural networks, Adaboost, KNN, Logistic regression, Naïve Bayes, Linear SVM	22 attributes of patient data	-	Ahmed et. al. (2021)
36	2021 2nd International Conference on Intelligent Engineering and Management	Covid-Proof Smart systems	-	-	Unmanned air vehicle methods, augmented reality, robotics, image recognition, smart sensors	Developing model	-	Shahina and Kaaber (2021)
37	International Journal of Hospitality Management	Comparative study of deep learning models for analyzing restaurant reviews	112412 restaurant reviews in USA	On the web sites (Yelp.com)	Gradient boosting decision tree classifier, Random forest classifier, Bidirectional Long-short term memory (LSTM), Simple word-embedding model (SWEM)	Restaurant features (service, food, place, experience)	Term Frequency-Inverse Document Frequency (TF-IDF), dictionary-based sentiment analysis	Luo and Xu (2021)

continued on following page

Table 1. Continued

No	Name of Journal	Problem definition	Sampling	Data Collection Method	Types of Machine Learning	Variables	Data Analysis Technique	Authors
38	International Journal of Quality and Service Science	Critical success factors for lean six sigma in quality 4.0 for post-Covid 19 business	-	Questionnaire, scales	Various methods in combination with six sigma	Critical success factors for Lean Six Sigma: Top management commitment, Training on lean six sigma, Prior quality management system use e.g. ISO 9001/IATF 16949, Knowledge of the entire value stream, High volume, low variety set-up, Project management skills, Mechanism of feedback to processes, and corrective actions from data analysis, Funds/ resource availability, Skilled employees, Prior business improvement methodology use e.g. balanced scorecard/theory of inventive problem-solving (TRIZ), Employee involvement, Line balancing and production levelling practices, Change management culture	Cronbach's alpha, t-test and exploratory factor analysis.	Yadav et al., 2020
39	Proceedings of the 12th International Joint Conference on Knowledge Discovery, Knowledge Engineering and Knowledge Management	Personalised recommendation systems and the impact of covid-19	User information collected from e-trading web sites	Conceptual	Recommendation Systems using content-based filtering (CBF), collaborative filtering (CF) or hybrid approaches. Cluster analysis and deep learning algorithms, to improve the quality of predictions	discusses the impact of the COVID-19 pandemic on the Recommendation Systems landscape and focuses on new and atypical users	User ratings and preferences	Abdulrahman and Victor, 2020.
40	International Journal of Contemporary Hospitality Management	Revealing industry challenge and business response to Covid-19:	the hospitality industry 94,340 tweets of ordinary users and business owners	Web scraper	structural topic modeling	Whether a tweet has media, How many likes a tweet had received, How many times a tweet had been retweeted, The length of tweets	normalisation, stemming and character removing	Yang and Han, 2021

level in machine learning applications are firm performance, stock index, brand support, market size, social media reputation, being high-tech company or not, research and development expenses, crisis management performance, training on lean six sigma. The variables studied at the individual level are utilitarian motivation, hedonic motivation, loyalty, perceived quality, stress, customer sentiment, perceived togetherness, top management commitment, and project management skills.

As a result of the analysis of the articles examined with the help of the Scimat program, four outputs were obtained: 1. Strategic Diagram of Themes (Figure 1) 2. Cluster Network for theme "covid-19" (Figure 2). 3. Cluster Network for theme "decision making" (Figure 3). 4. 2. Cluster Network for theme "prediction" (Figure 4).

When the strategic diagram is examined, it is seen that the terms prediction and decision making are grouped together with the term Covid-19 in the motor themes

Figure 1. Strategic diagram of themes analyzed by Scimat

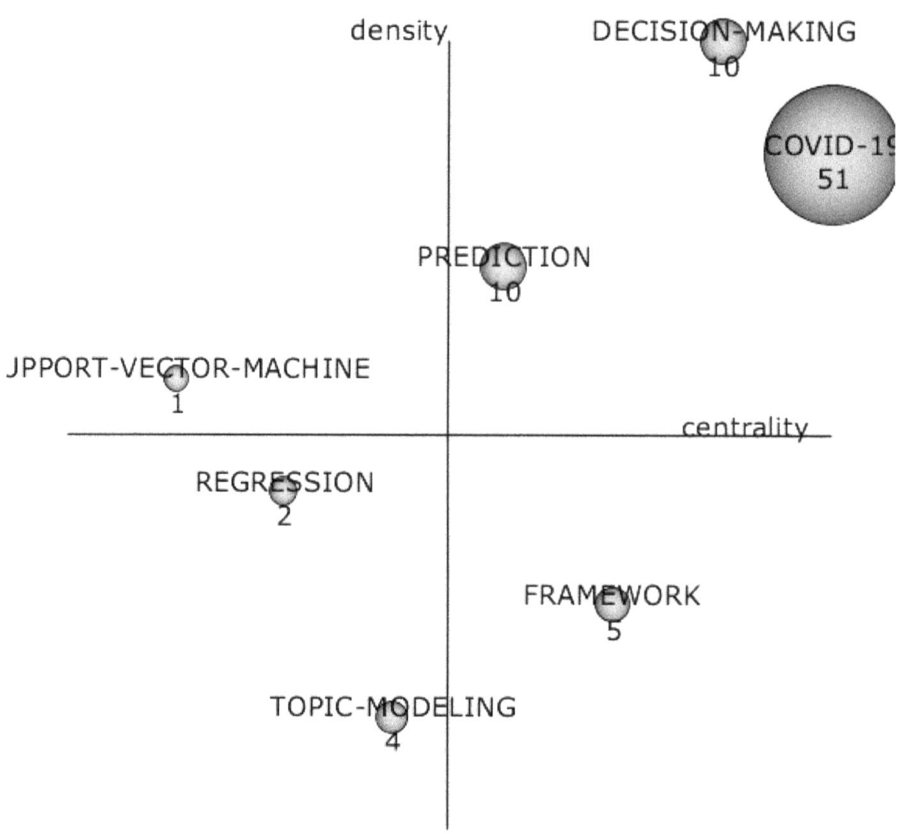

Figure 2. Cluster network for Covid-19 theme

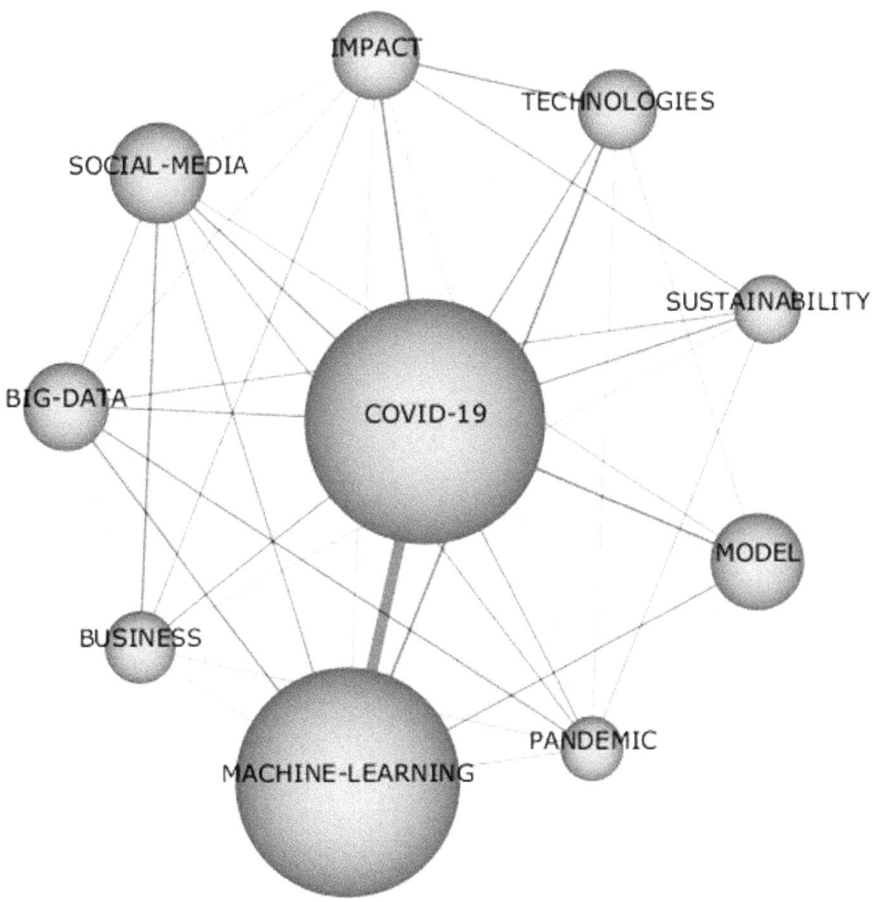

used in data analysis: dirichlet allocation, K-means, SEM, Higher order singular value decomposition, Bayesian structural equation modeling, cronbach alpha, t test, exploratory factor analysis for the scales, content analysis, sentiment analysis and space–time analysis have been used, followed by multivariate.

It has been observed that studies at the macroeconomic level are relatively few in the literature. Inflation rate and estimating stocks in the stock market in a financial perspective makes machine learning important as a smart working tool in the process of estimating the relationship between macroeconomic variables and business level.

It is seen that there are a wide range of contextual variables according to the models determined in the researches. The variables mostly examined at the organizational

Figure 3. Cluster network for decision-making theme

area. The emerging engine themes characterize the function of machine learning as a tool in smart working systems. They are the most studied and most advanced themes in the field. Two themes appeared in the emerging or decreasing themes section: Regression and topic modelling. These themes address the underlying statistics approaches and techniques for the machine learning tool. In the field of highly developed and isolated themes, the term support-vector- machine has emerged. This term can also be interpreted as a technical feature in the use of machine learning. The term framework, which emerged in the field of basic transformational themes, has a high centrality and low density feature. It is the theme with the highest relationship with other external themes. When the cluster network is examined, It has been observed that more studies are published with the term machine learning for the

Figure 4. Cluster network for prediction theme

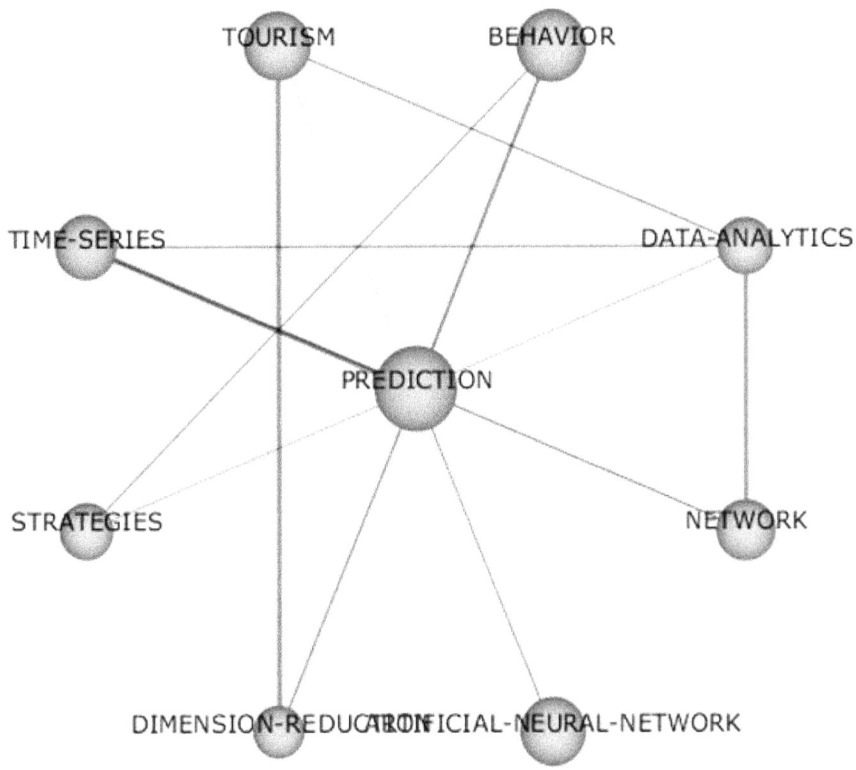

Covid-19 theme. In addition, it shows that the themes of big data, sustainability and social media are related to the Covid-19 term in the context of machine learning. For the decision making theme, the most related themes emerged as "management" and "performance". The relationship between information and adaptation draws attention in the context of decision making. Other themes working with decision making theme: logistics, system, digitalization, innovation, risk. For the prediction theme, time-series is grouped as the most commonly used term. It can be addressed as the most used technique in the prediction process. Data analytics, dimension reduction, artificial-neural-network specify the techniques in the machine learning infrastructure as other defined terms. Tourism is in the feature of the sector where the prediction theme is the most mention about. Behavior and strategy terms emphasize machine learning-themed research at individual level and organizational level, respectively.

4. CONCLUSION

Studies have shown that machine learning can be a tool for optimizing business resources and digitizing all processes. With the Covid-19 pandemic crisis, technological transformation has accelerated and machine learning has become an effective forecasting tool in the survival of businesses. Digitalization and technological transformation also draws attention to the replacement of human resources with machines. The human resources department is developing new job roles for employees as machine learning applications increase.

Research emphasizes that machine learning applications in different sectors bring along sectorial change and that the responsiveness of enterprises to these sectorial changes will also change on the basis of smart systems.

Machine learning applications, which will be widely used as a tool in smart systems, necessitate a change in organizational structures. A study on this subject draws attention to the lean organizational structure. The substitution of the machine with the human, the increase in the workforce qualifications and the reduction in the number of working personnel require designing leaner organizational structures. Machine learning applications accelerate this trend on the basis of smart systems.

5. ORIGINALITY

Industry 4.0 and Industry 5.0 have significantly changed the way of executing jobs in organizations depending on technological advancement. The comfort that new technologies provide in human life, for example, home-office work, e-commerce, online work, and education change the business context for the employees. It is seen that the majority of the studies examined are published in the fields of information management systems and the service sector. The research questions addressed in the studies were generally changing roles during and after the covid-19 pandemic, system development, diagnosis of senior management trends, and the reactions of businesses to the Covid-19 process. It is apparent that there are a wide range of contextual variables according to the models determined in the researches. In practice, it will be an valuable input for the smart-working system strategies to be developed for all business function systems the organization. With the onset of the pandemic, the interest in the effective use of resources by firms can play a role in ensuring sustainability, depending on the development of smart working systems on machine learning tool.

REFERENCES

Abdulrahman, R., & Viktor, H. L. (2020). Personalised recommendation systems and the impact of covid-19: Perspectives, opportunities and challenges. *Proceedings of the 12th International Joint Conference on Knowledge Discovery, Knowledge Engineering and Knowledge Management*, (*vol.* 1, pp. 295-301). Scitepress. 10.5220/0010145702950301

Attah-Boakye, R., Adams, K., Hernandez-Perdomo, E., Yu, H., & Johansson, J. (2023). Resource Re-orchestration and firm survival in crisis periods: The role of business models of technology MNEs during COVID-19. *Technovation*, *125*, 102769. doi:10.1016/j.technovation.2023.102769

Bamel, U., Talwar, S., Pereira, V., Corazza, L., & Dhir, A. (2023). Disruptive digital innovations in healthcare: Knowing the past and anticipating the future. *Technovation*, *125*, 102785. doi:10.1016/j.technovation.2023.102785

Bughin, J. (2023). Are you resilient? Machine learning prediction of corporate rebound out of the Covid-19 pandemic. *MDE. Managerial and Decision Economics*, *44*(3), 1547–1564. doi:10.1002/mde.3764

Chaves-Maza, M., & Martel, E. M. F. (2020). *Entrepreneurship support ways after the COVID-19 crisis*. Entrepreneurship Sustain. doi:10.9770/jesi.2020.8.2(40)

Donthu, N., & Gustafsson, A. (2020). Effects of COVID-19 on business and research. *Journal of Business Research*, *117*, 284–289. doi:10.1016/j.jbusres.2020.06.008 PMID:32536736

Fan, W., Wu, X., Shi, X. Y., Zhang, C., Wai Hung, I., Kai Leung, Y., & Zeng, L. S. (2023). Support vector regression model for flight demand forecasting. *International Journal of Engineering Business Management*, *15*, 18479790231174318. doi:10.1177/18479790231174318

Funk, S., Gilad, E., Watkins, C., & Jansen, V. A. (2009). The spread of awareness and its impact on epidemic outbreaks. *Proceedings of the National Academy of Sciences of the United States of America*, *106*(16), 6872–6877. doi:10.1073/pnas.0810762106 PMID:19332788

Hauzenberger, N., Huber, F., & Klieber, K. (2023). Real-time inflation forecasting using non-linear dimension reduction techniques. *International Journal of Forecasting*, *39*(2), 901–921. doi:10.1016/j.ijforecast.2022.03.002

Hu, H., Xu, J., Liu, M., & Lim, M. K. (2023). Vaccine supply chain management: An intelligent system utilizing blockchain, IoT and machine learning. *Journal of Business Research*, *156*, 113480. doi:10.1016/j.jbusres.2022.113480 PMID:36506475

Luo, Y., & Xu, X. (2021). Comparative study of deep learning models for analyzing online restaurant reviews in the era of the COVID-19 pandemic. *International Journal of Hospitality Management*, *94*, 102849. doi:10.1016/j.ijhm.2020.102849 PMID:34785843

McKinsey, G. L., Lizama, C. O., Keown-Lang, A. E., Niu, A., Santander, N., Larpthaveesarp, A., & Arnold, T. D. (2020). A new genetic strategy for targeting microglia in development and disease. *elife, 9*, e54590.

Minbaeva, D. (2021). Disrupted HR? *Human Resource Management Review*, *31*(4), 100820. doi:10.1016/j.hrmr.2020.100820

Nilashi, M., Abumalloh, R. A., Minaei-Bidgoli, B., Abdu Zogaan, W., Alhargan, A., Mohd, S., Syed Azhar, S. N. F., Asadi, S., & Samad, S. (2021). Revealing travellers' satisfaction during COVID-19 outbreak: Moderating role of service quality. *Journal of Retailing and Consumer Services*, *64*, 102783. doi:10.1016/j.jretconser.2021.102783

Pal, S., Biswas, B., Gupta, R., Kumar, A., & Gupta, S. (2023). Exploring the factors that affect user experience in mobile-health applications: A text-mining and machine-learning approach. *Journal of Business Research*, *156*, 113484. doi:10.1016/j.jbusres.2022.113484 PMID:36475057

Pal, T. (2023). The Exploratory Study of Machine Learning on Applications, Challenges, and Uses in the Financial Sector. In *Advanced Machine Learning Algorithms for Complex Financial Applications* (pp. 156–165). IGI Global. doi:10.4018/978-1-6684-4483-2.ch010

Riswantini, D., Nugraheni, E., Arisal, A., Khotimah, P.H., Munandar, D., & Suwarningsih, W. (2021). Big data research in fighting COVID-19: Contributions and techniques. *Big Data and Cognitive Computing*, *5*(3).

Shahina, F. A. C., & Kabeer, S. (2021). Covid-Proof' Smart World. *Proceedings of 2021 2nd International Conference on Intelligent Engineering and Management*. Scitepress.

Su, Y., Du, J., Biscaia, R., & Inoue, Y. (2021). We are in this together: Sport brand involvcmcnt and fans' well-bein. *European Sport Management Quarterly*.

Yadav, H., Kar, A. K., & Kashiramka, S. (2021). How does entrepreneurial orientation and SDG orientation of CEOs evolve before and during a pandemic. *Journal of Enterprise Information Management*.

Yadav, N., Shankar, R., & Singh, S. P. (2021). Critical success factors for lean six sigma in quality 4.0. *International Journal of Quality and Service Sciences*, *13*(1), 123–156. doi:10.1108/IJQSS-06-2020-0099

Yang, M., & Han, C. (2020). Revealing industry challenge and business response to Covid-19: A text mining approach. *International Journal of Contemporary Hospitality Management*, *33*(4), 1230–1248. doi:10.1108/IJCHM-08-2020-0920

Zhang, A., Prang, K. H., Devlin, N., Scott, A., & Kelaher, M. (2020). The impact of price transparency on consumers and providers: A scoping review. *Health Policy (Amsterdam)*, *124*(8), 819–825. doi:10.1016/j.healthpol.2020.06.001 PMID:32576391

Chapter 7
Smart Working Strategies Unlocking Innovation and Entrepreneurship With Resilience, Agility, and Dynamic Capabilities

Ayse Asli Yilmaz
https://orcid.org/0000-0003-1784-7307
Atilim University, Turkey

ABSTRACT

The rise of smart working has revolutionized the way organizations operate, presenting new strategies and courses of action for innovation and entrepreneurial growth. This book chapter proposes research into the strategies and management practices that organizations can employ within the framework of resilience, agility, and dynamic capabilities to unlock and harness innovation capabilities and entrepreneurial opportunities in the context of smart working. By examining the interplay between these concepts, this chapter seeks to uncover practical insights and provide guidance for organizations in maximizing the potential of smart working for innovation and entrepreneurship.

1. INTRODUCTION

Smart working has emerged as a catalyst for fostering innovation and creating entrepreneurial opportunities in organizations. It refers to a flexible work approach

DOI: 10.4018/978-1-7998-8797-3.ch007

that leverages technology and enables employees to work remotely, collaborate efficiently, and achieve a better work-life balance (Doherty & Burke, 2019). It involves the use of digital tools, virtual communication platforms, and cloud-based solutions to facilitate seamless collaboration and productivity regardless of physical location. Smart working encompasses various forms such as telecommuting, remote work, and virtual teams, allowing organizations to tap into a global talent pool and embrace diverse perspectives (Albrecht et al., 2019).

Smart working has been recognized as a driver of innovation capabilities within organizations. It provides employees with the flexibility and autonomy to explore new ideas, experiment, and engage in creative problem-solving (Kowalkiewicz et al., 2020). By breaking down geographical barriers and promoting collaboration among remote teams, smart working fosters a culture of innovation and knowledge sharing (Bentley et al., 2019). Moreover, smart working enables organizations to tap into entrepreneurial opportunities by leveraging the skills and expertise of remote workers and facilitating the rapid development and implementation of innovative ideas (Raghupathi et al., 2020).

While smart working offers significant opportunities for innovation and entrepreneurship, it also poses certain challenges. One key challenge is the need for effective communication and collaboration tools to ensure seamless virtual interactions among team members (Arazy et al., 2020). Organizations must invest in reliable technology infrastructure and establish protocols for virtual meetings, project management, and information sharing to overcome these challenges. Additionally, ensuring data security and privacy in a smart working environment is crucial to protect sensitive information (Caniëls & Semeijn, 2020).

To leverage smart working for innovation and entrepreneurial opportunities, organizations should focus on creating a supportive and inclusive culture that encourages creativity, risk-taking, and continuous learning (Huczynski et al., 2021). Providing training and development programs to enhance digital literacy and remote collaboration skills among employees is essential for harnessing the full potential of smart working (Oksanen et al., 2019). Furthermore, organizations should establish clear performance metrics and reward systems that recognize and incentivize innovative and entrepreneurial behaviors in a smart working context (Davenport et al., 2020). This section provides a comprehensive review of the literature on the definition and characteristics of smart working, explores the linkages between smart working, innovation capabilities, and entrepreneurial opportunities, and discusses the key challenges and opportunities in leveraging smart working for innovation and entrepreneurship. the study's "Background and significance of the chapter," "Research objectives and relevance of the topic," and "Overview of the chapter structure" will be described in detail for the target audience.

In the light of all, this chapter is designed that will be a roadmap for organizations and decision makers for smart working strategies through unlocking innovation and entrepreneurship with resilience, agility, and dynamic capabilities.

This journey starts from the comprehension of organizational dynamic capabilities and situational awareness Then, it is time to proceed the organizations towards innovation that has no boundaries. For this reason, the question of how organizations can employ strategies and management practices based on resilience, agility, and dynamic capabilities to enhance innovation skills and embrace entrepreneurial opportunities in the context of smart working is the research question. Therefore, this chapter aims to illustrate the importance of knowledge smart working strategies through unlocking innovation and entrepreneurship with resilience, agility, and dynamic capabilities particularly the correspondence between aspects of knowledge management and open innovation. As a result, this chapter is designed in a logical sequence. First, the relationship among resilience, agility, and dynamic capabilities in the organizations is discussed. The strategies for enhancing innovation capabilities in smart working is then presented. Finally, the conclusion is provided.

2. RESILIENCE, AGILITY, AND DYNAMIC CAPABILITIES

Resilience, agility, and dynamic capabilities are critical concepts that organizations need to embrace in today's dynamic and uncertain business environment. This section provides a comprehensive review of the literature on resilience, agility, and dynamic capabilities, exploring their theoretical foundations and discussing their role in managing disruptions, fostering innovation, and seizing entrepreneurial opportunities. Resilience, agility, and dynamic capabilities are indeed critical concepts in today's fast-paced and uncertain business environment. These concepts help organizations adapt, thrive, and maintain a competitive edge.

Resilience refers to an organization's ability to withstand disruptions, bounce back from adversity, and continue operating effectively. It involves identifying and managing risks, building robust systems, and fostering a culture of adaptability and learning (Zolnowski & Mueller, 2019). Agility refers to an organization's capacity to respond quickly and effectively to changes in its external environment. It involves the ability to make swift decisions, adjust strategies, and reconfigure resources to capitalize on emerging opportunities or mitigate threats (Teece, 2018). Dynamic capabilities are an organization's capacity to integrate, build, and reconfigure internal and external competencies to address rapidly changing environments. It encompasses the ability to sense opportunities, seize them, and continually renew strategic resources and capabilities (Teece,2007). These concepts are interconnected and mutually reinforcing. Resilience provides a foundation for agility and dynamic capabilities by ensuring that an organization can withstand shocks and disruptions. Agility enables organizations to respond swiftly to change, while dynamic capabilities help them to innovate and adapt in a rapidly evolving environment (Doz & Kosonen, 2010).

When it comes to the understanding resilience and its role in managing disruptions and fostering innovation this requires more scrutinized. Resilience is the ability of organizations to effectively respond, adapt, and recover from disruptions or adversity (Mehralian et al., 2021). Resilient organizations are equipped with the capabilities to absorb shocks, quickly recover, and even transform in the face of challenges (Doern et al., 2020). Therefore, resilience enables organizations to identify opportunities within crises, foster innovation, and develop new competitive advantages (Hamel, 2020). It involves proactive risk management, robust infrastructure, and a culture of learning and adaptation (Wilden et al., 2019). Decision makers must comprehend agility as a driver of adaptability, responsiveness, and entrepreneurial opportunities. Agility refers to the ability of organizations to sense, seize, and capitalize on opportunities in a rapidly changing environment (Teece, 2018). Agile organizations are characterized by their ability to quickly respond to market shifts, adapt their strategies, and make timely decisions (Sambamurthy et al., 2020). Agile practices enable organizations to foster innovation, enhance customer responsiveness, and create entrepreneurial opportunities (Senge et al., 2012). Agile organizations embrace experimentation, cross-functional collaboration, and iterative approaches to problem-solving (Rigby et al., 2016). Dynamic Capabilities could be thought as enablers of learning, renewal, and innovation. Because dynamic capabilities represent an organization's ability to integrate, build, and reconfigure its resources and competencies to adapt to the changing business landscape (Teece et al., 2016). These capabilities involve sensing market opportunities, seizing them through effective resource allocation, and continuously reconfiguring the organization's capabilities to sustain competitive advantage (Helfat et al., 2007). Dynamic capabilities provide organizations to engage in continuous learning, promote innovation, and pursue entrepreneurial opportunities (Zollo et al., 2019). They involve the ability to sense changes, seize opportunities, and transform resources and processes (Helfat, 2021). To leverage resilience, agility, and dynamic capabilities, organizations must foster a culture that values adaptability, innovation, and learning (Birkenshaw et al., 2019). They need to invest in building organizational structures and processes that promote flexibility, collaboration, and information sharing (Eisenhardt et al., 2016). Additionally, organizations should cultivate a mindset that embraces change, encourages experimentation, and supports entrepreneurial initiatives (Burgelman et al., 2018).

The strategies for enhancing innovation capabilities in smart working, in particular, developing a culture of innovation in smart working organizations, leveraging digital technologies and collaborative platforms for innovation in remote teams/ subgroups, and best practices and strategies for fostering innovation capabilities in smart working environment are needed to be understood. Because in today's rapidly evolving business landscape, organizations are increasingly adopting smart working practices to enhance their innovation capabilities. Creating a culture of innovation is crucial for organizations to foster creativity, collaboration, and idea generation in the context of smart working. This involves cultivating an environment that encourages risk-taking, embraces diverse perspectives, and rewards experimentation (Dahlander et al., 2020). Smart working organizations can promote innovation by providing employees with autonomy, encouraging knowledge sharing, and fostering a mindset that values continuous improvement and learning (O'Reilly et al., 2019). When it comes to leveraging digital technologies and collaborative platforms for innovation in remote teams/subgroups, digital technologies and collaborative platforms play a vital role in facilitating innovation in smart working environments. These tools enable remote teams and subgroups to collaborate effectively, share ideas, and co-create solutions (Chesbrough et al., 2018). Cloud-based project management tools, virtual meeting platforms, and online ideation platforms can enhance communication, knowledge sharing, and the generation of innovative ideas (Bughin et al., 2018). Leveraging these technologies allows organizations to overcome geographical barriers and tap into the diverse expertise of their distributed workforce. Best Practices and Strategies for Fostering Innovation Capabilities in Smart Working Environments have significant contributions. Several best practices and strategies can be implemented to foster innovation capabilities in smart working environments. These include:

Encouraging cross-functional collaboration: Promoting collaboration across different functions and departments enables the exchange of diverse perspectives and knowledge, leading to innovative outcomes (West et al., 2019). Smart working organizations can establish virtual collaboration spaces and encourage interdisciplinary teams to work together on innovation projects.

Supporting continuous learning and professional development: Providing employees with opportunities for skill development and learning is crucial for fostering innovation. Organizations can offer virtual training programs, online courses, and webinars to enhance employees' knowledge and capabilities (Eisenbeiss et al., 2020). Additionally, creating a supportive environment for knowledge sharing and feedback can encourage a culture of continuous learning and improvement.

Embracing user-centered design and co-creation: Involving end-users and stakeholders in the innovation process is essential for developing user-centric solutions. Smart working organizations can leverage virtual co-creation methods, such as online focus groups and virtual user testing, to gather insights and feedback from users (Bogers et al., 2017). This approach ensures that innovative solutions meet the needs and preferences of the target audience.

Implementing resilience, agility, and dynamic capabilities in the context of smart working can greatly enhance an organization's innovation capabilities.

By combining these strategies with a focus on innovation, organizations can leverage digital technologies and best practices to maximize the potential of their distributed workforce and foster a culture of creativity. To promote innovation within a distributed workforce, organizations need to create an environment that encourages experimentation, collaboration, and continuous learning. This involves empowering employees to take risks, sharing knowledge and ideas across teams and departments, and recognizing and rewarding innovative efforts (Amabile & Pratt, 2016). Digital technologies play a crucial role in enabling innovation within a distributed workforce. Cloud-based collaboration tools, project management platforms, and virtual communication platforms facilitate seamless collaboration and knowledge sharing among remote teams. These technologies provide a foundation for fostering creativity and innovation across geographically. Organizations can enhance their innovation capabilities by adopting and implementing best practices in smart working. This involves establishing clear goals and objectives, developing effective communication channels, providing appropriate training and support for remote teams, and regularly evaluating and improving processes. (Battistelli & Montani, 2019).

By combining resilience, agility, and dynamic capabilities with a focus on innovation, organizations can create a dynamic and adaptive environment that unleashes the creative potential of their distributed workforce.

3. MANAGEMENT APPROACHES FOR SEIZING ENTREPRENEURIAL OPPORTUNITIES IN SMART WORKING

The emergence of smart working has provided organizations with new avenues for identifying and capitalizing on entrepreneurial opportunities. So, the comprehension on the management approaches for effectively seizing entrepreneurial opportunities in the context of smart working, including identifying opportunities, promoting startup formation and growth, and implementing effective management practices are required by the decision makers.Identifying and evaluating entrepreneurial opportunities is a crucial step in the entrepreneurial process. In the context of smart working, organizations can leverage various approaches to identify opportunities. These include conducting market research, analysing emerging trends and technologies, monitoring customer needs and preferences, and engaging in open innovation practices (Chesbrough, 2006). Additionally, smart working organizations can encourage employees to contribute ideas and participate in innovation challenges to uncover entrepreneurial opportunities within the organization (Bogers et al., 2017). It is important for organizations to establish processes and mechanisms for evaluating the feasibility and potential of these opportunities, considering factors such as market demand, resource availability, and competitive landscape (Shane and Venkataraman, 2000). In addition, smart working environments offer unique advantages for promoting startup formation and growth. Organizations can support entrepreneurial employees in their startup endeavours by providing access to resources, networks, and mentorship programs (Van der Zwan et al., 2019). Additionally, organizations can foster a culture of intrapreneurship, encouraging employees to develop and pursue their entrepreneurial ideas within the organization (Antoncic and Hisrich, 2003). Creating flexible work arrangements, providing seed funding, and offering shared office spaces or incubator programs can facilitate the establishment and growth of startups in a smart working context (Gianiodis et al., 2019). Effective management practices play a critical role in leveraging entrepreneurial opportunities in smart working environments. Key practices include:

Empowering employees: Providing employees with autonomy and decision-making authority enables them to seize entrepreneurial opportunities. Organizations can empower employees by delegating responsibilities, encouraging risk-taking, and providing support and resources to pursue entrepreneurial initiatives (Bos-Nehles et al., 2021).

Building cross-functional teams: Forming cross-functional teams with diverse skills and perspectives enhances the capability to identify and pursue entrepreneurial opportunities. Collaborative teamwork enables the integration of different expertise and facilitates innovation and creativity (Eisenbeiss et al., 2020).

Emphasizing learning and adaptability: Smart working organizations should prioritize continuous learning and adaptability to navigate the dynamic business landscape. Learning-oriented cultures, training programs, and feedback mechanisms enable employees to develop the skills and knowledge necessary to identify and seize entrepreneurial opportunities (Rosing et al., 2011).

Implementing these management approaches enables organizations to effectively seize entrepreneurial opportunities in the context of smart working. By identifying and evaluating opportunities, promoting startup formation and growth, and implementing effective management practices, organizations can foster an entrepreneurial ecosystem that thrives in a smart working environment. So, it is time to explore the "Synergies and interdependencies between resilience, agility, and dynamic capabilities," "Strategies for integrating and optimizing these capabilities to enhance innovation and entrepreneurship in smart working," and "Real-world case studies showcasing successful implementation and management of resilience, agility, and dynamic capabilities in smart working environments." In today's dynamic and uncertain business landscape, organizations need to adopt a holistic approach that integrates resilience, agility, and dynamic capabilities to thrive and adapt to change. Understanding resilience and its role in managing disruptions and fostering innovation in smart working are required to be understood. Resilience refers to an organization's ability to withstand and recover from disruptions, while also adapting and transforming in response to changing circumstances. In the context of smart working, organizations need to build resilience to effectively manage remote work arrangements, technological disruptions, and market uncertainties (Sutcliffe et al., 2016). Resilience enables organizations to maintain business continuity, mitigate risks, and seize innovation opportunities by fostering a culture of adaptability and learning (Hermann et al., 2019). In addition, exploring agility as a driver of adaptability, responsiveness, and entrepreneurial opportunities in smart working are to be scrutinized.

Agility is the capability of organizations to quickly respond and adapt to changes in their environment. In a smart working context, agility plays a crucial role in enabling organizations to exploit emerging opportunities and respond to market demands. Agile organizations embrace iterative processes, decentralized decision-making, and cross-functional collaboration to enhance their responsiveness and capture entrepreneurial opportunities (Teece, 2018). By fostering a culture of experimentation, agility allows organizations to explore new ideas and innovate rapidly in the digital age (Rigby et al., 2016). Dynamic capabilities refer to an organization's ability to sense, seize, and transform resources and capabilities in response to changing market conditions. In the context of smart working, dynamic capabilities enable organizations to continuously learn, renew their strategies, and innovate to stay competitive (Teece, 2007). Organizations with strong dynamic capabilities effectively leverage digital technologies, develop new competencies, and adapt their business models to capitalize on entrepreneurial opportunities in the digital economy (Tushman and O'Reilly, 2017). So, it is considered as the dynamic capabilities might be enablers of learning, renewal, and innovation in the context of smart working. When it comes to the strategies for integrating and optimizing resilience, agility, and dynamic capabilities in smart working, integrating resilience, agility, and dynamic capabilities requires organizations to adopt strategies. These strategies that align these concepts and enable their synergistic interaction. Strategies include fostering a culture of flexibility and adaptability, developing agile and cross-functional teams, investing in technological infrastructure and capabilities, and promoting continuous learning and knowledge sharing (Helfat et al., 2019).

By integrating and optimizing these capabilities, organizations can enhance their ability to respond to disruptions, exploit opportunities, and drive innovation in the context of smart working. Real-world case studies showcasing successful implementation and management of resilience, agility, and dynamic capabilities in smart working environments further emphasize the practical implications of this holistic approach (Liu et al., 2019; Sanchez-Rodriguez et al., 2020). These case studies provide insights into the strategies, challenges, and outcomes of integrating resilience, agility, and dynamic capabilities in organizations across different industries and contexts. Therefore, the integration of resilience, agility, and dynamic capabilities offers organizations a holistic approach to navigate the complexities and uncertainties of the smart working landscape. By understanding the role of resilience in managing disruptions, embracing agility as a driver of adaptability, and leveraging dynamic capabilities for learning and innovation, organizations can enhance their ability to thrive in the digital age.

4. IMPLICATIONS FOR ORGANIZATIONS AND MANAGEMENT

As the subject deepens, it becomes evident how important understanding practical implications for organizations in enhancing innovation capabilities and seizing entrepreneurial opportunities in smart working, managerial strategies for developing and sustaining resilience, agility, and dynamic capabilities in a smart working context, and policy recommendations for supporting and promoting smart working as a platform for innovation and entrepreneurship relationships are.

The implications for organizations and management in the context of smart working are multifaceted and require careful consideration to maximize the benefits and address the challenges associated with this work arrangement. This literature review examines the practical implications for organizations and management in enhancing innovation capabilities and seizing entrepreneurial opportunities in the realm of smart working.Smart working offers organizations a range of practical implications for enhancing their innovation capabilities and capitalizing on entrepreneurial opportunities. One key implication is the need to develop a culture of innovation that fosters creativity, collaboration, and risk-taking (Cai et al., 2019). Organizations should create an environment that encourages idea generation, experimentation, and learning from failures to foster a culture of continuous innovation.

Leveraging digital technologies and collaborative platforms is another critical implication for organizations in smart working environments. Digital tools and platforms enable remote teams and subgroups to collaborate effectively, share knowledge, and leverage collective intelligence (Alipour et al., 2020). Organizations should invest in technologies that support virtual collaboration, communication, and knowledge management to facilitate innovation in distributed work settings. Best practices and strategies play a vital role in fostering innovation capabilities in smart working environments. Organizations can implement strategies such as open innovation, crowdsourcing, and design thinking methodologies to stimulate idea generation and accelerate the innovation process (Wonglimpiyarat, 2018). By embracing these best practices, organizations can tap into diverse perspectives and leverage external knowledge to drive innovation. To develop and sustain resilience, agility, and dynamic capabilities in a smart working context, effective managerial strategies are crucial. Managers should focus on creating a supportive and inclusive work environment that promotes employee well-being, engagement, and work-life balance (Kelliher & Anderson, 2010). This includes providing the necessary resources, training, and support for employees to adapt to the challenges of smart working. Promoting a culture of learning and continuous improvement is another essential managerial strategy. Managers should encourage employees to engage in ongoing skill development, knowledge sharing, and learning from both successes and failures (Nembhard & Edmondson, 2006). Learning-oriented organizations are better equipped to adapt to changing circumstances and seize entrepreneurial opportunities in smart working.

Policy recommendations are crucial for supporting and promoting smart working as a platform for innovation and entrepreneurship. Policymakers should consider providing incentives and support for organizations to invest in digital infrastructure, technology adoption, and training programs for employees to enhance their digital competencies (European Commission, 2020). Policies that encourage collaboration between academia, industry, and government can foster innovation ecosystems and promote knowledge exchange in smart working contexts.

Furthermore, policymakers can play a role in creating a regulatory framework that supports flexible work arrangements while ensuring employee rights, fair compensation, and work-life balance (International Labour Organization, 2017). Clear guidelines and regulations related to data security, privacy, and intellectual property rights are also important to build trust and confidence in smart working environments. Therefore, organizations and management need to navigate the practical implications of smart working to enhance innovation capabilities and seize entrepreneurial opportunities. By fostering a culture of innovation, leveraging digital technologies, adopting best practices, and implementing effective managerial strategies, organizations can maximize the potential of smart working. Additionally, policy recommendations that support digital infrastructure, skill development, and flexible work arrangements can further facilitate innovation and entrepreneurship in the context of smart working. In fact, this is a broad topic that can be applied to various sectors such as;

Information Technology (IT) Sector: In the IT sector, smart working strategies can enable remote collaboration, flexible work arrangements, and virtual teaming. This allows IT professionals to work on projects seamlessly, regardless of their geographical location. Smart working strategies also foster a culture of innovation and entrepreneurship by providing employees with the flexibility to experiment, explore new technologies, and develop creative solutions (Bosch-Sijtsema, & Vartiainen, 2017).

Creative Industries: In creative industries such as design, advertising, and media, smart working strategies enable professionals to work remotely, collaborate virtually, and leverage digital tools for creativity and innovation. This flexibility allows creative individuals and teams to explore new ideas, engage in cross-disciplinary collaborations, and adapt quickly to changing client needs, fostering entrepreneurship and dynamic capabilities (Calza & Corno, 2020).

Healthcare Sector: Smart working strategies in the healthcare sector can include telemedicine, remote patient monitoring, and virtual consultations. These strategies enhance the resilience and agility of healthcare organizations by allowing them to provide care remotely, reach underserved populations, and respond swiftly to emergencies or crises. They also create opportunities for innovation and entrepreneurship in digital health solutions and personalized medicine. Reference: Ohannessian, R., & Duong, T. A. (2020). Ongoing clinical trials for the management of the COVID-19 pandemic. Frontiers in Pharmacology, 11, 1196.

Manufacturing Sector: In the manufacturing sector, smart working strategies can incorporate technologies such as the Internet of Things (IoT), automation, and data analytics. These strategies enhance resilience by enabling remote monitoring of production processes, real-time supply chain management, and agile responses to disruptions. They also foster innovation and entrepreneurship through the development of smart products, predictive maintenance solutions, and agile manufacturing systems. Reference: Pillai, R. G., & Jain, P. K. (2019). Manufacturing 4.0: A bibliometric analysis and systematic literature review. Technological Forecasting and Social Change, 142, 70-85.

CONCLUSION

Smart working strategies that leverage resilience, agility, and dynamic capabilities have the power to unlock innovation and entrepreneurship within organizations. By fostering a culture of innovation, harnessing digital technologies, and implementing best practices, organizations can tap into the full potential of their distributed workforce. Resilience ensures the ability to withstand disruptions and bounce back from adversity, while agility enables organizations to adapt quickly to changes in the external environment. Dynamic capabilities allow organizations to continuously integrate and reconfigure their resources to address evolving challenges and seize emerging opportunities. By embracing these concepts and approaches, organizations can create a dynamic and adaptable environment that fosters creativity, collaboration, and innovation. This, in turn, enables them to stay ahead of the curve, drive growth, and thrive in today's rapidly changing business landscape.

This book chapter highlights the significance of smart working as a catalyst for innovation and entrepreneurial opportunities. It provides valuable insights into the theoretical frameworks, strategies, and management approaches that organizations can employ to enhance innovation capabilities and seize entrepreneurial opportunities in the context of smart working. The interplay between resilience, agility, and dynamic capabilities is crucial in creating a holistic approach to leverage the potential of smart working for innovation and entrepreneurship. However, there are several areas that require further exploration and future research.

Firstly, the impact of emerging technologies on smart working practices and their influence on innovation and entrepreneurship needs to be investigated in greater detail. Understanding how these technologies can be effectively integrated into smart working environments and their implications for innovation and entrepreneurial outcomes is critical.

Secondly, socio-cultural factors and their influence on innovation and entrepreneurship in smart working settings require deeper examination. Investigating how national and organizational cultures, as well as social norms, shape behaviours, collaboration, and risk-taking in remote work arrangements can provide valuable insights for organizations and policymakers.

Thirdly, ethical, and legal implications associated with smart working, such as data privacy, cybersecurity, and fair compensation, need to be addressed in future research. Developing frameworks and guidelines for responsible and sustainable smart working practices will help organizations create an environment that fosters innovation and entrepreneurship while ensuring ethical standards are met.

Additionally, exploring human resource management practices specific to smart working, such as talent management, employee engagement, and motivation strategies, can contribute to effective people management in remote work environments. Understanding how organizations can attract, develop, and retain talent in the context of smart working is essential for sustaining innovation and entrepreneurship.

Furthermore, future research should focus on collaborative innovation in virtual teams within the smart working context. Investigating factors that facilitate effective collaboration, knowledge sharing, and innovation in virtual teams can enhance organizations' understanding of teamwork dynamics and leadership approaches in remote work arrangements. It is important to acknowledge some limitations of the current literature review. The field of smart working is still relatively new and rapidly evolving, which may limit the availability of comprehensive studies. Additionally, the literature review primarily focuses on the positive aspects of smart working, and there is a need for more research examining potential challenges and drawbacks associated with remote work arrangements.

In conclusion, future research in smart working should address the gaps identified in this literature review, including the impact of emerging technologies, socio-cultural factors, ethical and legal implications, human resource management practices, and collaborative innovation in virtual teams. By exploring these areas, researchers can contribute to the development of effective strategies, policies, and practices that harness the potential of smart working for innovation and entrepreneurship, ultimately benefiting organizations, employees, and society as a whole. As the field of smart working continues to evolve, there are several promising avenues for future research that can expand our understanding of innovation, entrepreneurship, resilience, agility, and dynamic capabilities in this context. This literature review explores some key areas for future research in the realm of smart working.

The Impact of Emerging Technologies on Smart Working: Future research should explore the implications of emerging technologies, such as artificial intelligence, blockchain, and virtual reality, on smart working practices and their influence on innovation and entrepreneurship (Fang et al., 2020). Understanding how these technologies can be effectively integrated into smart working environments and how they shape innovation capabilities and entrepreneurial opportunities is a critical area of exploration.

Socio-Cultural Factors and Smart Working: Investigating the socio-cultural factors that influence innovation and entrepreneurship in smart working settings is another important avenue for future research. Factors such as national culture, organizational culture, and social norms can impact individuals' willingness to take risks, share knowledge, and collaborate in remote work arrangements (Cramton et al., 2017). Examining how these factors influence innovation outcomes and entrepreneurial behaviors can provide valuable insights for organizations and policymakers.

Ethical and Legal Implications of Smart Working: With the increasing adoption of smart working practices, it is crucial to address the ethical and legal implications associated with remote work arrangements. Future research should explore issues such as data privacy, cybersecurity, intellectual property rights, and fair compensation in smart working contexts (Baruch & Nicholson, 2017). Understanding the ethical challenges and developing frameworks for responsible and sustainable smart working can guide organizations and policymakers in creating conducive environments for innovation and entrepreneurship.

Human Resource Management Practices in Smart Working: Investigating human resource management practices that are effective in supporting innovation and entrepreneurial activities in smart working settings is a promising area for future research. Topics such as talent management, employee engagement, performance evaluation, and motivation strategies specific to smart working can contribute to the development of effective people management practices (Golden et al., 2020). Understanding how organizations can attract, develop, and retain talent in a remote work environment can have significant implications for innovation and entrepreneurship.

Collaborative Innovation in Virtual Teams: Virtual teams play a crucial role in smart working, and exploring how collaboration and innovation unfold in these teams is essential. Future research should investigate factors that facilitate effective collaboration, knowledge sharing, and innovation in virtual teams, such as team dynamics, communication technologies, and leadership styles (Martins et al., 2016). Understanding how virtual teams can overcome challenges and leverage their diversity to drive innovation can inform organizations' strategies in smart working environments.

In conclusion, future research in smart working should focus on understanding the impact of emerging technologies, socio-cultural factors, ethical and legal implications, human resource management practices, and collaborative innovation in virtual teams. By delving into these areas, researchers can provide valuable insights for organizations, policymakers, and practitioners, enabling them to navigate the complexities of smart working and leverage its full potential for innovation and entrepreneurship.

REFERENCES

Albrecht, S. L., Bakker, A. B., Gruman, J. A., Macey, W. H., & Saks, A. M. (2019). Employee engagement, human resource management practices and competitive advantage: An integrated approach. *Journal of Organizational Effectiveness: People and Performance*, *6*(1), 34–50.

Alipour, M., Karimi-Alaghehband, F., & Gupta, H. (2020). Leveraging the impacts of digital transformation on knowledge management in remote work environments: A COVID-19 perspective. *Journal of Innovation & Knowledge*, *5*(4), 267–274.

Amabile, T. M., & Pratt, M. G. (2016). The Dynamic Componential Model of Creativity and Innovation in Organizations: Making Progress, Making Meaning. *Research in Organizational Behavior*, *36*, 157–183. doi:10.1016/j.riob.2016.10.001

Antoncic, B., & Hisrich, R. D. (2003). Clarifying the intrapreneurship concept. *Journal of Small Business and Enterprise Development*, *10*(1), 7–24. doi:10.1108/14626000310461187

Arazy, O., Daxenberger, J., Nov, O., & Yeo, L. (2020). Factors shaping and being shaped by virtual work. *Journal of the Association for Information Systems*, *21*(2), 327–341.

Baruch, Y., & Nicholson, N. (2017). Smart working, digitalization and the implications for HRM: A research agenda. *International Journal of Human Resource Management*, *28*(18), 2471–2492.

Battistelli, A., & Montani, F. (2019). Smart Working: Mind the Gap between Policy Discourse and Practice. *Frontiers in Psychology*, *10*, 1–9.

Bentley, T. A., Teo, S. T. T., McLeod, L., Tan, F. T., Bosua, R., & Gloet, M. (2019). Creating better virtual teams: A longitudinal study of the effects of trust and collaboration on performance. *Journal of Business Research, 96*, 238–250.

Birkenshaw, J., Hamel, G., & Mol, M. J. (2019). Managing joint ventures: Addressing the execution challenge. *Harvard Business Review, 97*(4), 80–89.

Bogers, M., Hadar, R., & Bilberg, A. (2017). Additive manufacturing for consumer-centric business models: Implications for supply chains in consumer goods manufacturing. *Technological Forecasting and Social Change, 124*, 214–224.

Bogers, M., Hadar, R., & Bilberg, A. (2017). Additive manufacturing for consumer-centric business models: Implications for supply chains in consumer goods manufacturing. *Technological Forecasting and Social Change, 124*, 214–224.

Bos-Nehles, A. C., Renkema, M., Groeneveld, S., & Van Riemsdijk, M. J. (2021). Shifting the entrepreneurial mindset: Antecedents of employee entrepreneurial behavior. *European Management Review, 18*(1), 47–63.

Bosch-Sijtsema, P., & Vartiainen, M. (2017). The concept of smart work: A critique. *New Technology, Work and Employment, 32*(3), 195–211.

Broadway Business.Teece, D. J. (2018). Business models and dynamic capabilities. *Long Range Planning, 51*(1), 40–49. doi:10.1016/j.lrp.2017.06.007

Bughin, J., Catlin, T., Hirt, M., & Willmott, P. (2018). *Why Digital Strategies Fail*. McKinsey Quarterly. https://www.mckinsey.com/business-functions/mckinsey-digital/our-insights/why-digital-strategies-fail

Bughin, J., Hazan, E., Ramaswamy, S., Chui, M., Allas, T., Dahlström, P., & Trench, M. (2018). *Artificial intelligence: The next digital frontier?* McKinsey Global Institute.

Burgelman, R. A., Christensen, C. M., & Wheelwright, S. C. (2018). *Strategic management of technology and innovation*. McGraw-Hill.

Cai, Y., Song, S., & Landry, M. (2019). Promoting creativity and innovation in organizations: A state-of-the-art review and future directions. *Journal of Innovation & Knowledge, 4*(3), 123–130.

Calza, F., & Corno, F. (2020). Creativity and innovation in creative industries: A systematic literature review. *Creativity and Innovation Management, 29*(1), 25–41.

Caniëls, M. C., & Semeijn, J. H. (2020). Ensuring data privacy and security in remote work: A systematic review and implications for future research. *Journal of Business Research, 117*, 463–478.

Chesbrough, H., Vanhaverbeke, W., & West, J. (2018). *New frontiers in open innovation*. Oxford University Press.

Chesbrough, H. W. (2006). *Open business models: How to thrive in the new innovation landscape*. Harvard Business Press.

Cramton, C. D., Orvis, K. L., & Wilson, J. M. (2017). Beyond teams: New research perspectives on the interplay of boundaries and teamwork. *The Journal of Applied Psychology*, *102*(3), 324–332. PMID:28125264

Dahlander, L., Piezunka, H., & Gann, D. M. (2020). Open to suggestions: How organizations elicit suggestions through proactive and reactive attention. *Academy of Management Journal*, *63*(2), 448–479.

Davenport, T. H., Harris, J. G., & Shapiro, J. (2020). *Competing on talent analytics*. Harvard Business Review Press.

Doern, R., Goss, D., & Neely, A. (2020). Special Issue on 'SMEs and the COVID-19 pandemic'. *International Small Business Journal*, *38*(6), 473–476.

Doherty, N., & Burke, R. (2019). *Flexibility in the workplace: Implications of flexible work arrangements for individuals, teams, and organizations*. Routledge.

Doz, Y. L., & Kosonen, M. (2010). Embedding Strategic Agility: A Leadership Agenda for Accelerating Business Model Renewal. *Long Range Planning*, *43*(2-3), 370–382. doi:10.1016/j.lrp.2009.07.006

Eisenbeiss, S. A., Knippenberg, D. V., & Boerner, S. (2020). Transformational leadership and team innovation: Integrating team climate principles. *The Journal of Applied Psychology*, *105*(9), 1021–1037. PMID:19025260

Eisenbeiss, S. A., Knippenberg, D. V., & Boerner, S. (2020). Transformational leadership and team innovation: Integrating team climate principles. *The Journal of Applied Psychology*, *105*(9), 1021–1037. PMID:19025260

Eisenhardt, K. M., Furr, N. R., & Bingham, C. B. (2016). Crossroads—microfoundations of performance: Balancing efficiency and flexibility in dynamic environments. *Organization Science*, *27*(6), 1394–1406.

European Commission. (2020). *The European Commission's contribution to the future of work*. EC. https://ec.europa.eu/commission/presscorner/detail/en/IP_20_2349

Fang, Y., Qureshi, I., Sun, H., McCole, P., Ramsey, E., & Lim, K. H. (2020). Trust, satisfaction, and online repurchase intention: The moderating role of perceived effectiveness of e-commerce institutional mechanisms. *Management Information Systems Quarterly*, *44*(2), 471–502.

Gianiodis, P. T., Pyeon, J., & Li, S. (2019). Hybrid incubators: The role of smart workspaces in startup development. *Technological Forecasting and Social Change*, *149*, 119734.

Golden, T. D., Veiga, J. F., & Simsek, Z. (2020). Telecommuting's differential impact on work-family conflict: Is there no place like home? *The Journal of Applied Psychology*, *105*(11), 1234–1245. PMID:32969707

Hamel, G. (2020). The quest for resilience. *Harvard Business Review*, *98*(5), 50–59. PMID:12964393

Helfat, C. E. (2021). Dynamic capabilities: Foundations, theories, and research opportunities. *Industrial and Corporate Change*, *30*(1), 3–30.

Helfat, C. E., Finkelstein, S., Mitchell, W., Peteraf, M. A., Singh, H., Teece, D., & Winter, S. G. (2007). *Dynamic capabilities: Understanding strategic change in organizations*. Blackwell Publishing.

Helfat, C. E., Finkelstein, S., Mitchell, W., Peteraf, M. A., Singh, H., Teece, D., & Winter, S. G. (2019). *Dynamic capabilities: Understanding strategic change in organizations*. John Wiley & Sons.

Hermann, M., Pentek, T., & Otto, B. (2019). Design principles for industrie 4.0 scenarios: A literature review. *Technological Forecasting and Social Change*, *144*, 75–99.

Huczynski, A. A., Buchanan, D. A., & Huczynski, A. A. (2021). *Organizational behaviour: An introductory text*. Pearson.

International Labour Organization. (2017). Guidelines for the promotion of decent work in e-commerce. ILO. https://www.ilo.org/wcmsp5/groups/public/---ed_protect/---protrav/---travail/documents/publication/wcms_623375.pdf

Kelliher, C., & Anderson, D. (2010). Doing more with less? Flexible working practices and the intensification of work. *Human Relations*, *63*(1), 83–106. doi:10.1177/0018726709349199

Kowalkiewicz, R., Zhou, J., Ma, M., & Filieri, R. (2020). From crowdsourcing to smart working: A review and agenda for future research. *Journal of Management Information Systems*, *37*(1), 9–52.

Liu, Y., Wei, L., Fan, J., Zhou, H., & Zhou, S. (2019). Agile manufacturing: A systematic review. *International Journal of Production Research, 57*(13), 4075–4097.

Martins, L. L., Gilson, L. L., & Maynard, M. T. (2016). Virtual teams: What do we know and where do we go from here? *Journal of Management, 43*(6), 1437–1473.

Mehralian, G., O'Cass, A., & Nguyen, B. (2021). Understanding resilient organizations: A systematic review and synthesis. *Journal of Business Research, 136*, 615–632.

Nembhard, I. M., & Edmondson, A. C. (2006). Making it safe: The effects of leader inclusiveness and professional status on psychological safety and improvement efforts in health care teams. *Journal of Organizational Behavior, 27*(7), 941–966. doi:10.1002/job.413

O'Reilly, C. A., Doerr, B., & Chatman, J. A. (2019). See how they think: The effects of cognitive and affective perspective taking on empathy in negotiations. *The Journal of Applied Psychology, 104*(5), 635–652.

Oksanen, A., Syrek, C. J., Salmela-Aro, K., de Bloom, J., & Korpela, K. (2019). How the 21st-century workforce shapes global value chains: Work characteristics and the fear of job loss. *The Academy of Management Perspectives, 33*(4), 403–424.

Raghupathi, W., Xiang, X., & Sun, S. (2020). Smart working in a digital world: Opportunities and challenges for organizations. *International Journal of Information Management, 50*, 106145.

Rigby, D. K., Sutherland, J., & Takeuchi, H. (2016). Embracing agile. *Harvard Business Review, 94*(5), 40–50.

Rigby, D. K., Sutherland, J., & Takeuchi, H. (2016). Embracing agile. *Harvard Business Review, 94*(5), 40–50.

Rosing, K., Frese, M., & Bausch, A. (2011). Explaining the heterogeneity of the leadership-innovation relationship: Ambidextrous leadership. *The Leadership Quarterly, 22*(5), 956–974. doi:10.1016/j.leaqua.2011.07.014

Sambamurthy, V., Bharadwaj, A., & Grover, V. (2020). Shaping agility through digital options: Reconceptualizing the role of information technology in contemporary firms. *Management Information Systems Quarterly, 44*(1), 1–22. doi:10.2307/25148665

Sanchez-Rodriguez, C., Stölzle, W., & Zerfass, A. (2020). Agile and stakeholder-oriented organizational culture: The case of BMW. *Journal of Communication Management (London), 24*(1), 61–81.

Senge, P. M., Smith, B., Kruschwitz, N., Laur, J., & Schley, S. (2012). *The necessary revolution: How individuals and organizations are working together to create a sustainable world.*

Shane, S., & Venkataraman, S. (2000). The promise of entrepreneurship as a field of research. *Academy of Management Review, 25*(1), 217–226. doi:10.5465/amr.2000.2791611

Sutcliffe, K. M., Vogus, T. J., & Dane, E. (2016). Organizing for resilience. *Harvard Business Review, 94*(9), 52–59.

Teece, D. J. (2007). Explicating dynamic capabilities: The nature and microfoundations of (sustainable) enterprise performance. *Strategic Management Journal, 28*(13), 1319–1350. doi:10.1002mj.640

Teece, D. J. (2018). Profiting from innovation in the digital economy: Enabling technologies, standards, and licensing models in the wireless world. *Research Policy, 47*(8), 1367–1387. doi:10.1016/j.respol.2017.01.015

Teece, D. J. (2018). Business Models and Dynamic Capabilities. *Long Range Planning, 51*(1), 40–49. doi:10.1016/j.lrp.2017.06.007

Teece, D. J., Pisano, G., & Shuen, A. (2016). *Dynamic capabilities and strategic management: Organizing for innovation and growth.* Oxford University Press.

Tushman, M. L., & O'Reilly, C. A. (2017). Ambidextrous organizations: Managing evolutionary and revolutionary change. *California Management Review, 59*(4), 5–23.

Van der Zwan, P., Verheul, I., & Thurik, R. (2019). The entrepreneurial ladder's rungs and the impact of entrepreneurial experience on subsequent entry into self-employment. *Small Business Economics, 53*(2), 383–404.

West, M. A., Sacramento, C. A., & Fay, D. (2019). Creativity and innovation implementation in work groups: The paradoxical role of demands. *Journal of Organizational Behavior, 40*(5), 559–575.

Wilden, R., Devinney, T. M., & Dowling, G. R. (2019). The architecture of dynamic capability research: Identifying the building blocks of a configurational approach. *Journal of Management, 45*(1), 26–60.

Wonglimpiyarat, J. (2018). Enhancing organizational innovation: The roles of knowledge management and organizational culture. *Journal of Innovation & Knowledge, 3*(4), 204–209.

Zollo, M., Heavey, C., & Meier, D. (2019). Dynamic capabilities: Foundations, processes, and prospects. *Journal of Management Studies*, *56*(8), 1465–1480.

Zolnowski, A., & Mueller, F. (2019). Developing Organizational Resilience: A Review of Theory and Research Findings. *International Journal of Disaster Risk Science*, *10*(4), 543–555.

Glossary

Employee Creativity: The development of novel and useful ideas within the corporate environment (e.g., solving problems, improving processes, developing products and processes).

Extrinsic Motivation: A human behavior driven by personal added value (e.g., rewards).

Individual Absorptive Capacity: An individual's ability to identify, assimilate, and advocate valuable knowledge within a firm.

Information System: A software or hardware related system that supports the, e.g., capturing, transferring, and transforming of data.

Information Technology: A term for electronic data processing and the hardware and software infrastructure used for this purpose.

Intrinsic Motivation: A human behavior driven by pure interest or pleasure.

Knowledge Management System: A type of information system that is applied to manage firms' internal and external knowledge.

Remote Working: A work setup in which employees work in sites or locations that are not their firms' offices, and they have no direct personal contact with colleagues but can communicate with them via enabling technology (e.g., computer or mobile phones and related software).

Compilation of References

Abbasianchavari, A., & Moritz, A. (2021). The impact of role models on entrepreneurial intentions and behavior: A review of the literature. *Management Review Quarterly*, *71*(1), 1–40. doi:10.100711301-019-00179-0

Abdellatif, S., Shomotova, A., Trabelsi, S., Husain, S., Alsalhi, N., & Eltahir, M. (2023). Transition to Distance Learning: Student Experience and Communication during the COVID-19 Pandemic in the United Arab Emirates. *Sustainability (Basel)*, *15*(8), 6456. doi:10.3390u15086456

Abdulrahman, R., & Viktor, H. L. (2020). Personalised recommendation systems and the impact of covid-19: Perspectives, opportunities and challenges. *Proceedings of the 12th International Joint Conference on Knowledge Discovery, Knowledge Engineering and Knowledge Management*, (*vol.* 1, pp. 295-301). Scitepress. 10.5220/0010145702950301

Abulibdeh, A. (2020). Can COVID-19 mitigation measures promote telework practices? *Journal of Labor and Society*, *23*(4), 551–576. doi:10.1111/wusa.12498

Adekoya, O. D., Adisa, T. A., & Aiyenitaju, O. (2022). Going forward: Remote working in the post-COVID-19 era. Employee Relations. *International Journal (Toronto, Ont.)*, *44*(6), 1410–1427.

Afonso, P., Fonseca, M., & Teodoro, T. (2022). Evaluation of anxiety, depression and sleep quality in full-time teleworkers. *Journal of Public Health (Oxford, England)*, *44*(4), 797–804. doi:10.1093/pubmed/fdab164 PMID:34036369

Ahmadi, A., & Soga, L. R. (2022). To be or not to be: Latent entrepreneurship, the networked agent, and the fear factor. *Technological Forecasting and Social Change*, *174*, 121281. doi:10.1016/j.techfore.2021.121281

Ahmad, N. A., Sham, F. M., & Ismail, A. (2021). Technology-Based Support in Organizations and the Impact on Affective Commitment. *Social Sciences*, *11*(8), 1263–1274.

Akpan, I. J., Soopramanien, D., & Kwak, D.-H. (2020). Cutting-edge technologies for small business and innovation in the era of COVID-19 global health pandemic. *Journal of Small Business and Entrepreneurship*, 1–11. doi:10.1080/08276331.2020.1799294

Alavi, M., & Leidner, D. E. (2001). Review: Knowledge management and knowledge management systems: Conceptual foundations and research issues. *Management Information Systems Quarterly*, *25*(1), 107–136. doi:10.2307/3250961

Albrecht, S. L., Bakker, A. B., Gruman, J. A., Macey, W. H., & Saks, A. M. (2019). Employee engagement, human resource management practices and competitive advantage: An integrated approach. *Journal of Organizational Effectiveness: People and Performance*, *6*(1), 34–50.

Aldholay, A. H., Isaac, O., Abdullah, Z., & Ramayah, T. (2018). The role of transformational leadership as a mediating variable in DeLone and McLean information system success model: The context of online learning usage in Yemen. *Telematics and Informatics*, *35*(5), 1421–1437. doi:10.1016/j.tele.2018.03.012

Alfonso, G. J. (2015). Olien and distance e-Learning: New dimensions in teaching, learning, research, and extension for higher education institutions. *The International Journal on Olien and Distance e-Learning*, *1*(1-2), 2-4.

Alipour, M., Karimi-Alaghehband, F., & Gupta, H. (2020). Leveraging the impacts of digital transformation on knowledge management in remote work environments: A COVID-19 perspective. *Journal of Innovation & Knowledge*, *5*(4), 267–274.

Al-Kofahi, M. K., Hassan, H., & Mohamad, R. (2020). Information systems success model: A review of literature. *International Journal of Innovation. Creativity and Change*, *12*(10), 104–128.

Allen, T. D., Golden, T. D., & Shockley, K. M. (2015). How effective is telecommuting? Assessing the status of our scientific findings. *Psychological Science in the Public Interest*, *16*(2), 40–68. doi:10.1177/1529100615593273 PMID:26403188

Al-Mawee, W., Kwayu, K. M., & Gharaibeh, T. (2021). Student's perspective on DL during COVID-19 pandemic: A case study of Western Michigan University, United States. *International Journal of Educational Research Open*, *2*, 100080. doi:10.1016/j.ijedro.2021.100080 PMID:35059670

Alrowwad, A. A., Abualoush, S. H., & Masa'deh, R. E. (2020). Innovation and intellectual capital as intermediary variables among transformational leadership, transactional leadership, and organizational performance. *Journal of Management Development*, *39*(2), 196–222. doi:10.1108/JMD-02-2019-0062

Altowairiki, N. (2021). Online Collaborative Learning: Analyzing the Process through Living the Experience. [IJTE]. *International Journal of Technology in Education*, *4*(3), 413–427. doi:10.46328/ijte.95

Alvarado Valenzuela, J. F., Wakkee, I., Martens, J., & Grijsbach, P. (2020). Lessons from entrepreneurial failure through vicarious learning. *Journal of Small Business and Entrepreneurship*, 1–25.

Amabile, T. M. (1988). A model of creativity and innovation in organizations. *Research in Organizational Behavior*, *10*, 123–167.

Amabile, T. M. (1993). Motivational synergy: Toward new conceptualizations of intrinsic and extrinsic motivation in the workplace. *Human Resource Management Review, 3*(3), 185–201. doi:10.1016/1053-4822(93)90012-S

Amabile, T. M., & Pratt, M. G. (2016). The dynamic componential model of creativity and innovation in organizations: Making progress, making meaning. *Research in Organizational Behavior, 36*, 157–183. doi:10.1016/j.riob.2016.10.001

Amankwah-Amoah, J., Khan, Z., Wood, G., & Knight, G. (2021). COVID-19 and digitalization: The great acceleration. *Journal of Business Research, 136*, 602–611. doi:10.1016/j.jbusres.2021.08.011 PMID:34538980

Amidon, O. (2010). Undergraduate student online learning readiness. *International Journal of Education and Research, 5*(2), 44–54.

Andersen, C. L., & West, R. E. (2021). We Overwhelm Them with Hope": How Online Mentors Can Support Online Learners. *Online Learning : the Official Journal of the Online Learning Consortium, 25*(4), 388–415. doi:10.24059/olj.v25i4.2440

Anderson, T., & Rivera, V. P. (2020). A critical look at educational technology from a distance education perspective. *Digital Education Review* (37): 208-229. . hdl: doi:10.1344/der.2020.37.208-229

Anderson, N., Potočnik, K., & Zhou, J. (2014). Innovation and creativity in organizations: A state-of-the-science review, prospective commentary, and guiding framework. *Journal of Management, 40*(5), 1297–1333. doi:10.1177/0149206314527128

Anderson, T., & Dron, J. (2011). Three generations of distance education pedagogy. *International Review of Research in Open and Distance Learning, 12*(3), 80–97. doi:10.19173/irrodl.v12i3.890

AngeliciM.ProfetaP. (2020). Smart-Working: Work Flexibility Without Constraints. (Working Paper No. 8165). CESifo. https://ssrn.com/abstract=3556304 doi:10.2139/ssrn.3556304

Antoncic, B., & Hisrich, R. D. (2003). Clarifying the intrapreneurship concept. *Journal of Small Business and Enterprise Development, 10*(1), 7–24. doi:10.1108/14626000310461187

Aravind, V. K., Krishnaram, V. D., & Thasneem, Z. (2012). Boundary crossings and violations in clinical settings. *Indian Journal of Psychological Medicine, 34*(1), 21–24. doi:10.4103/0253-7176.96151 PMID:22661802

Arazy, O., Daxenberger, J., Nov, O., & Yeo, L. (2020). Factors shaping and being shaped by virtual work. *Journal of the Association for Information Systems, 21*(2), 327–341.

Attah-Boakye, R., Adams, K., Hernandez-Perdomo, E., Yu, H., & Johansson, J. (2023). Resource Re-orchestration and firm survival in crisis periods: The role of business models of technology MNEs during COVID-19. *Technovation, 125*, 102769. doi:10.1016/j.technovation.2023.102769

Autor, D. H. (2015). Why are there still so many jobs? The history and future of workplace automation. *The Journal of Economic Perspectives, 29*(3), 3–30. doi:10.1257/jep.29.3.3

Aw, E. C. X., & Labrecque, L. I. (2020). Celebrity endorsement in social media contexts: Understanding the role of parasocial interactions and the need to belong. *Journal of Consumer Marketing*, *37*(7), 895–908. doi:10.1108/JCM-10-2019-3474

Aw, E. C. X., Tan, G. W. H., Chuah, S. H. W., Ooi, K. B., & Hajli, N. (2022). Be my friend! Cultivating parasocial relationships with social media influencers: Findings from PLS-SEM and fsQCA. *Information Technology & People*.

Babatunde, S., & El-Gohary, H. (2019). Necessity of mentoring in entrepreneurship education: Reflection by practitioners. *Journal of Professional Issues in Engineering Education and Practice*, *145*(1), 02518007. doi:10.1061/(ASCE)EI.1943-5541.0000399

Badwan, A. R., Tamvada, J. P., & Rentocchini, F. (2022). Evaluating mentorship-based learning in entrepreneurship education. *International Review of Entrepreneurship*, *20*, 69–86.

Bakare, O. D. (2023). Emerging Technologies as a Panacea for Sustainable Provision of Library Services in Nigeria. In *Global Perspectives on Sustainable Library Practices* (pp. 1–21). IGI Global.

Bakare, O. D., & Ademakinwa, M. A. (2021). The Impact of Covid - 19 on Mentorship of Graduate Students in Nigerian Universities. *Journal of the Nigerian Pastoral Counselling Association*, *1*(1), 15–19.

Bakare, O. D., & Okuonghae, N. (2022). Information Managers as Change Agents in achievingSustainable Development in the 21st Century. *Journal of Environmental Science and Economics*, *1*(2), 68–78.

Bakare, O. D., & Okuonghae, N. (2023). Digital Technologies and Resources for Learning Under Lockdown. In *Impact of Disruptive Technologies on the Socio-Economic Development of Emerging Countries* (pp. 87–103). IGI Global. doi:10.4018/978-1-6684-6873-9.ch006

Bakare, O. D., Oladokun, T., Quadri, G. O., & Idowu-Davies, T. O. (2023). ChatGPT and Other Generative Artificial Intelligence (AI) Tools in Tcaching and Learning as Integrative Pathways to Contemporary University Education. In *Creative AI Tools and Ethical Implications in Teaching and Learning* (pp. 168–180). IGI Global. doi:10.4018/979-8-3693-0205-7.ch009

Baker, E., Avery, G. C., & Crawford, J. (2006). Home alone: The role of technology in telecommuting. *Information Resources Management Journal*, *19*(4), 1–22. doi:10.4018/irmj.2006100101

Balaban, D. C., Szambolics, J., & Chirică, M. (2022). Parasocial relations and social media influencers' persuasive power. Exploring the moderating role of product involvement. *Acta Psychologica*, *230*, 103731. doi:10.1016/j.actpsy.2022.103731 PMID:36057200

Bamel, U., Talwar, S., Pereira, V., Corazza, L., & Dhir, A. (2023). Disruptive digital innovations in healthcare: Knowing the past and anticipating the future. *Technovation*, *125*, 102785. doi:10.1016/j.technovation.2023.102785

Bareket-Bojmel, L., Hochman, G., & Ariely, D. (2017). It's (not) all about the Jacksons: Testing different types of short-term bonuses in the field. *Journal of Management*, *43*(2), 534–554. doi:10.1177/0149206314535441

Barile, S., & Polese, F. (2010). Smart service systems and viable service systems: Applying systems theory to service science. *Service Science*, *2*(1–2), 21–40. doi:10.1287erv.2.1_2.21

Baruch, Y., & Nicholson, N. (2017). Smart working, digitalization and the implications for HRM: A research agenda. *International Journal of Human Resource Management*, *28*(18), 2471–2492.

Bashir, F., & Warraich, N. F. (2023). Systematic literature review of Semantic Web for distance learning. *Interactive Learning Environments*, *31*(1), 527–543. doi:10.1080/10494820.2020.1799023

Battilana, J., & Casciaro, T. (2013). The network secrets of great change agents. *Harvard Business Review*, *91*(7), 62–68. PMID:24730170

Battistelli, A., & Montani, F. (2019). Smart Working: Mind the Gap between Policy Discourse and Practice. *Frontiers in Psychology*, *10*, 1–9.

Beck, S., Bergenholtz, C., Bogers, M., Brasseur, T. M., Conradsen, M. L., Di Marco, D., Distel, A. P., Dobusch, L., Dörler, D., Effert, A., Fecher, B., Filiou, D., Frederiksen, L., Gillier, T., Grimpe, C., Gruber, M., Haeussler, C., Heigl, F., Hoisl, K., & Xu, S. M. (2020). The open innovation in science research field: A collaborative conceptualisation approach. *Industry and Innovation*, 1–50.

Bednar, P. M., & Welch, C. (2020). Socio-Technical Perspectives on Smart Working: Creating Meaningful and Sustainable Systems. *Information Systems Frontiers*, *22*(2), 281–298. doi:10.100710796-019-09921-1

Bentley, T. A., Teo, S. T. T., McLeod, L., Tan, F. T., Bosua, R., & Gloet, M. (2019). Creating better virtual teams: A longitudinal study of the effects of trust and collaboration on performance. *Journal of Business Research*, *96*, 238–250.

Berman, S. J. (2012). Digital transformation: Opportunities to create new business models. *Strategy and Leadership*, *40*(2), 16–24. doi:10.1108/10878571211209314

Betti, N., & Sarens, G. (2021). Understanding the internal audit function in a digitalised business environment. *Journal of Accounting & Organizational Change*, *17*(2), 197–216. doi:10.1108/JAOC-11-2019-0114

Bird, L. (2021). The role of startups in improving smart working. Entrepreneur: What It Means to Be One and How to Get Started. Investopedia.

Birkenshaw, J., Hamel, G., & Mol, M. J. (2019). Managing joint ventures: Addressing the execution challenge. *Harvard Business Review*, *97*(4), 80–89.

Blight, M. G., Ruppel, E. K., & Schoenbauer, K. V. (2017). Sense of community on Twitter and Instagram: Exploring the roles of motives and parasocial relationships. *Cyberpsychology, Behavior, and Social Networking*, *20*(5), 314–319. doi:10.1089/cyber.2016.0505 PMID:28498041

Bogers, M., Hadar, R., & Bilberg, A. (2017). Additive manufacturing for consumer-centric business models: Implications for supply chains in consumer goods manufacturing. *Technological Forecasting and Social Change*, *124*, 214–224.

Boorsma, B., & Mitchell, S. (2011). Work-life innovation smart work—A paradigm shift transforming how, where, and when work gets done. *Cisco IBSG Point of View*. https://www.cisco.com/c/dam/en_us/about/ac79/docs/ps/Work- Life_ Innovation_Smart_Work.pdf

Bosch-Sijtsema, P., & Vartiainen, M. (2017). The concept of smart work: A critique. *New Technology, Work and Employment*, *32*(3), 195–211.

Bos-Nehles, A. C., Renkema, M., Groeneveld, S., & Van Riemsdijk, M. J. (2021). Shifting the entrepreneurial mindset: Antecedents of employee entrepreneurial behavior. *European Management Review*, *18*(1), 47–63.

Brand, M. J., Croonen, E. P., & Leenders, R. T. (2018). Entrepreneurial networking: A blessing or a curse? Differential effects for low, medium and high performing franchisees. *Small Business Economics*, *50*(4), 783–805. doi:10.100711187-017-9895-1

Brestovanský, M., & Sekerešová, D. (2022). Parasocial Interaction Does Not Function as a Relationship Mediator between the Influencer's Online Content and the Adolescent's Prosocial Moral Reasoning and Behaviour. *Communication Today, 13*(1).

Briscoe, P. (2019). Virtual mentor partnerships between practising and preservice teachers: Helping to enhance professional growth and well-being. *International Journal of Mentoring and Coaching in Education*, *8*(4), 235–254. doi:10.1108/IJMCE-02-2019-0023

Broadway Business.Teece, D. J. (2018). Business models and dynamic capabilities. *Long Range Planning*, *51*(1), 40–49. doi:10.1016/j.lrp.2017.06.007

Brodie, J., Van Saane, S. H., & Osowska, R. (2017). Help wanted: Exploring the value of entrepreneurial mentoring at start-up. *Industry and Higher Education*, *31*(2), 122–131. doi:10.1177/0950422217691666

Brunetti, F., Matt, D. T., Bonfanti, A., De Longhi, A., Pedrini, G., & Orzes, G. (2020). Digital transformation challenges: Strategies emerging from a multi-stakeholder approach. *The TQM Journal*, *32*(4), 697–724. doi:10.1108/TQM-12-2019-0309

Buffer. (2021). *State of Remote Work 2021*. Buffer. https://buffer.com/state-of-remote-work/2021

Bughin, J., Catlin, T., Hirt, M., & Willmott, P. (2018). *Why Digital Strategies Fail*. McKinsey Quarterly. https://www.mckinsey.com/business-functions/mckinsey-digital/our-insights/why-digital-strategies-fail

Bughin, J. (2023). Are you resilient? Machine learning prediction of corporate rebound out of the Covid-19 pandemic. *MDE. Managerial and Decision Economics*, *44*(3), 1547–1564. doi:10.1002/mde.3764

Bughin, J., Hazan, E., Ramaswamy, S., Chui, M., Allas, T., Dahlstrom, P., & Trench, M. (2017). *Artificial intelligence: The next digital frontier?* McKinsey Global Institute.

Burgelman, R. A., Christensen, C. M., & Wheelwright, S. C. (2018). *Strategic management of technology and innovation*. McGraw-Hill.

Burns, S. T. (2019). Students' ethical decision-making when considering boundary crossings with counselor educators. *Counseling and Values, 64*(1), 53–71. doi:10.1002/cvj.12094

Caesens, G., Stinglhamber, F., & Luypaert, G. (2014). The impact of work engagement and workaholism on well-being: The role of work-related social support. *Career Development International, 19*(7), 813–835. doi:10.1108/CDI-09-2013-0114

Cai, Y., Song, S., & Landry, M. (2019). Promoting creativity and innovation in organizations: A state-of-the-art review and future directions. *Journal of Innovation & Knowledge, 4*(3), 123–130.

Calza, F., & Corno, F. (2020). Creativity and innovation in creative industries: A systematic literature review. *Creativity and Innovation Management, 29*(1), 25–41.

Caniëls, M. C., & Semeijn, J. H. (2020). Ensuring data privacy and security in remote work: A systematic review and implications for future research. *Journal of Business Research, 117*, 463–478.

Cao, Q., Thompson, M. A., & Triche, J. (2013). Investigating the role of business processes and knowledge management systems on performance: A multi-case study approach. *International Journal of Production Research, 51*(18), 5565–5575. doi:10.1080/00207543.2013.789145

Cao, X., Ali, A., Pitafi, A. H., Khan, A. N., & Waqas, M. (2021). A socio-technical system approach to knowledge creation and team performance: Evidence from China. *Information Technology & People, 34*(7), 1976–1996. doi:10.1108/ITP-10-2019-0536

Carillo, K., Scornavacca, E., & Za, S. (2017). The role of media dependency in predicting continuance intention to use ubiquitous media systems. *Information & Management, 54*(3), 317–335. doi:10.1016/j.im.2016.09.002

Carpenter, J. P., Shelton, C. C., & Schroeder, S. E. (2022). The education influencer: A new player in the educator professional landscape. *Journal of Research on Technology in Education*, 1–16. doi:10.1080/15391523.2022.2119452

Casale, S., Akbari, M., Bocci Benucci, S., Seydavi, M., & Fioravanti, G. (2022). Interpersonally-Based Fears and Problematic Social Networking Site Use: The Moderating Role of Online Social Support. *International Journal of Mental Health and Addiction*, 1–13. doi:10.100711469-022-00908-9

Cascio, W. F., & Montealegre, R. (2016). How technology is changing work and organizations. *Annual Review of Organizational Psychology and Organizational Behavior, 3*(1), 349–375. doi:10.1146/annurev-orgpsych-041015-062352

Cerasoli, C. P., Nicklin, J. M., & Ford, M. T. (2014). Intrinsic motivation and extrinsic incentives jointly predict performance: A 40-year meta-analysis. *Psychological Bulletin, 140*(4), 980–1008. doi:10.1037/a0035661 PMID:24491020

Chatterjee, D., & Corral, J. (2017). How to write well-defined learning objectives. *The Journal of Education in Perioperative Medicine : JEPM, 19*(4). PMID:29766034

Chaves-Maza, M., & Martel, E. M. F. (2020). *Entrepreneurship support ways after the COVID-19 crisis*. Entrepreneurship Sustain. doi:10.9770/jesi.2020.8.2(40)

Chen, L., Zhao, X., Tang, O., Price, L., Zhang, S., & Zhu, W. (2017). Supply chain collaboration for sustainability: A literature review and future research agenda. *International Journal of Production Economics*, *194*(April), 73–87. doi:10.1016/j.ijpe.2017.04.005

Chen, M. H., & Wang, M. C. (2008). Social networks and a new venture's innovative capability: The role of trust within entrepreneurial teams. *R & D Management*, *38*(3), 253–264. doi:10.1111/j.1467-9310.2008.00515.x

Chesbrough, H. W. (2006). *Open business models: How to thrive in the new innovation landscape*. Harvard Business Press.

Chesbrough, H., Vanhaverbeke, W., & West, J. (2018). *New frontiers in open innovation*. Oxford University Press.

Cheung, J. H., Burns, D. K., Sinclair, R. R., & Sliter, M. (2017). Amazon Mechanical Turk in organizational psychology: An evaluation and practical recommendations. *Journal of Business and Psychology*, *32*(4), 347–361. doi:10.100710869-016-9458-5

Cho, Y. J., & Perry, J. L. (2012). Intrinsic motivation and employee attitudes: Role of managerial trustworthiness, goal directedness, and extrinsic reward expectancy. *Review of Public Personnel Administration*, *32*(4), 382–406. doi:10.1177/0734371X11421495

Chung, H., & Van der Lippe, T. (2020). Flexible working, work–life balance, and gender equality: Introduction. *Social Indicators Research*, *151*(2), 365–381. doi:10.100711205-018-2025-x PMID:33029036

Chwialkowska, A. (2019). How sustainability influencers drive green lifestyle adoption on social media: The process of green lifestyle adoption explained through the lenses of the minority influence model and social learning theory. *Management of Sustainable Development*, *11*(1), 33–42.

Cioffi, R., Travaglioni, M., Piscitelli, G., Petrillo, A., & De Felice, F. (2020). Artificial intelligence and machine learning applications in smart production: Progress, trends, and directions. *Sustainability (Basel)*, *12*(2), 492–515. doi:10.3390u12020492

Cohen, W. M., & Levinthal, D. A. (1989). Innovation and learning: The two faces of R&D. *Economic Journal (London)*, *99*(397), 569–596. doi:10.2307/2233763

Cohen, W. M., & Levinthal, D. A. (1990). Absorptive capacity: A new perspective on learning and innovation. *Administrative Science Quarterly*, *35*(1), 128. doi:10.2307/2393553

Collins, C. J., & Smith, K. G. (2006). Knowledge exchange and combination: The role of human resource practices in the performance of high-technology firms. *Academy of Management Journal*, *49*(3), 544–560. doi:10.5465/amj.2006.21794671

Coombs, C., Hislop, D., Taneva, S. K., & Barnard, S. (2020). The strategic impacts of Intelligent Automation for knowledge and service work: An interdisciplinary review. *The Journal of Strategic Information Systems*, *29*(4), 101600. doi:10.1016/j.jsis.2020.101600

Cramton, C. D., Orvis, K. L., & Wilson, J. M. (2017). Beyond teams: New research perspectives on the interplay of boundaries and teamwork. *The Journal of Applied Psychology*, *102*(3), 324–332. PMID:28125264

Crow, D., & Millot, A. (2020, June 12). *Working from home can save energy and reduce emissions. But how much?* [Commentary]. International Energy Agency. https://www.iea.org/commentaries/working-from-home-can-save-energy-and-reduce-emissions-but-how-much

Da Silva, N., & Davis, A. R. (2011). Absorptive capacity at the individual level: Linking creativity to innovation in academia. *Review of Higher Education*, *34*(3), 355–379. doi:10.1353/rhe.2011.0007

Dahlander, L., Piezunka, H., & Gann, D. M. (2020). Open to suggestions: How organizations elicit suggestions through proactive and reactive attention. *Academy of Management Journal*, *63*(2), 448–479.

Daim, T. U., Ha, A., Reutiman, S., Hughes, B., Pathak, U., Bynum, W., & Bhatla, A. (2012). Exploring the communication breakdown in global virtual teams. *International Journal of Project Management*, *30*(2), 199–212. doi:10.1016/j.ijproman.2011.06.004

Davenport, T. H., Harris, J. G., & Shapiro, J. (2020). *Competing on talent analytics*. Harvard Business Review Press.

Davis, F. D., Bagozzi, R. P., & Warshaw, P. R. (1992). Extrinsic and intrinsic motivation to use computers in the workplace. *Journal of Applied Social Psychology*, *22*(14), 1111–1132. doi:10.1111/j.1559-1816.1992.tb00945.x

Deci, E. L., & Ryan, R. M. (1987). The support of autonomy and the control of behavior. *Journal of Personality and Social Psychology*, *53*(6), 1024–1037. doi:10.1037/0022-3514.53.6.1024 PMID:3320334

Deci, E. L., Spiegel, N. H., Ryan, R. M., Koestner, R., & Kauffman, M. (1982). Effects of performance standards on teaching styles: Behavior of controlling teachers. *Journal of Educational Psychology*, *74*(6), 852–859. doi:10.1037/0022-0663.74.6.852

Deng, X., Doll, W. J., & Cao, M. (2008). Exploring the absorptive capacity to innovation / productivity link for individual engineers engaged in IT enabled work. *Information & Management*, *45*(2), 75–87. doi:10.1016/j.im.2007.12.001

Doern, R., Goss, D., & Neely, A. (2020). Special Issue on 'SMEs and the COVID-19 pandemic'. *International Small Business Journal*, *38*(6), 473–476.

Doherty, N., & Burke, R. (2019). *Flexibility in the workplace: Implications of flexible work arrangements for individuals, teams, and organizations*. Routledge.

Donthu, N., & Gustafsson, A. (2020). Effects of COVID-19 on business and research. *Journal of Business Research, 117*, 284–289. doi:10.1016/j.jbusres.2020.06.008 PMID:32536736

Doz, Y. L., & Kosonen, M. (2010). Embedding Strategic Agility: A Leadership Agenda for Accelerating Business Model Renewal. *Long Range Planning, 43*(2-3), 370–382. doi:10.1016/j.lrp.2009.07.006

Dron, J., & Anderson, T. (2014). *Teaching Crowds: Learning and Social Media*. AU Press.

Dutton, H., Bullen, P., & Deane, K. L. (2019). "It is OK to let them know you are human too": Mentor self-disclosure in formal youth mentoring relationships. *Journal of Community Psychology, 47*(4), 943–963. doi:10.1002/jcop.22165 PMID:30714171

Dwivedi, Y. K., Hughes, L., Baabdullah, A. M., Ribeiro-Navarrete, S., Giannakis, M., Al-Debei, M. M., Dennehy, D., Metri, B., Buhalis, D., Cheung, C. M. K., Conboy, K., Doyle, R., Dubey, R., Dutot, V., Felix, R., Goyal, D. P., Gustafsson, A., Hinsch, C., Jebabli, I., & Wamba, S. F. (2022). Metaverse beyond the hype: Multidisciplinary perspectives on emerging challenges, opportunities, and agenda for research, practice and policy. *International Journal of Information Management, 66*, 102542. doi:10.1016/j.ijinfomgt.2022.102542

Dwivedi, Y. K., Ismagilova, E., Hughes, D. L., Carlson, J., Filieri, R., Jacobson, J., Jain, V., Karjaluoto, H., Kefi, H., Krishen, A. S., Kumar, V., Rahman, M. M., Raman, R., Rauschnabel, P. A., Rowley, J., Salo, J., Tran, G. A., & Wang, Y. (2021). Setting the future of digital and social media marketing research: Perspectives and research propositions. *International Journal of Information Management, 59*, 102168. doi:10.1016/j.ijinfomgt.2020.102168

Efthymiou, I. P. (2017). *Wellness: A new word for Ancient Ideas*. Xlibris UK, Efthymiou, I. P., (2020). Non-Cognitive Skills and AI: A New Era of Learning and Development. *International Case Studies Journal, 9*(10), 42–46.

Eisenbeiss, S. A., Knippenberg, D. V., & Boerner, S. (2020). Transformational leadership and team innovation: Integrating team climate principles. *The Journal of Applied Psychology, 105*(9), 1021–1037. PMID:19025260

Eisenberger, R., & Shanock, L. (2003). Rewards, intrinsic motivation, and creativity: A case study of conceptual and methodological isolation. *Creativity Research Journal, 15*(2 & 3), 121–130. doi:10.1080/10400419.2003.9651404

Eisenhardt, K. M., Furr, N. R., & Bingham, C. B. (2016). Crossroads—microfoundations of performance: Balancing efficiency and flexibility in dynamic environments. *Organization Science, 27*(6), 1394–1406.

Elmorshidy, A. (2018). The impact of knowledge management systems on innovation: An empirical investigation in Kuwait. *VINE Journal of Information and Knowledge Management Systems, 48*(3), 388–403. doi:10.1108/VJIKMS-12-2017-0089

ElSaheli-Elhage, R. (2021). Access to Students and Parents and Levels of Preparedness of Educators during the COVID-19 Emergency Transition to e-Learning. [IJonSE]. *International Journal on Studies in Education*, *3*(2), 61–69. doi:10.46328/ijonse.35

Enkel, E., Heil, S., Hengstler, M., & Wirth, H. (2017). Exploratory and exploitative innovation: To what extent do the dimensions of individual level absorptive capacity contribute? *Technovation*, *60–61*(August), 29–38. doi:10.1016/j.technovation.2016.08.002

European Commission. (2020). *The European Commission's contribution to the future of work*. EC. https://ec.europa.eu/commission/presscorner/detail/en/IP_20_2349

Fang, Y., Qureshi, I., Sun, H., McCole, P., Ramsey, E., & Lim, K. H. (2020). Trust, satisfaction, and online repurchase intention: The moderating role of perceived effectiveness of e-commerce institutional mechanisms. *Management Information Systems Quarterly*, *44*(2), 471–502.

Fan, W., Wu, X., Shi, X. Y., Zhang, C., Wai Hung, I., Kai Leung, Y., & Zeng, L. S. (2023). Support vector regression model for flight demand forecasting. *International Journal of Engineering Business Management*, *15*, 18479790231174318. doi:10.1177/18479790231174318

Fernández-Díaz, J. R., Gutiérrez-Ortega, M., Llamas-Salguero, F., & Cantón-Mayo, I. (2021). Creativity and resilience as predictors of career success. *Sustainability (Basel)*, *13*(8), 4489. doi:10.3390u13084489

Fischer, C., Baker, R., Li, Q., Orona, G., & Warschauer, M. (2022). Increasing success in Higher Education: The relationships of online course taking with college completion and time-to-degree. *Educational Evaluation and Policy Analysis*, *44*(3), 355–379. . ISSN 0162-3737. S2CID 244498785. doi:10.3102/01623737211055768

Freeport, M. (2020). *Challenges of working remotely from a business perspective*.

Frentzel-Beyme, L., Holtze, M., Szczuka, J. M., & Krämer, N. C. (2022). Posting from the Past-A Longitudinal Study of the Potentials of Parasocial Interaction with a Historical Figure for History Education.

Fujita, K., Inoue, A., Kuzuya, M., Uno, C., Huang, C. H., Umegaki, H., & Onishi, J. (2021). Mental Health Status of the Older Adults in Japan During the COVID-19 Pandemic. *Journal of the American Medical Directors Association*, *22*(1), 220–221. doi:10.1016/j.jamda.2020.11.023 PMID:33321080

Funk, S., Gilad, E., Watkins, C., & Jansen, V. A. (2009). The spread of awareness and its impact on epidemic outbreaks. *Proceedings of the National Academy of Sciences of the United States of America*, *106*(16), 6872–6877. doi:10.1073/pnas.0810762106 PMID:19332788

Gaddefors, J., & Anderson, A. R. (2017). Entrepreneurship and context: when entrepreneurship is greater than entrepreneurs. *International Journal of Entrepreneurial Behavior & Research*. *23*(2), 267–278.. doi:10.1108/IJEBR-01-2016-0040

Gagné, M., & Deci, E. L. (2005). Self-determination theory and work motivation. *Journal of Organizational Behavior*, *26*(4), 331–362. doi:10.1002/job.322

Gajendran, R. S., & Harrison, D. A. (2007). The good, the bad, and the unknown about telecommuting: Meta-analysis of psychological mediators and individual consequences. *The Journal of Applied Psychology*, *92*(6), 1524–1541. doi:10.1037/0021-9010.92.6.1524 PMID:18020794

Gerard, L., Bradford, A., & Linn, M. C. (2022). Supporting Teachers to Customize Curriculum for Self-Directed Learning. *Journal of Science Education and Technology*, *31*(5), 660–679. doi:10.100710956-022-09985-w

Gianiodis, P. T., Pyeon, J., & Li, S. (2019). Hybrid incubators: The role of smart workspaces in startup development. *Technological Forecasting and Social Change*, *149*, 119734.

Gibbs, S., Singh, R. P., Butler, J. S., & Scott, C. (2018). *The role of networking, entrepreneurial environments, and support systems in the creation, survival and success of ventures founded by minority, women, and immigrant entrepreneurs*. New England Journal of Entrepreneurship. doi:10.1108/NEJE-10-2018-018

Gibson, C. B., Huang, L., Kirkman, B. L., & Shapiro, D. L. (2014). Where global and virtual meet: The value of examining the intersection of these elements in twenty-first-century teams. *Annual Review of Organizational Psychology and Organizational Behavior*, *1*(1), 217–244. doi:10.1146/annurev-orgpsych-031413-091240

Gig Economy Data Hub. (2021). *What is the gig economy*? Gig Economy Data Shop. https://www.gigeconomydata.org/

Gil-Quintana, J., & Vida de León, E. (2021). Educational influencers on instagram: Analysis of educational channels, audiences, and economic performance. *Publications / MDPI*, *9*(4), 43. doi:10.3390/publications9040043

Giorgi, G., Lecca, L. I., Alessio, F., Finstad, G. L., Bondanini, G., Lulli, L. G., Arcangeli, G., & Mucci, N. (2020). COVID-19-related mental health effects in the workplace: A narrative review. *International Journal of Environmental Research and Public Health*, *17*(21), 7857. doi:10.3390/ijerph17217857 PMID:33120930

Golden, T. D., & Veiga, J. F. (2005). The impact of extent of telecommuting on job satisfaction: Resolving inconsistent findings. *Journal of Management*, *31*(2), 301–318. doi:10.1177/0149206304271768

Golden, T. D., Veiga, J. F., & Simsek, Z. (2020). Telecommuting's differential impact on work-family conflict: Is there no place like home? *The Journal of Applied Psychology*, *105*(11), 1234–1245. PMID:32969707

Gong, Y., Cheung, S. Y., Wang, M., & Huang, J. C. (2012). Unfolding the proactive process for creativity: Integration of the employee proactivity, information exchange, and psychological safety perspectives. *Journal of Management*, *38*(5), 1611–1633. doi:10.1177/0149206310380250

Görög, G. (2018). The Definitions of Sharing Economy: A Systematic Literature Review. *Management (18544223)*, *13*(2).

Grant, R. M. (1996). Toward a knowledge-based theory of the firm. *Strategic Management Journal, 17*(S2), 109–122. doi:10.1002mj.4250171110

Griffiths, R. F. (2003). *Time management in telework and other autonomous work environments*. Kansas State University.

Guenard, R. (2021). The COVID-19 pandemic, one year later. *Inform (Champaign, Ill.)*, 6–11.

Guinez-Cabrera, N., & Aqueveque, C. (2021). Entrepreneurial influencers and influential entrepreneurs: Two sides of the same coin. *International Journal of Entrepreneurial Behaviour & Research, 28*(1), 231–254. doi:10.1108/IJEBR-08-2020-0563

Gulbahar, Y., & Kalelioglu, F. (2015). Competencies for e-Instructors: How to qualify and guarantee sustainability. *Contemporary Educational Technology, 6*(2), 140–154.

Gurcan, F., & Cagiltay, N. E. (2023). Research trends on distance learning: A text mining-based literature review from 2008 to 2018. *Interactive Learning Environments, 31*(2), 1007–1028. doi:10.1080/10494820.2020.1815795

Hager, F. W. (2018). Links between telecommuting, social support and mental well-being among teleworkers. In *Links between telecommuting, social support and mental well-being among teleworkers*. Hager, Frank W. doi:10.20472/BM.2018.6.2.003

Hamari, J., Sjöklint, M., & Ukkonen, A. (2016). The sharing economy: Why people participate in collaborative consumption. *Journal of the Association for Information Science and Technology, 67*(9), 2047–2059. doi:10.1002/asi.23552

Hamel, G. and Breen, B. (2007). The Future of Management. *Human Resource Management International, 16*(6)

Hamel, G. (2020). The quest for resilience. *Harvard Business Review, 98*(5), 50–59. PMID:12964393

Hansen, J. M., & Levin, M. A. (2016). The effect of apathetic motivation on employees' intentions to use social media for businesses. *Journal of Business Research, 69*(12), 6058–6066. doi:10.1016/j.jbusres.2016.06.009

Hardill, I., & Green, A. (2003). Remote working – Altering the spatial contours of work and home in the new economy. *New Technology, Work and Employment, 18*(3), 212–222. doi:10.1111/1468-005X.00122

Hausberg, J. P., & Leeflang, P. S. H. (2019). Absorbing integration: Empirical evidence on the mediating role of absorptive capacity between functional-/cross-functional integration and innovation performance. *International Journal of Innovation Management, 23*(6), 1–37. doi:10.1142/S1363919619500567

Hauzenberger, N., Huber, F., & Klieber, K. (2023). Real-time inflation forecasting using non-linear dimension reduction techniques. *International Journal of Forecasting, 39*(2), 901–921. doi:10.1016/j.ijforecast.2022.03.002

Heidari, E., Mehrvarz, M., Marzooghi, R., & Stoyanov, S. (2021). The role of digital informal learning in the relationship between students' digital competence and academic engagement during the COVID-19 pandemic. *Journal of Computer Assisted Learning*, *37*(4), 1154–1166. doi:10.1111/jcal.12553 PMID:34230741

Helfat, C. E. (2021). Dynamic capabilities: Foundations, theories, and research opportunities. *Industrial and Corporate Change*, *30*(1), 3–30.

Helfat, C. E., Finkelstein, S., Mitchell, W., Peteraf, M. A., Singh, H., Teece, D., & Winter, S. G. (2007). *Dynamic capabilities: Understanding strategic change in organizations*. Blackwell Publishing.

Hermann, M., Pentek, T., & Otto, B. (2019). Design principles for industrie 4.0 scenarios: A literature review. *Technological Forecasting and Social Change*, *144*, 75–99.

Hill, E. J., Ferris, M., & Märtinson, V. (2003). Does it matter where you work? A comparison of how three work venues (traditional office, virtual office, and home office) influence aspects of work and personal/family life. *Journal of Vocational Behavior*, *63*(2), 220–241. doi:10.1016/S0001-8791(03)00042-3

Himanen, L., Geurts, A., Foster, A. S., & Rinke, P. (2019). Data-driven materials science: Status, challenges, and perspectives. *Advancement of Science*, *6*(21), 1900808. doi:10.1002/advs.201900808 PMID:31728276

Hoel, A., & Dahl, T. I. (2019). Why bother? Student motivation to participate in student evaluations of teaching. *Assessment & Evaluation in Higher Education*, *44*(3), 361–378. https://books.google.com.my/books?hl=en&lr=&id=r7UwEAAAQBAJ&oi=fnd&pg=PA87&ots=64I7nkx6U9&sig=IykWo_0CLJRq6QUih_jjv2GZCH s&redir_esc=y#v=onepage&q=para&f=false. doi:10.1080/02602938.2018.1511969

Hopkins, J. L., & McKay, J. (2019). Investigating 'anywhere working'as a mechanism for alleviating traffic congestion in smart cities. *Technological Forecasting and Social Change*, *142*, 258–272. doi:10.1016/j.techfore.2018.07.032

Hotho, J. J., Becker-Ritterspach, F., & Saka-Helmhout, A. (2012). Enriching absorptive capacity through social interaction. *British Journal of Management*, *23*(3), 383–401.

Hu, B., Zheng, Q., Wu, J., Tang, Z., Zhu, J., Wu, S., & Ling, Y. (2021). Role of Education and Mentorship in Entrepreneurial Behavior: Mediating Role of Self-Efficacy. *Frontiers in Psychology*, *12*, 5042. doi:10.3389/fpsyg.2021.775227 PMID:34917001

Huczynski, A. A., Buchanan, D. A., & Huczynski, A. A. (2021). *Organizational behaviour: An introductory text*. Pearson.

Hu, H., Xu, J., Liu, M., & Lim, M. K. (2023). Vaccine supply chain management: An intelligent system utilizing blockchain, IoT and machine learning. *Journal of Business Research*, *156*, 113480. doi:10.1016/j.jbusres.2022.113480 PMID:36506475

Hwang, N. K., Shim, S. H., & Cheon, H. W. (2023). Digital learning designs in occupational therapy education: A scoping review. *BMC Medical Education*, *23*(1), 1–19. doi:10.118612909-022-03955-x PMID:36604723

Iapichino, A., De Rosa, A., & Liberace, P. (2018). Smart organizations, new skills, and smart working to manage companies' digital transformation. *Digitized Labor: The Impact of the Internet on Employment*, 215-227. doi:10.1007/978-3-319-78420-5_13

International Labour Organization. (2017). Guidelines for the promotion of decent work in e-commerce. ILO. https://www.ilo.org/wcmsp5/groups/public/---ed_protect/---protrav/---travail/documents/publication/wcms_623375.pdf

International Labour Organization. (2019). *Working anytime, anywhere: The effects on the world of work*. ILO. https://www.ilo.org/global/publications/books/WCMS_544138/lang--en/index.htm

Iqbal, H. (2020). E-mentoring: an effective platform for distance learning. *e-mentor. Czasopismo naukowe Szkoły Głównej Handlowej w Warszawie, 84*(2), 54-61.

Ishay, Y.B. (2019). *Revisiting "Work from Home" from an Organizational Perspective*. Research Gate.

Jabri, M. M. (1991). The development of conceptually independent subscales in the measurement of modes of problem solving. *Educational and Psychological Measurement*, *51*(4), 975–983. doi:10.1177/0013164491051004l7

Jansen, J. J. P., Van Den Bosch, F. A. J., & Volberda, H. W. (2005). Managing potential and realized absorptive capacity: How do organizational antecedents matter? *Academy of Management Journal*, *48*(6), 999–1015. doi:10.5465/amj.2005.19573106

Jarzyna, C. L. (2021). Parasocial interaction, the COVID-19 quarantine, and digital age media. *Human Arenas*, *4*(3), 413–429. doi:10.100742087-020-00156-0

Jedlicka, J. S., Brown, S. W., Bunch, A. E., & Jaffe, L. E. (2002). A comparison of distance education instructional methods in occupational therapy. *Journal of Allied Health*, *31*(4), 247–251. PMID:12491955

Jeske, D. (2022). Remote workers' experiences with electronic monitoring during covid-19: Implications and recommendations. *International Journal of Workplace Health Management*, *15*(3), 393–409. doi:10.1108/IJWHM-02-2021-0042

Jiang, H., & Luo, Y. (2018). Crafting employee trust: From authenticity, transparency to engagement. *Journal of Communication Management (London)*, *22*(2), 138–160. doi:10.1108/JCOM-07-2016-0055

John, S. P., Walford, R., & Purayidathil, J. (2022). Factors affecting the adoption of social media in marketing of higher education: An empirical analysis. *FIIB Business Review*, *11*(4), 422–437. doi:10.1177/23197145211072198

Johnston, D., Rockhill, C., & Pastore, D. (2021). The effectiveness of podcasts in sport management education part two: A qualitative analysis. *Journal of Hospitality, Leisure, Sport and Tourism Education, 29*, 100338. doi:10.1016/j.jhlste.2021.100338

Kang, M., & Lee, M. J. (2017). Absorptive capacity, knowledge sharing, and innovative behaviour of R&D employees. *Technology Analysis and Strategic Management, 29*(2), 219–232. doi:10.1080/09537325.2016.1211265

Kaplan, A. M., & Haenlein, M. (2016). Higher education and the digital revolution: About MOOCs, SPOCs, social media, and the Cookie Monster. *Business Horizons, 59*(4), 441–450. doi:10.1016/j.bushor.2016.03.008

Kaufman, M. R., Wright, K., Simon, J., Edwards, G., Thrul, J., & DuBois, D. L. (2022). Mentoring in the time of COVID-19: An analysis of online focus groups with mentors to youth. *American Journal of Community Psychology, 69*(1-2), 33–45. doi:10.1002/ajcp.12543 PMID:34318506

Kees, J., Berry, C., Burton, S., & Sheehan, K. (2017). An analysis of data quality: Professional panels, student subject pools, and Amazon's Mechanical Turk. *Journal of Advertising, 46*(1), 141–155. doi:10.1080/00913367.2016.1269304

Keith, M. G., Harms, P. D., & Long, A. C. (2020). Worker health and well-being in the gig economy: A proposed framework and research agenda. *Entrepreneurial and small business stressors, experienced stress, and well-being, 18*(1), 1-33. doi:10.1108/S1479-355520200000018002

Kelliher, C., & Anderson, D. (2010). Doing more with less? Flexible working practices and the intensification of work. *Human Relations, 63*(1), 83–106. doi:10.1177/0018726709349199

Kern, L., Harrison, J. R., Custer, B. E., & Mehta, P. D. (2019). Factors that enhance the quality of relationships between mentors and mentees during Check & Connect. *Behavioral Disorders, 44*(3), 148–161. doi:10.1177/0198742918779791

Khalifa, M., Yan, A. Y., & Ning, K. S. (2008). Knowledge management systems success: A contingency perspective. *Journal of Knowledge Management, 12*(1), 119–132. doi:10.1108/13673270810852430

Kim, J., Kim, J., & Yang, H. (2019). Loneliness and the use of social media to follow celebrities: A moderating role of social presence. *The Social Science Journal, 56*(1), 21–29. doi:10.1016/j.soscij.2018.12.007

Kim, J., & Kim, M. (2022). Rise of Social Media Influencers as a New Marketing Channel: Focusing on the Roles of Psychological Well-Being and Perceived Social Responsibility among Consumers. *International Journal of Environmental Research and Public Health, 19*(4), 2362. doi:10.3390/ijerph19042362 PMID:35206553

Klyver, K., & Arenius, P. (2022). Networking, social skills and launching a new business: A 3-year study of nascent entrepreneurs. *Entrepreneurship Theory and Practice, 46*(5), 1256–1283. doi:10.1177/1042258720967063

Kobia, M., & Sikalieh, D. (2010). Towards a search for the meaning of entrepreneurship. *Journal of European Industrial Training*, *34*(2), 110–127. doi:10.1108/03090591011023970

Ko, D. G., Kirsch, L. J., & King, W. R. (2005). Antecedents of knowledge transfer from consultants to clients in enterprise system implementations. *Management Information Systems Quarterly*, *29*(1), 59–85. doi:10.2307/25148668

Kossek, E. E., Lautsch, B. A., & Eaton, S. C. (2006). Telecommuting, control, and boundary management: Correlates of policy use and practice, job control, and work–family effectiveness. *Journal of Vocational Behavior*, *68*(2), 347–367. doi:10.1016/j.jvb.2005.07.002

Kostopoulos, K., Papalexandris, A., Papachroni, M., & Ioannou, G. (2011). Absorptive capacity, innovation, and financial performance. *Journal of Business Research*, *64*(12), 1335–1343. doi:10.1016/j.jbusres.2010.12.005

Kowalkiewicz, R., Zhou, J., Ma, M., & Filieri, R. (2020). From crowdsourcing to smart working: A review and agenda for future research. *Journal of Management Information Systems*, *37*(1), 9–52.

Kowert, R., & Daniel, E. Jr. (2021). The one-and-a-half sided parasocial relationship: The curious case of live streaming. *Computers in Human Behavior Reports*, *4*, 100150. doi:10.1016/j.chbr.2021.100150

Kreiterling, C. (2023). Digital innovation and entrepreneurship: A review of challenges in competitive markets. *Journal of Innovation and Entrepreneurship*, *12*(1), 49. doi:10.118613731-023-00320-0

Kurian, P. S., & Nair, S. S. K. (2023). Alumni mentoring: An approach to build community of learners. In *SHS Web of Conferences* (*Vol. 156*, p. 08003). EDP Sciences.

Kuvaas, B., Buch, R., Gagné, M., Dysvik, A., & Forest, J. (2016). Do you get what you pay for? Sales incentives and implications for motivation and changes in turnover intention and work effort. *Motivation and Emotion*, *40*(5), 667–680. doi:10.100711031-016-9574-6

Kuvaas, B., & Dysvik, A. (2009). Perceived investment in employee development, intrinsic motivation and work performance. *Human Resource Management Journal*, *19*(3), 217–236. doi:10.1111/j.1748-8583.2009.00103.x

Kuzin, D. V. (2018). Global competences and challenges for entrepreneurship educators. *Journal of Entrepreneurship Education*, *21*(2S), 1–11.

Lake, A. (2016). *Smart flexibility: Moving smart and flexible working from theory to practice*. CRC Press. doi:10.4324/9781315609379

Lall, S. A., Chen, L. W., & Mason, D. P. (2022). Digital platforms and entrepreneurial support: A field experiment in online mentoring. *Small Business Economics*, 1–24.

Lane, P. J., Koka, B. R., & Pathak, S. (2006). The reification of absorptive capacity: A critical review and rejuvenation of the construct. *Academy of Management Review*, *31*(4), 833–863. doi:10.5465/amr.2006.22527456

Larose, S., Tarabulsy, G. M., Boisclair-Châteauvert, G., & Karcher, M. (2019). When insecure attachment dispositions affect mentoring relationship quality: An exploration of interactive mentoring contexts. *Journal of Relationships Research, 10*, e6. doi:10.1017/jrr.2019.1

Lattacher, W., & Wdowiak, M. A. (2020). Entrepreneurial learning from failure. A systematic review. *International Journal of Entrepreneurial Behaviour & Research, 26*(5), 1093–1131. doi:10.1108/IJEBR-02-2019-0085

Lazar, I., Osoian, C., & Ratiu, P. I. (2010). The role of work-life balance practices in order to improve organizational performance. *European Research Studies, 13*(1), 202–214. doi:10.35808/ersj/267

Lee, J., Bagheri, B., & Kao, H. A. (2015). A cyber-physical systems architecture for industry 4.0-based manufacturing systems. *Manufacturing Letters, 3*(1), 18–23. doi:10.1016/j.mfglet.2014.12.001

Lee, Y., Tao, W., Li, J. Y. Q., & Sun, R. (2020). Enhancing employees' knowledge sharing through diversity-oriented leadership and strategic internal communication during the COVID-19 outbreak. *Journal of Knowledge Management.*

Liao, S. H., Fei, W. C., & Chen, C. C. (2007). Knowledge sharing, absorptive capacity, and innovation capability: An empirical study of Taiwan's knowledge-intensive industries. *Journal of Information Science, 33*(3), 340–359. doi:10.1177/0165551506070739

Li, C. T. (2019). Mentor-spotting: Recommending expert mentors to mentees for live trouble-shooting in Codementor. *Knowledge and Information Systems, 61*(2), 799–820. doi:10.100710115-018-1298-3

Liebers, N., & Schramm, H. (2019). Parasocial interactions and relationships with media characters–an inventory of 60 years of research. *Communication Research Trends, 38*(2), 4–31.

Lim, J. S., Choe, M. J., Zhang, J., & Noh, G. Y. (2020). The role of wishful identification, emotional engagement, and parasocial relationships in repeated viewing of live-streaming games: A social cognitive theory perspective. *Computers in Human Behavior, 108*, 106327. doi:10.1016/j.chb.2020.106327

Lin, T. C., & Huang, C. C. (2008). Understanding knowledge management system usage antecedents: An integration of social cognitive theory and task technology fit. *Information & Management, 45*(6), 410–417. doi:10.1016/j.im.2008.06.004

Liu, D., Jiang, K., Shalley, C. E., Keem, S., & Zhou, J. (2016). Motivational mechanisms of employee creativity: A meta-analytic examination and theoretical extension of the creativity literature. *Organizational Behavior and Human Decision Processes, 137*, 236–263. doi:10.1016/j.obhdp.2016.08.001

Liu, F., Ma, J., & Li, R. (2019). Which role model is more effective in entrepreneurship education? An investigation of storytelling on individual's entrepreneurial intention. *Frontiers in Psychology, 10*, 837. doi:10.3389/fpsyg.2019.00837 PMID:31068853

Liu, Y., Wei, L., Fan, J., Zhou, H., & Zhou, S. (2019). Agile manufacturing: A systematic review. *International Journal of Production Research*, *57*(13), 4075–4097.

Lock, J., & Redmond, P. (2021). Embedded experts in online collaborative learning: A case study. *The Internet and Higher Education*, *48*, 100773. doi:10.1016/j.iheduc.2020.100773

Lou, C., & Kim, H. K. (2019). Fancying the new rich and famous? Explicating the roles of influencer content, credibility, and parental mediation in adolescents' parasocial relationship, materialism, and purchase intentions. *Frontiers in Psychology*, *10*, 2567. doi:10.3389/fpsyg.2019.02567 PMID:31803110

Lukosch, S., Billinghurst, M., Alem, L., & Kiyokawa, K. (2015). Collaboration in augmented reality. [CSCW]. *Computer Supported Cooperative Work*, *24*(6), 515–525. doi:10.100710606-015-9239-0

Luo, Y., & Xu, X. (2021). Comparative study of deep learning models for analyzing online restaurant reviews in the era of the COVID-19 pandemic. *International Journal of Hospitality Management*, *94*, 102849. doi:10.1016/j.ijhm.2020.102849 PMID:34785843

Lu, Y., & Ramamurthy, K. (2011). Understanding the link between information technology capability and organizational agility: An empirical examination. *Management Information Systems Quarterly*, *35*(4), 931–954. doi:10.2307/41409967

MacInnis, D. J., & Jaworski, B. J. (1989). Information processing from advertisements: Toward an integrative framework. *Journal of Marketing*, *53*(4), 1–23. doi:10.1177/002224298905300401

Madjar, N., Oldham, G. R., & Pratt, M. G. (2002). There's no place like home? The contributions of work and nonwork creativity support to employees' creative performance. *Academy of Management Journal*, *45*(4), 757–767. doi:10.2307/3069309

Malhotra, A., Majchrzak, A., & Rosen, B. (2007). Leading virtual teams. *The Academy of Management Perspectives*, *21*(1), 60–70. doi:10.5465/amp.2007.24286164

Malik, A. A., Masood, T., & Bilberg, A. (2020). Virtual reality in manufacturing: Immersive and collaborative artificial-reality in design of human-robot workspace. *International Journal of Computer Integrated Manufacturing*, *33*(1), 22–37. doi:10.1080/0951192X.2019.1690685

Manolopoulos, D. (2006). What motivates R&D professionals? Evidence from decentralized laboratories in Greece. *International Journal of Human Resource Management*, *17*(4), 616–647. doi:10.1080/09585190600581394

Martins, L. L., Gilson, L. L., & Maynard, M. T. (2016). Virtual teams: What do we know and where do we go from here? *Journal of Management*, *43*(6), 1437–1473.

Masson, M. (2014). Benefits of TED Talks. *Canadian Family Physician Medecin de Famille Canadien*, *60*(12), 1080. PMID:25500595

McKinsey, G. L., Lizama, C. O., Keown-Lang, A. E., Niu, A., Santander, N., Larpthaveesarp, A., & Arnold, T. D. (2020). A new genetic strategy for targeting microglia in development and disease. *elife, 9*, e54590.

McLaughlin, C., & Wohn, D. Y. (2021). Predictors of parasocial interaction and relationships in live streaming. *Convergence (London), 27*(6), 1714–1734. doi:10.1177/13548565211027807

McReynolds, M. R., Termini, C. M., Hinton, A. O. Jr, Taylor, B. L., Vue, Z., Huang, S. C., Roby, R. A. S., Shuler, H., & Carter, C. S. (2020). The art of virtual mentoring in the twenty-first century for STEM majors and beyond. *Nature Biotechnology, 38*(12), 1477–1482. doi:10.103841587-020-00758-7 PMID:33273732

Mehralian, G., O'Cass, A., & Nguyen, B. (2021). Understanding resilient organizations: A systematic review and synthesis. *Journal of Business Research, 136*, 615–632.

Memon, J., Rozan, M. Z. A., Ismail, K., Uddin, M., & Daud, D. (2015). Mentoring an entrepreneur: Guide for a mentor. *SAGE Open, 5*(1), 2158244015569666. doi:10.1177/2158244015569666

Meyer, J. P., Becker, T. E., & Vandenberghe, C. (2004). Employee commitment and motivation: A conceptual analysis and integrative model. *The Journal of Applied Psychology, 89*(6), 991–1007. doi:10.1037/0021-9010.89.6.991 PMID:15584837

Minbaeva, D. B., Makela, K., & Rabbiosi, L. (2007). *Individual absorptive capacity and knowledge transfer.* Unpublished Paper, Copenhagen Business School.

Minbaeva, D. (2021). Disrupted HR? *Human Resource Management Review, 31*(4), 100820. doi:10.1016/j.hrmr.2020.100820

Minbaeva, D. B., Pedersen, T., Björkman, I., Fey, C. F., & Park, H. J. (2003). MNC knowledge transfer, subsidiary absorptive capacity, and HRM. *Journal of International Business Studies, 34*(6), 586–599. doi:10.1057/palgrave.jibs.8400056

Mishra, A., Agarwal A., & Agarwal V. (2020). Work from Home: The Modus Operandi During COVID-19. *Horizon, 2*(s), 67-74.

Molino, M., Ingusci, E., Signore, F., Manuti, A., Giancaspro, M. L., Russo, V., Zito, M., & Cortese, C. G. (2020). Wellbeing costs of technology use during Covid-19 remote working: An investigation using the Italian translation of the technostress creators scale. *Sustainability (Basel), 12*(15), 1–20. doi:10.3390u12155911

Montag, T., Maertz, C. P. Jr, & Baer, M. (2012). A critical analysis of the workplace creativity criterion space. *Journal of Management, 38*(4), 1362–1386. doi:10.1177/0149206312441835

Moore, H. F., & Gheisari, M. (2019). A review of virtual and mixed reality applications in construction safety literature. *Safety (Basel, Switzerland), 5*(3), 51–70. doi:10.3390afety5030051

Moss, J. (2021). Beyond burned out. *Harvard Business Review.* https://hbr.org/2021/02/beyond-burned-out

Mumford, M. D., & Hunter, S. T. (2005). Innovation in organizations: A multi-level perspective on creativity. *Research in Multi-Level Issues*, *4*(05), 9–73. doi:10.1016/S1475-9144(05)04001-4

Mumu, J. R., Tahmid, T., & Azad, M. A. K. (2021). Job satisfaction and intention to quit: A bibliometric review of work-family conflict and research agenda. *Applied Nursing Research*, *59*, 151334. doi:10.1016/j.apnr.2020.151334 PMID:33947506

Myers, S. (2021). Instagram source effects: The impact of familiarity and likeability on influencer outcomes. *Journal of Marketing Development and Competitiveness*, *15*(3), 50–55.

Nabi, G., Walmsley, A., & Akhtar, I. (2021). Mentoring functions and entrepreneur development in the early years of university. *Studies in Higher Education*, *46*(6), 1159–1174. doi:10.1080/03075079.2019.1665009

Nembhard, I. M., & Edmondson, A. C. (2006). Making it safe: The effects of leader inclusiveness and professional status on psychological safety and improvement efforts in health care teams. *Journal of Organizational Behavior*, *27*(7), 941–966. doi:10.1002/job.413

Ng, C. F. (2021). The Physical Learning Environment of Online Distance Learners in Higher Education – A Conceptual Model. *Frontiers in Psychology*, *12*, 635117. doi:10.3389/fpsyg.2021.635117 PMID:34650464

Nguyen, T. (2015). The effectiveness of online learning. *Journal of Online Learning and Teaching*, *11*(2), 309–319.

Nguyen, T. D., Nguyen, T. M., & Cao, T. H. (2015). Information systems success: A literature review. *Springer International Publishing Switzerland*, *9446*, 242–256.

Nilashi, M., Abumalloh, R. A., Minaei-Bidgoli, B., Abdu Zogaan, W., Alhargan, A., Mohd, S., Syed Azhar, S. N. F., Asadi, S., & Samad, S. (2021). Revealing travellers' satisfaction during COVID-19 outbreak: Moderating role of service quality. *Journal of Retailing and Consumer Services*, *64*, 102783. doi:10.1016/j.jretconser.2021.102783

Niu, S., Lu, Z., Zhang, A. X., Cai, J., Griggio, C. F., & Heuer, H. (2023, April). Building Credibility, Trust, and Safety on Video-Sharing Platforms. In *Extended Abstracts of the 2023 CHI Conference on Human Factors in Computing Systems* (pp. 1-7).

Nowiński, W., & Haddoud, M. Y. (2019). The role of inspiring role models in enhancing entrepreneurial intention. *Journal of Business Research*, *96*, 183–193. doi:10.1016/j.jbusres.2018.11.005

O'Reilly, C. A., Doerr, B., & Chatman, J. A. (2019). See how they think: The effects of cognitive and affective perspective taking on empathy in negotiations. *The Journal of Applied Psychology*, *104*(5), 635–652.

Oblinger, D. G. (2000). The Nature and Purpose of Distance Education. *Technology (Elmsford, N.Y.)*.

Oksanen, A., Syrek, C. J., Salmela-Aro, K., de Bloom, J., & Korpela, K. (2019). How the 21st-century workforce shapes global value chains: Work characteristics and the fear of job loss. *The Academy of Management Perspectives*, *33*(4), 403–424.

Oldham, G. R., & Cummings, A. (1996). Employee creativity: Personal and contextual factors at work. *Academy of Management Journal*, *39*(3), 607–634. doi:10.2307/256657

Oliveira, T., & Martins, M. (2012). Literature review of information technology adoption models at firm level. *The Australasian Journal of Construction Economics and Building*, *14*(1), 110–121.

Ouvrein, G., Pabian, S., Giles, D., Hudders, L., & De Backer, C. (2021). The web of influencers. A marketing-audience classification of (potential) social media influencers. *Journal of Marketing Management*, *37*(13-14), 1313–1342. doi:10.1080/0267257X.2021.1912142

Oztemel, E., & Gursev, S. (2020). Literature review of Industry 4.0 and related technologies. *Journal of Intelligent Manufacturing*, *31*(1), 127–182. doi:10.100710845-018-1433-8

Pal, S., Biswas, B., Gupta, R., Kumar, A., & Gupta, S. (2023). Exploring the factors that affect user experience in mobile-health applications: A text-mining and machine-learning approach. *Journal of Business Research*, *156*, 113484. doi:10.1016/j.jbusres.2022.113484 PMID:36475057

Pal, T. (2023). The Exploratory Study of Machine Learning on Applications, Challenges, and Uses in the Financial Sector. In *Advanced Machine Learning Algorithms for Complex Financial Applications* (pp. 156–165). IGI Global. doi:10.4018/978-1-6684-4483-2.ch010

Pech, M., & Vrchota, J. (2020). Classification of small-and medium-sized enterprises based on the level of industry 4.0 implementation. *Applied Sciences (Basel, Switzerland)*, *10*(15), 5150. doi:10.3390/app10155150

Penrose, E. (1959). *The Theory of the Growth of the Firm*. Oxford University Press.

Penttinen, V., Ciuchita, R., & Čaić, M. (2022). YouTube it before you buy it: The role of parasocial interaction in consumer-to-consumer video reviews. *Journal of Interactive Marketing*, *57*(4), 561–582. doi:10.1177/10949968221102825

Petter, S., DeLone, W., & McLean, E. (2008). Measuring information systems success: Models, dimensions, measures, and interrelationships. *European Journal of Information Systems*, *17*(3), 236–263. doi:10.1057/ejis.2008.15

Pocek, J., Politis, D., & Gabrielsson, J. (2021). Entrepreneurial learning in extra-curricular start-up programs for students. *International Journal of Entrepreneurial Behaviour & Research*, *28*(2), 325–345. doi:10.1108/IJEBR-04-2020-0206

Podgorski, D., Majchrzycka, K., Dąbrowska, A., Gralewicz, G., & Okrasa, M. (2017). Towards a conceptual framework of OSH risk management in smart working environments based on smart PPE, ambient intelligence and the Internet of Things technologies. *International Journal of Occupational Safety and Ergonomics*, *23*(1), 1–20. doi:10.1080/10803548.2016.1214431 PMID:27441587

Pouri, M. J., & Hilty, L. M. (2021). The digital sharing economy: A confluence of technical and social sharing. *Environmental Innovation and Societal Transitions*, *38*(1), 127–139. doi:10.1016/j.eist.2020.12.003

Prastyaningtyas, E. W., Sutrisno, S., Soeprajitno, E. D., Ausat, A. M. A., & Suherlan, S. (2023). Analysing the Role of Mentors in Entrepreneurship Education: Effective Support and Assistance. *Journal of Education*, *5*(4), 14571–14577.

Price, D. (1976). A general theory of bibliometric and other cumulative advantage processes. *Journal of the American Society for Information Science*, *27*(5), 292–306. doi:10.1002/asi.4630270505

Radović-Marković, M., Stevanović, M., & Milojević, N. (2021) Remote Working in Terms of Covid-19. *International Journal of Entrepreneurship, 25* (1). ISSN 1939-4675

Raghupathi, W., Xiang, X., & Sun, S. (2020). Smart working in a digital world: Opportunities and challenges for organizations. *International Journal of Information Management*, *50*, 106145.

Rammstedt, B., & John, O. P. (2007). Measuring personality in one minute or less: A 10-item short version of the Big Five Inventory in English and German. *Journal of Research in Personality*, *41*(1), 203–212. doi:10.1016/j.jrp.2006.02.001

Ratten, V., & Jones, P. (2021). Covid-19 and entrepreneurship education: Implications for advancing research and practice. *International Journal of Management Education*, *19*(1), 100432. doi:10.1016/j.ijme.2020.100432

Ratten, V., & Rashid, S. (2021). Entrepreneurship Education and digital marketing: What does the future hold? In *Developing Digital Marketing* (pp. 87–101). Emerald Publishing Limited. doi:10.1108/978-1-80071-348-220211006

Ren, X., & Xu, H. (2023). Flexible working during the COVID-19 pandemic: Gains and strains in a Chinese state-owned organisation. *Journal of Asia Business Studies*, *17*(1), 75–96. doi:10.1108/JABS-03-2022-0109

Rigby, D. K., Sutherland, J., & Takeuchi, H. (2016). Embracing agile. *Harvard Business Review*, *94*(5), 40–50.

Riswantini, D., Nugraheni, E., Arisal, A., Khotimah, P.H., Munandar, D., & Suwarningsih, W. (2021). Big data research in fighting COVID-19: Contributions and techniques. *Big Data and Cognitive Computing*, *5*(3).

Roberto, R., Penna, M., Felici, B., & Rao, M. (2023). Smart working and flexible work arrangements: opportunities and risks for sustainable communities. In *Intelligent Environments* (pp. 243–283). North-Holland. doi:10.1016/B978-0-12-820247-0.00001-1

Rosing, K., Frese, M., & Bausch, A. (2011). Explaining the heterogeneity of the leadership-innovation relationship: Ambidextrous leadership. *The Leadership Quarterly*, *22*(5), 956–974. doi:10.1016/j.leaqua.2011.07.014

Rudeloff, C., & Damms, J. (2023). Entrepreneurs as influencers: The impact of parasocial interactions on communication outcomes. *Journal of Research in Marketing and Entrepreneurship*, *25*(2), 328–346. doi:10.1108/JRME-04-2022-0052

Ryan, R. M., & Deci, E. L. (2020). Intrinsic and extrinsic motivation from a self-determination theory perspective: Definitions, theory, practices, and future directions. *Contemporary Educational Psychology*, *61*, 61. doi:10.1016/j.cedpsych.2020.101860

Sadeghi, M. (2019). A shift from classroom to distance learning: Advantages and limitations. *International Journal of Research in English Education*, *4*(1), 80–88. doi:10.29252/ijree.4.1.80

Sambamurthy, V., Bharadwaj, A., & Grover, V. (2020). Shaping agility through digital options: Reconceptualizing the role of information technology in contemporary firms. *Management Information Systems Quarterly*, *44*(1), 1–22. doi:10.2307/25148665

Samoylenko, N., Zharko, L., & Glotova, A. (2022). Designing Online Learning Environment: ICT Tools and Teaching Strategies. *Athens Journal of Education*, *9*(1), 49–62. doi:10.30958/aje.9-1-4

Sanchez-Rodriguez, C., Stölzle, W., & Zerfass, A. (2020). Agile and stakeholder-oriented organizational culture: The case of BMW. *Journal of Communication Management (London)*, *24*(1), 61–81.

Sarabipour, S., Hainer, S. J., Arslan, F. N., De Winde, C. M., Furlong, E., Bielczyk, N., Jadavji, N. M., Shah, A. P., & Davla, S. (2022). Building and sustaining mentor interactions as a mentee. *The FEBS Journal*, *289*(6), 1374–1384. doi:10.1111/febs.15823 PMID:33818917

Sasaki, N., Kuroda, R., Tsuno, K., & Kawakami, N. (2020). Workplace responses to COVID-19 associated with mental health and work performance of employees in Japan. *Journal of Occupational Health*, *62*(1), e12134. doi:10.1002/1348-9585.12134 PMID:32529654

Savić, D. (2020). COVID-19 and work from home: Digital transformation of the workforce. [TGJ]. *Grey Journal*, *16*(2), 101–104.

Scherer, H., Diaz, S., Iannone, N., McCarty, M., Branch, S., & Kelly, J. (2022). "Leave Britney alone!": Parasocial relationships and empathy. *The Journal of Social Psychology*, *162*(1), 128–142. doi:10.1080/00224545.2021.1997889 PMID:34850669

Schiller, R. (2020). *A perspective on working from home: The good and the bad (But mostly good)*. Benefits Pro.

Schmidtner, M., Doering, C., & Timinger, H. (2021). Agile Working During COVID-19 Pandemic. *IEEE Engineering Management Review*, *49*(2), 18–32. doi:10.1109/EMR.2021.3069940

Schor, J. B., & Attwood-Charles, W. (2017). The "sharing" economy: Labor, inequality, and social connection on for-profit platforms. *Sociology Compass*, *11*(8), e12493. doi:10.1111oc4.12493

Schou, P. K., Bucher, E., & Waldkirch, M. (2022). Entrepreneurial learning in online communities. *Small Business Economics*, *58*(4), 2087–2108. doi:10.100711187-021-00502-8

Schweisfurth, T. G., & Raasch, C. (2018). Absorptive capacity for need knowledge: Antecedents and effects for employee innovativeness. *Research Policy*, *47*(4), 687–699. doi:10.1016/j.respol.2018.01.017

Secundo, G., Gioconda, M. E. L. E., Del Vecchio, P., Gianluca, E. L. I. A., Margherita, A., & Valentina, N. D. O. U. (2021). Threat or opportunity? A case study of digital-enabled redesign of entrepreneurship education in the COVID-19 emergency. *Technological Forecasting and Social Change*, *166*, 120565. doi:10.1016/j.techfore.2020.120565 PMID:33518821

Seiders, K., Voss, G. B., Grewal, D., & Godfrey, A. L. (2005). Do satisfied customers buy more? Examining moderating influences in a retailing context. *Journal of Marketing*, *69*(4), 26–43. doi:10.1509/jmkg.2005.69.4.26

Semmer, N. K. (1982). Stress at work, stress in private life and psychological well-being. In W. Bachmann, & I. Udris (Eds.), Mental load and stress in activity: European approaches (pp. 42–55). Elsevier.

Senge, P. M., Smith, B., Kruschwitz, N., Laur, J., & Schley, S. (2012). *The necessary revolution: How individuals and organizations are working together to create a sustainable world.*

Seo, Y. W., Chae, S. W., & Lee, K. C. (2015). The impact of absorptive capacity, exploration, and exploitation on individual creativity: Moderating effect of subjective well-being. *Computers in Human Behavior*, *42*, 68–82. doi:10.1016/j.chb.2014.03.031

Shahina, F. A. C., & Kabeer, S. (2021). Covid-Proof' Smart World. *Proceedings of 2021 2nd International Conference on Intelligent Engineering and Management*. Scitepress.

Shalley, C. E., Zhou, J., & Oldham, G. R. (2004). The effects of personal and contextual characteristics on creativity: Where should we go from here? *Journal of Management*, *30*(6), 933–958. doi:10.1016/j.jm.2004.06.007

Shalley, C., Gilson, L., & Blum, T. (2009). Interactive effects of growth need strength, work context, and job complexity on self-reported creative performance. *Academy of Management Journal*, *52*(3), 489–505. doi:10.5465/amj.2009.41330806

Shane, S., & Venkataraman, S. (2000). The promise of entrepreneurship as a field of research. *Academy of Management Review*, *25*(1), 217–226. doi:10.5465/amr.2000.2791611

Sharifi, H., Colquhoun, G., Barclay, I., & Dann, Z. (2001). Agile manufacturing: A management and operational framework. *Proceedings of the Institution of Mechanical Engineers. Part B, Journal of Engineering Manufacture*, *215*(6), 857–869. doi:10.1243/0954405011518647

Sherrick, B., Smith, C., Jia, Y., Thomas, B., & Franklin, S. B. (2023). How Parasocial Phenomena Contribute to Sense of Community on Twitch. *Journal of Broadcasting & Electronic Media*, *67*(1), 47–67. doi:10.1080/08838151.2022.2151599

Shim, J. P., Warkentin, M., Courtney, J. F., Power, D. J., Sharda, R., & Carlsson, C. (2002). Past, present, and future of decision support technology. *Decision Support Systems*, *33*(2), 111–126. doi:10.1016/S0167-9236(01)00139-7

Simmering, M. J., Fuller, C. M., Richardson, H. A., Ocal, Y., & Atinc, G. M. (2015). Marker variable choice, reporting, and interpretation in the detection of common method variance: A review and demonstration. *Organizational Research Methods*, *18*(3), 473–511. doi:10.1177/1094428114560023

Smith, S. M., Roster, C. A., Golden, L. L., & Albaum, G. S. (2016). A multi-group analysis of online survey respondent data quality: Comparing a regular USA consumer panel to MTurk samples. *Journal of Business Research*, *69*(8), 3139–3148. doi:10.1016/j.jbusres.2015.12.002

Sobczak, A., & Ziora, L. (2021). The use of robotic process automation (RPA) as an element of smart city implementation: A case study of electricity billing document management at Bydgoszcz city Hall. *Energies*, *14*(16), 5191. doi:10.3390/en14165191

Soga, L. R., Bolade-Ogunfodun, Y., Mariani, M., Nasr, R., & Laker, B. (2022). Unmasking the other face of flexible working practices: A systematic literature review. *Journal of Business Research*, *142*, 648–662. doi:10.1016/j.jbusres.2022.01.024

Soomro, B. A., & Shah, N. (2019). Determining the impact of entrepreneurial orientation and organizational culture on job satisfaction, organizational commitment, and employee's performance. *South Asian Journal of Business Studies*, *8*(3), 266–282. doi:10.1108/SAJBS-12-2018-0142

Sorensen, C. (2004). The future role of trust in work–the key success factor for mobile productivity. *Tomorrow's Work Research Paper*.

Sörensen, A., Mitra, R., Hulthén, E., Hartmann, T., & Clausen, E. (2022). Bringing the entrepreneurial mindset into mining engineering education. *Mining, Metallurgy & Exploration*, *39*(4), 1333–1344. doi:10.100742461-022-00620-1

Soriani, A., & Bonafede, P. (2023). Metaverse and education: Which pedagogical perspectives for the school of tomorrow? *Journal of Inclusive Methodology and Technology in Learning and Teaching*, *3*(1).

Soto-Acosta, P., & Cegarra-Navarro, J. G. (2016). New ICTs for knowledge management in organizations. *Journal of Knowledge Management*, *20*(3), 417–422. doi:10.1108/JKM-02-2016-0057

Source. Michigan: Michigan Virtual University (March/April). Archived from the original on 18 July 2011. Retrieved 23 January 2011.

Spector, P. E. (1997). *Job satisfaction: Application, assessment, causes, and consequences* (Vol. 3). Sage. doi:10.4135/9781452231549

Spiess, J., T'Joens, Y., Dragnea, R., Spencer, P., & Philippart, L. (2014). Using big data to improve customer experience and business performance. *Bell Labs Technical Journal*, *18*(4), 3–17. doi:10.1002/bltj.21642

Stefanovic, D., Marjanovic, U., Delić, M., Culibrk, D., & Lalic, B. (2016). Assessing the success of e-government systems: An employee perspective. *Information & Management*, *53*(6), 717–726. doi:10.1016/j.im.2016.02.007

Stein, J. P., Linda Breves, P., & Anders, N. (2022). Parasocial interactions with real and virtual influencers: The role of perceived similarity and human-likeness. *New Media & Society*, 14614448221102900. doi:10.1177/14614448221102900

Sundararajan, A. (2017). *The sharing economy: The end of employment and the rise of crowd-based capitalism*. MIT press.

Sutcliffe, K. M., Vogus, T. J., & Dane, E. (2016). Organizing for resilience. *Harvard Business Review*, *94*(9), 52–59.

Su, Y., Du, J., Biscaia, R., & Inoue, Y. (2021). We are in this together: Sport brand involvement and fans' well-bein. *European Sport Management Quarterly*.

Taillon, B. J., Mueller, S. M., Kowalczyk, C. M., & Jones, D. N. (2020). Understanding the relationships between social media influencers and their followers: The moderating role of closeness. *Journal of Product and Brand Management*, *29*(6), 767–782. doi:10.1108/JPBM-03-2019-2292

Tamunomiebi, M. D., & Oyibo, C. (2020). Work-life balance and employee performance: A literature review. *European Journal of Business and Management Research*, *5*(2), 196–204. doi:10.24018/ejbmr.2020.5.2.196

Teece, D. J. (2007). Explicating dynamic capabilities: The nature and microfoundations of (sustainable) enterprise performance. *Strategic Management Journal*, *28*(13), 1319–1350. doi:10.1002mj.640

Teece, D. J. (2018). Profiting from innovation in the digital economy: Enabling technologies, standards, and licensing models in the wireless world. *Research Policy*, *47*(8), 1367–1387. doi:10.1016/j.respol.2017.01.015

Teece, D. J., Pisano, G., & Shuen, A. (2016). *Dynamic capabilities and strategic management: Organizing for innovation and growth*. Oxford University Press.

Teo, T. S. H., Lim, V. K. G., & Lai, R. Y. C. (1999). Intrinsic and extrinsic motivation in Internet usage. *Omega*, *27*(1), 25–37. doi:10.1016/S0305-0483(98)00028-0

Thakur, S. (2020). *Profitable Business Opportunities in Online Education Digital Nomad who loves to read & write startup stories, and tech news*.

Tibingana-Ahimbisibwe, B., Willis, S., Catherall, S., Butler, F., & Harrison, R. (2022). A systematic review of peer-assisted learning in fully online higher education distance learning programmes. *Open Learning*, *37*(3), 251–272. doi:10.1080/02680513.2020.1758651

Tinoco-Giraldo, H., Torrecilla Sanchez, E. M., & García-Peñalvo, F. J. (2020). E-mentoring in higher education: A structured literature review and implications for future research. *Sustainability (Basel)*, *12*(11), 4344. doi:10.3390u12114344

Tiven, M. B., Fuchs, E. R., Bazari, A., & MacQuarrie, A. (2018). Evaluating global digital education: Student outcomes framework. New York, NY: Bloomberg Philanthropies and the Organisation for Economic Co-operation and Development, 114.

Turkina, E. (2018). The importance of networking to entrepreneurship: Montreal's artificial intelligence cluster and its born-global firm element AI. *Journal of Small Business and Entrepreneurship*, *30*(1), 1–8. doi:10.1080/08276331.2017.1402154

Tushman, M. L., & O'Reilly, C. A. (2017). Ambidextrous organizations: Managing evolutionary and revolutionary change. *California Management Review*, *59*(4), 5–23.

Vallerand, R. J. (2000). Deci and Ryan's self-determination theory: A view from the hierarchical model of intrinsic and extrinsic motivation. *Psychological Inquiry*, *11*(4), 312–318.

van Astyne, M. W., Parker, G. G., & Choudary, S. P. (2016). Pipelines, platforms, and the new rules of strategy. *Harvard Business Review*, *94*(4), 16.

Van Der Voordt, T. J. (2004). Productivity and employee satisfaction in flexible workplaces. *Journal of Corporate Real Estate*, *6*(2), 133–148. doi:10.1108/14630010410812306

Van der Zwan, P., Verheul, I., & Thurik, R. (2019). The entrepreneurial ladder's rungs and the impact of entrepreneurial experience on subsequent entry into self-employment. *Small Business Economics*, *53*(2), 383–404.

Vassakis, K., Petrakis, E., & Kopanakis, I. (2018). Big data analytics: applications, prospects and challenges. *Mobile big data: A roadmap from models to technologies*, 10(1), 3-20. https://doi.org/ doi:10.1007/978-3-319-67925-9_1

Venkatesh, V., Morris, M. G., Davis, G. B., & Davis, F. D. (2003). User acceptance of information technology: Toward a unified view. *Management Information Systems Quarterly*, *27*(3), 425–478. doi:10.2307/30036540

Volberda, H. W., Foss, N. J., & Lyles, M. A. (2010). Absorbing the concept of absorptive capacity: How to realize its potential in the organization field. *Organization Science*, *21*(4), 931–951. doi:10.1287/orsc.1090.0503

von Krogh, G. (1998). Care in knowledge creation. *California Management Review*, *3*(3), 133–153. doi:10.2307/41165947

von Krogh, G. (2009). Individualist and collectivist perspectives on knowledge in organizations: Implications for information systems research. *The Journal of Strategic Information Systems*, *18*(3), 119–129. doi:10.1016/j.jsis.2009.08.001

Voss, G. B., Parasuraman, A., & Grewal, D. (1998). The roles of price, performance, and expectations in determining satisfaction in service exchanges. *Journal of Marketing*, *62*(4), 46–61. doi:10.1177/002224299806200404

Wang, B., Liu, Y., Qian, J., & Parker, S. K. (2021). Achieving Effective Remote Working During the COVID-19 Pandemic: A Work Design Perspective. *Applied Psychology*, *70*(1), 16–59. doi:10.1111/apps.12290 PMID:33230359

Wang, L., Liu, S., Liu, H., & Wang, X. V. (2020). Overview of human-robot collaboration in manufacturing. In *Proceedings of 5th International Conference on the Industry 4.0 Model for Advanced Manufacturing: AMP 2020* (pp. 15-58). Springer International Publishing. 10.1007/978-3-030-46212-3_2

Wang, W., Liu, L., Feng, Y., & Wang, T. (2014). Innovation with IS usage: Individual absorptive capacity as a mediator. *Industrial Management & Data Systems*, *114*(8), 1110–1130. doi:10.1108/IMDS-05-2014-0160

Webster, M. (2020). *Organizing Instruction and Study to Improve Student Learning. IES Practice Guide. NCER 2007-2004.* National Center for Education Research.

Weideman, M., & Hofmeyr, K. B. (2020). The influence of flexible work arrangements on employee engagement: An exploratory study. *SA Journal of Human Resource Management*, *18*(1), 1–18. doi:10.4102ajhrm.v18i0.1209

Weinstein, Y., & Sumeracki, M. A. (2019). Understanding how we learn: A visual guide. David Fulton, Routledge (p. 13).

West, M. A., Sacramento, C. A., & Fay, D. (2019). Creativity and innovation implementation in work groups: The paradoxical role of demands. *Journal of Organizational Behavior*, *40*(5), 559–575.

Wilden, R., Devinney, T. M., & Dowling, G. R. (2019). The architecture of dynamic capability research: Identifying the building blocks of a configurational approach. *Journal of Management*, *45*(1), 26–60.

Wilkesmann, U., Wilkesmann, M., & Virgillito, A. (2009). The absence of cooperation is not necessarily defection: Structural and motivational constraints of knowledge transfer in a social dilemma situation. *Organization Studies*, *30*(10), 1141–1164. doi:10.1177/0170840609344385

Wilson, D. (2023). Distance/remote learning engagement. *Journal of Resourceful and Distribution*, *1*(1), 78–86.

Wonglimpiyarat, J. (2018). Enhancing organizational innovation: The roles of knowledge management and organizational culture. *Journal of Innovation & Knowledge*, *3*(4), 204–209.

Wong, R. (2023). When no one can go to school: Does online learning meet students' basic learning needs? *Interactive Learning Environments*, *31*(1), 434–450. doi:10.1080/10494820.2020.1789672

Woods, M. (2021). Technology Impacts on Employee Engagement During Covid-19. In *Research and Innovation Forum 2021: Managing Continuity, Innovation, and Change in the Post-Covid World: Technology, Politics and Society* (pp. 45-58). Springer International Publishing. https://doi.org/10.1007/978-3-030-84311-3_5

Wu, J. H., & Wang, Y. M. (2006). Measuring KMS success: A respecification of the DeLone and McLean's model. *Information & Management*, *43*(6), 728–739. doi:10.1016/j.im.2006.05.002

Xinli, H. (2015). Effectiveness of information technology in reducing corruption in China A validation of the DeLone and McLean information systems success model. *The Electronic Library*, *33*(1), 52–64. doi:10.1108/EL-11-2012-0148

Yadav, H., Kar, A. K., & Kashiramka, S. (2021). How does entrepreneurial orientation and SDG orientation of CEOs evolve before and during a pandemic. *Journal of Enterprise Information Management*.

Yadav, N., Shankar, R., & Singh, S. P. (2021). Critical success factors for lean six sigma in quality 4.0. *International Journal of Quality and Service Sciences*, *13*(1), 123–156. doi:10.1108/IJQSS-06-2020-0099

Yang, M., & Han, C. (2020). Revealing industry challenge and business response to Covid-19: A text mining approach. *International Journal of Contemporary Hospitality Management*, *33*(4), 1230–1248. doi:10.1108/IJCHM-08-2020-0920

Ye, G., Hudders, L., De Jans, S., & De Veirman, M. (2021). The value of influencer marketing for business: A bibliometric analysis and managerial implications. *Journal of Advertising*, *50*(2), 160–178. doi:10.1080/00913367.2020.1857888

Yildiz, H. E., Murtic, A., Zander, U., & Richtnér, A. (2019). What fosters individual-level absorptive capacity in MNCs? An extended motivation–ability–opportunity framework. [). Springer Berlin Heidelberg.]. *MIR. Management International Review*, *59*(1), 93–129. doi:10.100711575-018-0367-x

Yukawa, M., Gansky, S. A., O'Sullivan, P., Teherani, A., & Feldman, M. D. (2020). A new mentor evaluation tool: Evidence of validity. *PLoS One*, *15*(6), e0234345. doi:10.1371/journal.pone.0234345 PMID:32544185

Zacher, H., & Frese, M. (2011). Maintaining a focus on opportunities at work: The interplay between age, job complexity, and the use of selection, optimization, and compensation strategies. *Journal of Organizational Behavior*, *32*(2), 291–318. doi:10.1002/job.683

Zahra, S. A., & George, G. (2002). Absorptive capacity: A review, reconceptualization, and extension. *Academy of Management Review*, *27*(2), 185–203. doi:10.2307/4134351

Zhang, A., Prang, K. H., Devlin, N., Scott, A., & Kelaher, M. (2020). The impact of price transparency on consumers and providers: A scoping review. *Health Policy (Amsterdam)*, *124*(8), 819–825. doi:10.1016/j.healthpol.2020.06.001 PMID:32576391

Zhang, X., & Bartol, K. M. (2010). Linking empowering leadership and employee creativity: The influence of psychological empowerment, intrinsic motivation, and creative process engagement. *Development and Learning in Organizations*, *24*(5), 4–9. doi:10.1108/dlo.2010.08124ead.007

Zhang, X., & Bartol, K. M. (2010). The influence of creative process engagement on employee creative performance and overall job performance: A curvilinear assessment. *The Journal of Applied Psychology*, *95*(5), 862–873. doi:10.1037/a0020173 PMID:20718512

Zhou, Q., Mao, J. Y., & Tang, F. (2020). Don't be afraid to fail because you can learn from it! How intrinsic motivation leads to enhanced self-development and benevolent leadership as a boundary condition. *Frontiers in Psychology*, *11*, 699. doi:10.3389/fpsyg.2020.00699 PMID:32425847

Zhu, F., Yu, W., Fan, S. X., & Jonathan, J. G. (2023). Should I stay or should I go? The impact of entrepreneurs' loneliness on business exit intentions through entrepreneurial passion. *Journal of Business Venturing Insights*, *19*, e00368. doi:10.1016/j.jbvi.2022.e00368

Zhu, Y. Q., Gardner, D. G., & Chen, H. G. (2016). Relationships between work team climate, individual motivation, and creativity. *Journal of Management*, *44*(5), 2094–2115. doi:10.1177/0149206316638161

Zollo, M., Heavey, C., & Meier, D. (2019). Dynamic capabilities: Foundations, processes, and prospects. *Journal of Management Studies*, *56*(8), 1465–1480.

Zolnowski, A., & Mueller, F. (2019). Developing Organizational Resilience: A Review of Theory and Research Findings. *International Journal of Disaster Risk Science*, *10*(4), 543–555.

Related References

To continue our tradition of advancing information science and technology research, we have compiled a list of recommended IGI Global readings. These references will provide additional information and guidance to further enrich your knowledge and assist you with your own research and future publications.

Abdul Razak, R., & Mansor, N. A. (2021). Instagram Influencers in Social Media-Induced Tourism: Rethinking Tourist Trust Towards Tourism Destination. In M. Dinis, L. Bonixe, S. Lamy, & Z. Breda (Eds.), *Impact of New Media in Tourism* (pp. 135-144). IGI Global. https://doi.org/10.4018/978-1-7998-7095-1.ch009

Abir, T., & Khan, M. Y. (2022). Importance of ICT Advancement and Culture of Adaptation in the Tourism and Hospitality Industry for Developing Countries. In C. Ramos, S. Quinteiro, & A. Gonçalves (Eds.), *ICT as Innovator Between Tourism and Culture* (pp. 30–41). IGI Global. https://doi.org/10.4018/978-1-7998-8165-0.ch003

Abtahi, M. S., Behboudi, L., & Hasanabad, H. M. (2017). Factors Affecting Internet Advertising Adoption in Ad Agencies. *International Journal of Innovation in the Digital Economy*, *8*(4), 18–29. doi:10.4018/IJIDE.2017100102

Afenyo-Agbe, E., & Mensah, I. (2022). Principles, Benefits, and Barriers to Community-Based Tourism: Implications for Management. In I. Mensah & E. Afenyo-Agbe (Eds.), *Prospects and Challenges of Community-Based Tourism and Changing Demographics* (pp. 1–29). IGI Global. doi:10.4018/978-1-7998-7335-8.ch001

Agbo, V. M. (2022). Distributive Justice Issues in Community-Based Tourism. In I. Mensah & E. Afenyo-Agbe (Eds.), *Prospects and Challenges of Community-Based Tourism and Changing Demographics* (pp. 107–129). IGI Global. https://doi.org/10.4018/978-1-7998-7335-8.ch005

Agrawal, S. (2017). The Impact of Emerging Technologies and Social Media on Different Business(es): Marketing and Management. In O. Rishi & A. Sharma (Eds.), *Maximizing Business Performance and Efficiency Through Intelligent Systems* (pp. 37–49). Hershey, PA: IGI Global. doi:10.4018/978-1-5225-2234-8.ch002

Ahmad, A., & Johari, S. (2022). Georgetown as a Gastronomy Tourism Destination: Visitor Awareness Towards Revisit Intention of Nasi Kandar Restaurant. In M. Valeri (Ed.), *New Governance and Management in Touristic Destinations* (pp. 71–83). IGI Global. https://doi.org/10.4018/978-1-6684-3889-3.ch005

Alkhatib, G., & Bayouq, S. T. (2021). A TAM-Based Model of Technological Factors Affecting Use of E-Tourism. *International Journal of Tourism and Hospitality Management in the Digital Age*, *5*(2), 50–67. https://doi.org/10.4018/IJTHMDA.20210701.oa1

Altinay Ozdemir, M. (2021). Virtual Reality (VR) and Augmented Reality (AR) Technologies for Accessibility and Marketing in the Tourism Industry. In C. Eusébio, L. Teixeira, & M. Carneiro (Eds.), *ICT Tools and Applications for Accessible Tourism* (pp. 277-301). IGI Global. https://doi.org/10.4018/978-1-7998-6428-8.ch013

Anantharaman, R. N., Rajeswari, K. S., Angusamy, A., & Kuppusamy, J. (2017). Role of Self-Efficacy and Collective Efficacy as Moderators of Occupational Stress Among Software Development Professionals. *International Journal of Human Capital and Information Technology Professionals*, *8*(2), 45–58. doi:10.4018/IJHCITP.2017040103

Aninze, F., El-Gohary, H., & Hussain, J. (2018). The Role of Microfinance to Empower Women: The Case of Developing Countries. *International Journal of Customer Relationship Marketing and Management*, *9*(1), 54–78. doi:10.4018/IJCRMM.2018010104

Antosova, G., Sabogal-Salamanca, M., & Krizova, E. (2021). Human Capital in Tourism: A Practical Model of Endogenous and Exogenous Territorial Tourism Planning in Bahía Solano, Colombia. In V. Costa, A. Moura, & M. Mira (Eds.), *Handbook of Research on Human Capital and People Management in the Tourism Industry* (pp. 282–302). IGI Global. https://doi.org/10.4018/978-1-7998-4318-4.ch014

Arsenijević, O. M., Orčić, D., & Kastratović, E. (2017). Development of an Optimization Tool for Intangibles in SMEs: A Case Study from Serbia with a Pilot Research in the Prestige by Milka Company. In M. Vemić (Ed.), *Optimal Management Strategies in Small and Medium Enterprises* (pp. 320–347). Hershey, PA: IGI Global. doi:10.4018/978-1-5225-1949-2.ch015

Aryanto, V. D., Wismantoro, Y., & Widyatmoko, K. (2018). Implementing Eco-Innovation by Utilizing the Internet to Enhance Firm's Marketing Performance: Study of Green Batik Small and Medium Enterprises in Indonesia. *International Journal of E-Business Research, 14*(1), 21–36. doi:10.4018/IJEBR.2018010102

Asero, V., & Billi, S. (2022). New Perspective of Networking in the DMO Model. In M. Valeri (Ed.), *New Governance and Management in Touristic Destinations* (pp. 105–118). IGI Global. https://doi.org/10.4018/978-1-6684-3889-3.ch007

Atiku, S. O., & Fields, Z. (2017). Multicultural Orientations for 21st Century Global Leadership. In N. Baporikar (Ed.), *Management Education for Global Leadership* (pp. 28–51). Hershey, PA: IGI Global. doi:10.4018/978-1-5225-1013-0.ch002

Atiku, S. O., & Fields, Z. (2018). Organisational Learning Dimensions and Talent Retention Strategies for the Service Industries. In N. Baporikar (Ed.), *Global Practices in Knowledge Management for Societal and Organizational Development* (pp. 358–381). Hershey, PA: IGI Global. doi:10.4018/978-1-5225-3009-1.ch017

Atsa'am, D. D., & Kuset Bodur, E. (2021). Pattern Mining on How Organizational Tenure Affects the Psychological Capital of Employees Within the Hospitality and Tourism Industry: Linking Employees' Organizational Tenure With PsyCap. *International Journal of Tourism and Hospitality Management in the Digital Age, 5*(2), 17–28. https://doi.org/10.4018/IJTHMDA.2021070102

Ávila, L., & Teixeira, L. (2018). The Main Concepts Behind the Dematerialization of Business Processes. In M. Khosrow-Pour, D.B.A. (Ed.), Encyclopedia of Information Science and Technology, Fourth Edition (pp. 888-898). Hershey, PA: IGI Global. https://doi.org/ doi:10.4018/978-1-5225-2255-3.ch076

Ayorekire, J., Mugizi, F., Obua, J., & Ampaire, G. (2022). Community-Based Tourism and Local People's Perceptions Towards Conservation: The Case of Queen Elizabeth Conservation Area, Uganda. In I. Mensah & E. Afenyo-Agbe (Eds.), *Prospects and Challenges of Community-Based Tourism and Changing Demographics* (pp. 56–82). IGI Global. https://doi.org/10.4018/978-1-7998-7335-8.ch003

Baleiro, R. (2022). Tourist Literature and the Architecture of Travel in Olga Tokarczuk and Patti Smith. In R. Baleiro & R. Pereira (Eds.), *Global Perspectives on Literary Tourism and Film-Induced Tourism* (pp. 202-216). IGI Global. https://doi.org/10.4018/978-1-7998-8262-6.ch011

Barat, S. (2021). Looking at the Future of Medical Tourism in Asia. *International Journal of Tourism and Hospitality Management in the Digital Age, 5*(1), 19–33. https://doi.org/10.4018/IJTHMDA.2021010102

Barbosa, C. A., Magalhães, M., & Nunes, M. R. (2021). Travel Instagramability: A Way of Choosing a Destination? In M. Dinis, L. Bonixe, S. Lamy, & Z. Breda (Eds.), *Impact of New Media in Tourism* (pp. 173-190). IGI Global. https://doi.org/10.4018/978-1-7998-7095-1.ch011

Bari, M. W., & Khan, Q. (2021). Pakistan as a Destination of Religious Tourism. In E. Alaverdov & M. Bari (Eds.), *Global Development of Religious Tourism* (pp. 1-10). IGI Global. https://doi.org/10.4018/978-1-7998-5792-1.ch001

Bartens, Y., Chunpir, H. I., Schulte, F., & Voß, S. (2017). Business/IT Alignment in Two-Sided Markets: A COBIT 5 Analysis for Media Streaming Business Models. In S. De Haes & W. Van Grembergen (Eds.), *Strategic IT Governance and Alignment in Business Settings* (pp. 82–111). Hershey, PA: IGI Global. doi:10.4018/978-1-5225-0861-8.ch004

Bashayreh, A. M. (2018). Organizational Culture and Organizational Performance. In W. Lee & F. Sabetzadeh (Eds.), *Contemporary Knowledge and Systems Science* (pp. 50–69). Hershey, PA: IGI Global. doi:10.4018/978-1-5225-5655-8.ch003

Bechthold, L., Lude, M., & Prügl, R. (2021). Crisis Favors the Prepared Firm: How Organizational Ambidexterity Relates to Perceptions of Organizational Resilience. In A. Zehrer, G. Glowka, K. Schwaiger, & V. Ranacher-Lackner (Eds.), *Resiliency Models and Addressing Future Risks for Family Firms in the Tourism Industry* (pp. 178–205). IGI Global. https://doi.org/10.4018/978-1-7998-7352-5.ch008

Bedford, D. A. (2018). Sustainable Knowledge Management Strategies: Aligning Business Capabilities and Knowledge Management Goals. In N. Baporikar (Ed.), *Global Practices in Knowledge Management for Societal and Organizational Development* (pp. 46–73). Hershey, PA: IGI Global. doi:10.4018/978-1-5225-3009-1.ch003

Bekjanov, D., & Matyusupov, B. (2021). Influence of Innovative Processes in the Competitiveness of Tourist Destination. In J. Soares (Ed.), *Innovation and Entrepreneurial Opportunities in Community Tourism* (pp. 243–263). IGI Global. https://doi.org/10.4018/978-1-7998-4855-4.ch014

Bharwani, S., & Musunuri, D. (2018). Reflection as a Process From Theory to Practice. In M. Khosrow-Pour, D.B.A. (Ed.), Encyclopedia of Information Science and Technology, Fourth Edition (pp. 1529-1539). Hershey, PA: IGI Global. doi:10.4018/978-1-5225-2255-3.ch132

Bhatt, G. D., Wang, Z., & Rodger, J. A. (2017). Information Systems Capabilities and Their Effects on Competitive Advantages: A Study of Chinese Companies. *Information Resources Management Journal*, *30*(3), 41–57. doi:10.4018/IRMJ.2017070103

Bhushan, M., & Yadav, A. (2017). Concept of Cloud Computing in ESB. In R. Bhadoria, N. Chaudhari, G. Tomar, & S. Singh (Eds.), *Exploring Enterprise Service Bus in the Service-Oriented Architecture Paradigm* (pp. 116–127). Hershey, PA: IGI Global. doi:10.4018/978-1-5225-2157-0.ch008

Bhushan, S. (2017). System Dynamics Base-Model of Humanitarian Supply Chain (HSCM) in Disaster Prone Eco-Communities of India: A Discussion on Simulation and Scenario Results. *International Journal of System Dynamics Applications*, *6*(3), 20–37. doi:10.4018/IJSDA.2017070102

Binder, D., & Miller, J. W. (2021). A Generations' Perspective on Employer Branding in Tourism. In V. Costa, A. Moura, & M. Mira (Eds.), *Handbook of Research on Human Capital and People Management in the Tourism Industry* (pp. 152–174). IGI Global. https://doi.org/10.4018/978-1-7998-4318-4.ch008

Birch Freeman, A. A., Mensah, I., & Antwi, K. B. (2022). Smiling vs. Frowning Faces: Community Participation for Sustainable Tourism in Ghanaian Communities. In I. Mensah & E. Afenyo-Agbe (Eds.), *Prospects and Challenges of Community-Based Tourism and Changing Demographics* (pp. 83–106). IGI Global. https://doi.org/10.4018/978-1-7998-7335-8.ch004

Biswas, A., & De, A. K. (2017). On Development of a Fuzzy Stochastic Programming Model with Its Application to Business Management. In S. Trivedi, S. Dey, A. Kumar, & T. Panda (Eds.), *Handbook of Research on Advanced Data Mining Techniques and Applications for Business Intelligence* (pp. 353–378). Hershey, PA: IGI Global. doi:10.4018/978-1-5225-2031-3.ch021

Boragnio, A., & Faracce Macia, C. (2021). "Taking Care of Yourself at Home": Use of E-Commerce About Food and Care During the COVID-19 Pandemic in the City of Buenos Aires. In M. Korstanje (Ed.), *Socio-Economic Effects and Recovery Efforts for the Rental Industry: Post-COVID-19 Strategies* (pp. 45–71). IGI Global. https://doi.org/10.4018/978-1-7998-7287-0.ch003

Borges, V. D. (2021). Happiness: The Basis for Public Policy in Tourism. In A. Perinotto, V. Mayer, & J. Soares (Eds.), *Rebuilding and Restructuring the Tourism Industry: Infusion of Happiness and Quality of Life* (pp. 1–25). IGI Global. https://doi.org/10.4018/978-1-7998-7239-9.ch001

Bücker, J., & Ernste, K. (2018). Use of Brand Heroes in Strategic Reputation Management: The Case of Bacardi, Adidas, and Daimler. In A. Erdemir (Ed.), *Reputation Management Techniques in Public Relations* (pp. 126–150). Hershey, PA: IGI Global. doi:10.4018/978-1-5225-3619-2.ch007

Buluk Eşitti, B. (2021). COVID-19 and Alternative Tourism: New Destinations and New Tourism Products. In M. Demir, A. Dalgıç, & F. Ergen (Eds.), *Handbook of Research on the Impacts and Implications of COVID-19 on the Tourism Industry* (pp. 786–805). IGI Global. https://doi.org/10.4018/978-1-7998-8231-2.ch038

Bureš, V. (2018). Industry 4.0 From the Systems Engineering Perspective: Alternative Holistic Framework Development. In R. Brunet-Thornton & F. Martinez (Eds.), *Analyzing the Impacts of Industry 4.0 in Modern Business Environments* (pp. 199–223). Hershey, PA: IGI Global. doi:10.4018/978-1-5225-3468-6.ch011

Buzady, Z. (2017). Resolving the Magic Cube of Effective Case Teaching: Benchmarking Case Teaching Practices in Emerging Markets – Insights from the Central European University Business School, Hungary. In D. Latusek (Ed.), *Case Studies as a Teaching Tool in Management Education* (pp. 79–103). Hershey, PA: IGI Global. doi:10.4018/978-1-5225-0770-3.ch005

Camillo, A. (2021). *Legal Matters, Risk Management, and Risk Prevention: From Forming a Business to Legal Representation.* IGI Global. doi:10.4018/978-1-7998-4342-9.ch004

Căpusneanu, S., & Topor, D. I. (2018). Business Ethics and Cost Management in SMEs: Theories of Business Ethics and Cost Management Ethos. In I. Oncioiu (Ed.), *Ethics and Decision-Making for Sustainable Business Practices* (pp. 109–127). Hershey, PA: IGI Global. doi:10.4018/978-1-5225-3773-1.ch007

Chan, R. L., Mo, P. L., & Moon, K. K. (2018). Strategic and Tactical Measures in Managing Enterprise Risks: A Study of the Textile and Apparel Industry. In K. Strang, M. Korstanje, & N. Vajjhala (Eds.), *Research, Practices, and Innovations in Global Risk and Contingency Management* (pp. 1–19). Hershey, PA: IGI Global. doi:10.4018/978-1-5225-4754-9.ch001

Charlier, S. D., Burke-Smalley, L. A., & Fisher, S. L. (2018). Undergraduate Programs in the U.S: A Contextual and Content-Based Analysis. In J. Mendy (Ed.), *Teaching Human Resources and Organizational Behavior at the College Level* (pp. 26–57). Hershey, PA: IGI Global. doi:10.4018/978-1-5225-2820-3.ch002

Chumillas, J., Güell, M., & Quer, P. (2022). The Use of ICT in Tourist and Educational Literary Routes: The Role of the Guide. In C. Ramos, S. Quinteiro, & A. Gonçalves (Eds.), *ICT as Innovator Between Tourism and Culture* (pp. 15–29). IGI Global. https://doi.org/10.4018/978-1-7998-8165-0.ch002

Dahlberg, T., Kivijärvi, H., & Saarinen, T. (2017). IT Investment Consistency and Other Factors Influencing the Success of IT Performance. In S. De Haes & W. Van Grembergen (Eds.), *Strategic IT Governance and Alignment in Business Settings* (pp. 176–208). Hershey, PA: IGI Global. doi:10.4018/978-1-5225-0861-8.ch007

Damnjanović, A. M. (2017). Knowledge Management Optimization through IT and E-Business Utilization: A Qualitative Study on Serbian SMEs. In M. Vemić (Ed.), *Optimal Management Strategies in Small and Medium Enterprises* (pp. 249–267). Hershey, PA: IGI Global. doi:10.4018/978-1-5225-1949-2.ch012

Daneshpour, H. (2017). Integrating Sustainable Development into Project Portfolio Management through Application of Open Innovation. In M. Vemić (Ed.), *Optimal Management Strategies in Small and Medium Enterprises* (pp. 370–387). Hershey, PA: IGI Global. doi:10.4018/978-1-5225-1949-2.ch017

Daniel, A. D., & Reis de Castro, V. (2018). Entrepreneurship Education: How to Measure the Impact on Nascent Entrepreneurs. In A. Carrizo Moreira, J. Guilherme Leitão Dantas, & F. Manuel Valente (Eds.), *Nascent Entrepreneurship and Successful New Venture Creation* (pp. 85–110). Hershey, PA: IGI Global. doi:10.4018/978-1-5225-2936-1.ch004

David, R., Swami, B. N., & Tangirala, S. (2018). Ethics Impact on Knowledge Management in Organizational Development: A Case Study. In N. Baporikar (Ed.), *Global Practices in Knowledge Management for Societal and Organizational Development* (pp. 19–45). Hershey, PA: IGI Global. doi:10.4018/978-1-5225-3009-1.ch002

De Uña-Álvarez, E., & Villarino-Pérez, M. (2022). Fostering Ecocultural Resources, Identity, and Tourism in Inland Territories (Galicia, NW Spain). In G. Fernandes (Ed.), *Challenges and New Opportunities for Tourism in Inland Territories: Ecocultural Resources and Sustainable Initiatives* (pp. 1-16). IGI Global. https://doi.org/10.4018/978-1-7998-7339-6.ch001

Delias, P., & Lakiotaki, K. (2018). Discovering Process Horizontal Boundaries to Facilitate Process Comprehension. *International Journal of Operations Research and Information Systems, 9*(2), 1–31. doi:10.4018/IJORIS.2018040101

Denholm, J., & Lee-Davies, L. (2018). Success Factors for Games in Business and Project Management. In *Enhancing Education and Training Initiatives Through Serious Games* (pp. 34–68). Hershey, PA: IGI Global. doi:10.4018/978-1-5225-3689-5.ch002

Deshpande, M. (2017). Best Practices in Management Institutions for Global Leadership: Policy Aspects. In N. Baporikar (Ed.), *Management Education for Global Leadership* (pp. 1–27). Hershey, PA: IGI Global. doi:10.4018/978-1-5225-1013-0.ch001

Deshpande, M. (2018). Policy Perspectives for SMEs Knowledge Management. In N. Baporikar (Ed.), *Knowledge Integration Strategies for Entrepreneurship and Sustainability* (pp. 23–46). Hershey, PA: IGI Global. doi:10.4018/978-1-5225-5115-7.ch002

Dezdar, S. (2017). ERP Implementation Projects in Asian Countries: A Comparative Study on Iran and China. *International Journal of Information Technology Project Management*, *8*(3), 52–68. doi:10.4018/IJITPM.2017070104

Domingos, D., Respício, A., & Martinho, R. (2017). Reliability of IoT-Aware BPMN Healthcare Processes. In C. Reis & M. Maximiano (Eds.), *Internet of Things and Advanced Application in Healthcare* (pp. 214–248). Hershey, PA: IGI Global. doi:10.4018/978-1-5225-1820-4.ch008

Dosumu, O., Hussain, J., & El-Gohary, H. (2017). An Exploratory Study of the Impact of Government Policies on the Development of Small and Medium Enterprises in Developing Countries: The Case of Nigeria. *International Journal of Customer Relationship Marketing and Management*, *8*(4), 51–62. doi:10.4018/IJCRMM.2017100104

Durst, S., Bruns, G., & Edvardsson, I. R. (2017). Retaining Knowledge in Smaller Building and Construction Firms. *International Journal of Knowledge and Systems Science*, *8*(3), 1–12. doi:10.4018/IJKSS.2017070101

Edvardsson, I. R., & Durst, S. (2017). Outsourcing, Knowledge, and Learning: A Critical Review. *International Journal of Knowledge-Based Organizations*, *7*(2), 13–26. doi:10.4018/IJKBO.2017040102

Edwards, J. S. (2018). Integrating Knowledge Management and Business Processes. In M. Khosrow-Pour, D.B.A. (Ed.), Encyclopedia of Information Science and Technology, Fourth Edition (pp. 5046-5055). Hershey, PA: IGI Global. doi:10.4018/978-1-5225-2255-3.ch437

Eichelberger, S., & Peters, M. (2021). Family Firm Management in Turbulent Times: Opportunities for Responsible Tourism. In A. Zehrer, G. Glowka, K. Schwaiger, & V. Ranacher-Lackner (Eds.), *Resiliency Models and Addressing Future Risks for Family Firms in the Tourism Industry* (pp. 103–124). IGI Global. https://doi.org/10.4018/978-1-7998-7352-5.ch005

Eide, D., Hjalager, A., & Hansen, M. (2022). Innovative Certifications in Adventure Tourism: Attributes and Diffusion. In R. Augusto Costa, F. Brandão, Z. Breda, & C. Costa (Eds.), *Planning and Managing the Experience Economy in Tourism* (pp. 161-175). IGI Global. https://doi.org/10.4018/978-1-7998-8775-1.ch009

Ejiogu, A. O. (2018). Economics of Farm Management. In *Agricultural Finance and Opportunities for Investment and Expansion* (pp. 56–72). Hershey, PA: IGI Global. doi:10.4018/978-1-5225-3059-6.ch003

Ekanem, I., & Abiade, G. E. (2018). Factors Influencing the Use of E-Commerce by Small Enterprises in Nigeria. *International Journal of ICT Research in Africa and the Middle East*, *7*(1), 37–53. doi:10.4018/IJICTRAME.2018010103

Ekanem, I., & Alrossais, L. A. (2017). Succession Challenges Facing Family Businesses in Saudi Arabia. In P. Zgheib (Ed.), *Entrepreneurship and Business Innovation in the Middle East* (pp. 122–146). Hershey, PA: IGI Global. doi:10.4018/978-1-5225-2066-5.ch007

El Faquih, L., & Fredj, M. (2017). Ontology-Based Framework for Quality in Configurable Process Models. *Journal of Electronic Commerce in Organizations*, *15*(2), 48–60. doi:10.4018/JECO.2017040104

Faisal, M. N., & Talib, F. (2017). Building Ambidextrous Supply Chains in SMEs: How to Tackle the Barriers? *International Journal of Information Systems and Supply Chain Management*, *10*(4), 80–100. doi:10.4018/IJISSCM.2017100105

Fernandes, T. M., Gomes, J., & Romão, M. (2017). Investments in E-Government: A Benefit Management Case Study. *International Journal of Electronic Government Research*, *13*(3), 1–17. doi:10.4018/IJEGR.2017070101

Figueira, L. M., Honrado, G. R., & Dionísio, M. S. (2021). Human Capital Management in the Tourism Industry in Portugal. In V. Costa, A. Moura, & M. Mira (Eds.), *Handbook of Research on Human Capital and People Management in the Tourism Industry* (pp. 1–19). IGI Global. doi:10.4018/978-1-7998-4318-4.ch001

Gao, S. S., Oreal, S., & Zhang, J. (2018). Contemporary Financial Risk Management Perceptions and Practices of Small-Sized Chinese Businesses. In I. Management Association (Ed.), Global Business Expansion: Concepts, Methodologies, Tools, and Applications (pp. 917-931). Hershey, PA: IGI Global. doi:10.4018/978-1-5225-5481-3.ch041

Garg, R., & Berning, S. C. (2017). Indigenous Chinese Management Philosophies: Key Concepts and Relevance for Modern Chinese Firms. In B. Christiansen & G. Koc (Eds.), *Transcontinental Strategies for Industrial Development and Economic Growth* (pp. 43–57). Hershey, PA: IGI Global. doi:10.4018/978-1-5225-2160-0.ch003

Gencer, Y. G. (2017). Supply Chain Management in Retailing Business. In U. Akkucuk (Ed.), *Ethics and Sustainability in Global Supply Chain Management* (pp. 197–210). Hershey, PA: IGI Global. doi:10.4018/978-1-5225-2036-8.ch011

Gera, R., Arora, S., & Malik, S. (2021). Emotional Labor in the Tourism Industry: Strategies, Antecedents, and Outcomes. In V. Costa, A. Moura, & M. Mira (Eds.), *Handbook of Research on Human Capital and People Management in the Tourism Industry* (pp. 73–91). IGI Global. https://doi.org/10.4018/978-1-7998-4318-4.ch004

Giacosa, E. (2018). The Increasing of the Regional Development Thanks to the Luxury Business Innovation. In L. Carvalho (Ed.), *Handbook of Research on Entrepreneurial Ecosystems and Social Dynamics in a Globalized World* (pp. 260–273). Hershey, PA: IGI Global. doi:10.4018/978-1-5225-3525-6.ch011

Glowka, G., Tusch, M., & Zehrer, A. (2021). The Risk Perception of Family Business Owner-Manager in the Tourism Industry: A Qualitative Comparison of the Intra-Firm Senior and Junior Generation. In A. Zehrer, G. Glowka, K. Schwaiger, & V. Ranacher-Lackner (Eds.), *Resiliency Models and Addressing Future Risks for Family Firms in the Tourism Industry* (pp. 126–153). IGI Global. https://doi.org/10.4018/978-1-7998-7352-5.ch006

Glykas, M., & George, J. (2017). Quality and Process Management Systems in the UAE Maritime Industry. *International Journal of Productivity Management and Assessment Technologies*, *5*(1), 20–39. doi:10.4018/IJPMAT.2017010102

Glykas, M., Valiris, G., Kokkinaki, A., & Koutsoukou, Z. (2018). Banking Business Process Management Implementation. *International Journal of Productivity Management and Assessment Technologies*, *6*(1), 50–69. doi:10.4018/IJPMAT.2018010104

Gomes, J., & Romão, M. (2017). The Balanced Scorecard: Keeping Updated and Aligned with Today's Business Trends. *International Journal of Productivity Management and Assessment Technologies*, *5*(2), 1–15. doi:10.4018/IJPMAT.2017070101

Gomes, J., & Romão, M. (2017). Aligning Information Systems and Technology with Benefit Management and Balanced Scorecard. In S. De Haes & W. Van Grembergen (Eds.), *Strategic IT Governance and Alignment in Business Settings* (pp. 112–131). Hershey, PA: IGI Global. doi:10.4018/978-1-5225-0861-8.ch005

Goyal, A. (2021). Communicating and Building Destination Brands With New Media. In M. Dinis, L. Bonixe, S. Lamy, & Z. Breda (Eds.), *Impact of New Media in Tourism* (pp. 1-20). IGI Global. https://doi.org/10.4018/978-1-7998-7095-1.ch001

Grefen, P., & Turetken, O. (2017). Advanced Business Process Management in Networked E-Business Scenarios. *International Journal of E-Business Research, 13*(4), 70–104. doi:10.4018/IJEBR.2017100105

Guasca, M., Van Broeck, A. M., & Vanneste, D. (2021). Tourism and the Social Reintegration of Colombian Ex-Combatants. In J. da Silva, Z. Breda, & F. Carbone (Eds.), *Role and Impact of Tourism in Peacebuilding and Conflict Transformation* (pp. 66-86). IGI Global. https://doi.org/10.4018/978-1-7998-5053-3.ch005

Haider, A., & Saetang, S. (2017). Strategic IT Alignment in Service Sector. In S. Rozenes & Y. Cohen (Eds.), *Handbook of Research on Strategic Alliances and Value Co-Creation in the Service Industry* (pp. 231–258). Hershey, PA: IGI Global. doi:10.4018/978-1-5225-2084-9.ch012

Hajilari, A. B., Ghadaksaz, M., & Fasghandis, G. S. (2017). Assessing Organizational Readiness for Implementing ERP System Using Fuzzy Expert System Approach. *International Journal of Enterprise Information Systems, 13*(1), 67–85. doi:10.4018/IJEIS.2017010105

Haldorai, A., Ramu, A., & Murugan, S. (2018). Social Aware Cognitive Radio Networks: Effectiveness of Social Networks as a Strategic Tool for Organizational Business Management. In H. Bansal, G. Shrivastava, G. Nguyen, & L. Stanciu (Eds.), *Social Network Analytics for Contemporary Business Organizations* (pp. 188–202). Hershey, PA: IGI Global. doi:10.4018/978-1-5225-5097-6.ch010

Hall, O. P. Jr. (2017). Social Media Driven Management Education. *International Journal of Knowledge-Based Organizations, 7*(2), 43–59. doi:10.4018/IJKBO.2017040104

Hanifah, H., Halim, H. A., Ahmad, N. H., & Vafaei-Zadeh, A. (2017). Innovation Culture as a Mediator Between Specific Human Capital and Innovation Performance Among Bumiputera SMEs in Malaysia. In N. Ahmad, T. Ramayah, H. Halim, & S. Rahman (Eds.), *Handbook of Research on Small and Medium Enterprises in Developing Countries* (pp. 261–279). Hershey, PA: IGI Global. doi:10.4018/978-1-5225-2165-5.ch012

Hartlieb, S., & Silvius, G. (2017). Handling Uncertainty in Project Management and Business Development: Similarities and Differences. In Y. Raydugin (Ed.), *Handbook of Research on Leveraging Risk and Uncertainties for Effective Project Management* (pp. 337–362). Hershey, PA: IGI Global. doi:10.4018/978-1-5225-1790-0.ch016

Hass, K. B. (2017). Living on the Edge: Managing Project Complexity. In Y. Raydugin (Ed.), *Handbook of Research on Leveraging Risk and Uncertainties for Effective Project Management* (pp. 177–201). Hershey, PA: IGI Global. doi:10.4018/978-1-5225-1790-0.ch009

Hawking, P., & Carmine Sellitto, C. (2017). Developing an Effective Strategy for Organizational Business Intelligence. In M. Tavana (Ed.), *Enterprise Information Systems and the Digitalization of Business Functions* (pp. 222–237). Hershey, PA: IGI Global. doi:10.4018/978-1-5225-2382-6.ch010

Hawking, P., & Sellitto, C. (2017). A Fast-Moving Consumer Goods Company and Business Intelligence Strategy Development. *International Journal of Enterprise Information Systems, 13*(2), 22–33. doi:10.4018/IJEIS.2017040102

Hawking, P., & Sellitto, C. (2017). Business Intelligence Strategy: Two Case Studies. *International Journal of Business Intelligence Research, 8*(2), 17–30. doi:10.4018/IJBIR.2017070102

Hee, W. J., Jalleh, G., Lai, H., & Lin, C. (2017). E-Commerce and IT Projects: Evaluation and Management Issues in Australian and Taiwanese Hospitals. *International Journal of Public Health Management and Ethics, 2*(1), 69–90. doi:10.4018/IJPHME.2017010104

Hernandez, A. A. (2018). Exploring the Factors to Green IT Adoption of SMEs in the Philippines. *Journal of Cases on Information Technology, 20*(2), 49–66. doi:10.4018/JCIT.2018040104

Hollman, A., Bickford, S., & Hollman, T. (2017). Cyber InSecurity: A Post-Mortem Attempt to Assess Cyber Problems from IT and Business Management Perspectives. *Journal of Cases on Information Technology, 19*(3), 42–70. doi:10.4018/JCIT.2017070104

Ibrahim, F., & Zainin, N. M. (2021). Exploring the Technological Impacts: The Case of Museums in Brunei Darussalam. *International Journal of Tourism and Hospitality Management in the Digital Age, 5*(1), 1–18. https://doi.org/10.4018/IJTHMDA.2021010101

Igbinakhase, I. (2017). Responsible and Sustainable Management Practices in Developing and Developed Business Environments. In Z. Fields (Ed.), *Collective Creativity for Responsible and Sustainable Business Practice* (pp. 180–207). Hershey, PA: IGI Global. doi:10.4018/978-1-5225-1823-5.ch010

Iwata, J. J., & Hoskins, R. G. (2017). Managing Indigenous Knowledge in Tanzania: A Business Perspective. In P. Jain & N. Mnjama (Eds.), *Managing Knowledge Resources and Records in Modern Organizations* (pp. 198–214). Hershey, PA: IGI Global. doi:10.4018/978-1-5225-1965-2.ch012

Jain, P. (2017). Ethical and Legal Issues in Knowledge Management Life-Cycle in Business. In P. Jain & N. Mnjama (Eds.), *Managing Knowledge Resources and Records in Modern Organizations* (pp. 82–101). Hershey, PA: IGI Global. doi:10.4018/978-1-5225-1965-2.ch006

James, S., & Hauli, E. (2017). Holistic Management Education at Tanzanian Rural Development Planning Institute. In N. Baporikar (Ed.), *Management Education for Global Leadership* (pp. 112–136). Hershey, PA: IGI Global. doi:10.4018/978-1-5225-1013-0.ch006

Janošková, M., Csikósová, A., & Čulková, K. (2018). Measurement of Company Performance as Part of Its Strategic Management. In R. Leon (Ed.), *Managerial Strategies for Business Sustainability During Turbulent Times* (pp. 309–335). Hershey, PA: IGI Global. doi:10.4018/978-1-5225-2716-9.ch017

Jean-Vasile, A., & Alecu, A. (2017). Theoretical and Practical Approaches in Understanding the Influences of Cost-Productivity-Profit Trinomial in Contemporary Enterprises. In A. Jean Vasile & D. Nicolò (Eds.), *Sustainable Entrepreneurship and Investments in the Green Economy* (pp. 28–62). Hershey, PA: IGI Global. doi:10.4018/978-1-5225-2075-7.ch002

Joia, L. A., & Correia, J. C. (2018). CIO Competencies From the IT Professional Perspective: Insights From Brazil. *Journal of Global Information Management, 26*(2), 74–103. doi:10.4018/JGIM.2018040104

Juma, A., & Mzera, N. (2017). Knowledge Management and Records Management and Competitive Advantage in Business. In P. Jain & N. Mnjama (Eds.), *Managing Knowledge Resources and Records in Modern Organizations* (pp. 15–28). Hershey, PA: IGI Global. doi:10.4018/978-1-5225-1965-2.ch002

K., I., & A, V. (2018). Monitoring and Auditing in the Cloud. In K. Munir (Ed.), *Cloud Computing Technologies for Green Enterprises* (pp. 318-350). Hershey, PA: IGI Global. https://doi.org/ doi:10.4018/978-1-5225-3038-1.ch013

Kabra, G., Ghosh, V., & Ramesh, A. (2018). Enterprise Integrated Business Process Management and Business Intelligence Framework for Business Process Sustainability. In A. Paul, D. Bhattacharyya, & S. Anand (Eds.), *Green Initiatives for Business Sustainability and Value Creation* (pp. 228–238). Hershey, PA: IGI Global. doi:10.4018/978-1-5225-2662-9.ch010

Kaoud, M. (2017). Investigation of Customer Knowledge Management: A Case Study Research. *International Journal of Service Science, Management, Engineering, and Technology*, *8*(2), 12–22. doi:10.4018/IJSSMET.2017040102

Katuu, S. (2018). A Comparative Assessment of Enterprise Content Management Maturity Models. In N. Gwangwava & M. Mutingi (Eds.), *E-Manufacturing and E-Service Strategies in Contemporary Organizations* (pp. 93–118). Hershey, PA: IGI Global. doi:10.4018/978-1-5225-3628-4.ch005

Khan, M. Y., & Abir, T. (2022). The Role of Social Media Marketing in the Tourism and Hospitality Industry: A Conceptual Study on Bangladesh. In C. Ramos, S. Quinteiro, & A. Gonçalves (Eds.), *ICT as Innovator Between Tourism and Culture* (pp. 213–229). IGI Global. https://doi.org/10.4018/978-1-7998-8165-0.ch013

Kinnunen, S., Ylä-Kujala, A., Marttonen-Arola, S., Kärri, T., & Baglee, D. (2018). Internet of Things in Asset Management: Insights from Industrial Professionals and Academia. *International Journal of Service Science, Management, Engineering, and Technology*, *9*(2), 104–119. doi:10.4018/IJSSMET.2018040105

Klein, A. Z., Sabino de Freitas, A., Machado, L., Freitas, J. C. Jr, Graziola, P. G. Jr, & Schlemmer, E. (2017). Virtual Worlds Applications for Management Education. In L. Tomei (Ed.), *Exploring the New Era of Technology-Infused Education* (pp. 279–299). Hershey, PA: IGI Global. doi:10.4018/978-1-5225-1709-2.ch017

Kővári, E., Saleh, M., & Steinbachné Hajmásy, G. (2022). The Impact of Corporate Digital Responsibility (CDR) on Internal Stakeholders' Satisfaction in Hungarian Upscale Hotels. In M. Valeri (Ed.), *New Governance and Management in Touristic Destinations* (pp. 35–51). IGI Global. https://doi.org/10.4018/978-1-6684-3889-3.ch003

Kożuch, B., & Jabłoński, A. (2017). Adopting the Concept of Business Models in Public Management. In M. Lewandowski & B. Kożuch (Eds.), *Public Sector Entrepreneurship and the Integration of Innovative Business Models* (pp. 10–46). Hershey, PA: IGI Global. doi:10.4018/978-1-5225-2215-7.ch002

Kumar, J., Adhikary, A., & Jha, A. (2017). Small Active Investors' Perceptions and Preferences Towards Tax Saving Mutual Fund Schemes in Eastern India: An Empirical Note. *International Journal of Asian Business and Information Management*, *8*(2), 35–45. doi:10.4018/IJABIM.2017040103

Latusi, S., & Fissore, M. (2021). Pilgrimage Routes to Happiness: Comparing the Camino de Santiago and Via Francigena. In A. Perinotto, V. Mayer, & J. Soares (Eds.), *Rebuilding and Restructuring the Tourism Industry: Infusion of Happiness and Quality of Life* (pp. 157–182). IGI Global. https://doi.org/10.4018/978-1-7998-7239-9.ch008

Lavassani, K. M., & Movahedi, B. (2017). Applications Driven Information Systems: Beyond Networks toward Business Ecosystems. *International Journal of Innovation in the Digital Economy*, *8*(1), 61–75. doi:10.4018/IJIDE.2017010104

Lazzareschi, V. H., & Brito, M. S. (2017). Strategic Information Management: Proposal of Business Project Model. In G. Jamil, A. Soares, & C. Pessoa (Eds.), *Handbook of Research on Information Management for Effective Logistics and Supply Chains* (pp. 59–88). Hershey, PA: IGI Global. doi:10.4018/978-1-5225-0973-8.ch004

Lechuga Sancho, M. P., & Martín Navarro, A. (2022). Evolution of the Literature on Social Responsibility in the Tourism Sector: A Systematic Literature Review. In G. Fernandes (Ed.), *Challenges and New Opportunities for Tourism in Inland Territories: Ecocultural Resources and Sustainable Initiatives* (pp. 169–186). IGI Global. https://doi.org/10.4018/978-1-7998-7339-6.ch010

Lederer, M., Kurz, M., & Lazarov, P. (2017). Usage and Suitability of Methods for Strategic Business Process Initiatives: A Multi Case Study Research. *International Journal of Productivity Management and Assessment Technologies*, *5*(1), 40–51. doi:10.4018/IJPMAT.2017010103

Lee, I. (2017). A Social Enterprise Business Model and a Case Study of Pacific Community Ventures (PCV). In V. Potocan, M. Üngan, & Z. Nedelko (Eds.), *Handbook of Research on Managerial Solutions in Non-Profit Organizations* (pp. 182–204). Hershey, PA: IGI Global. doi:10.4018/978-1-5225-0731-4.ch009

Leon, L. A., Seal, K. C., Przasnyski, Z. H., & Wiedenman, I. (2017). Skills and Competencies Required for Jobs in Business Analytics: A Content Analysis of Job Advertisements Using Text Mining. *International Journal of Business Intelligence Research*, *8*(1), 1–25. doi:10.4018/IJBIR.2017010101

Levy, C. L., & Elias, N. I. (2017). SOHO Users' Perceptions of Reliability and Continuity of Cloud-Based Services. In M. Moore (Ed.), *Cybersecurity Breaches and Issues Surrounding Online Threat Protection* (pp. 248–287). Hershey, PA: IGI Global. doi:10.4018/978-1-5225-1941-6.ch011

Levy, M. (2018). Change Management Serving Knowledge Management and Organizational Development: Reflections and Review. In N. Baporikar (Ed.), *Global Practices in Knowledge Management for Societal and Organizational Development* (pp. 256–270). Hershey, PA: IGI Global. doi:10.4018/978-1-5225-3009-1.ch012

Lewandowski, M. (2017). Public Organizations and Business Model Innovation: The Role of Public Service Design. In M. Lewandowski & B. Kożuch (Eds.), *Public Sector Entrepreneurship and the Integration of Innovative Business Models* (pp. 47–72). Hershey, PA: IGI Global. doi:10.4018/978-1-5225-2215-7.ch003

Lhannaoui, H., Kabbaj, M. I., & Bakkoury, Z. (2017). A Survey of Risk-Aware Business Process Modelling. *International Journal of Risk and Contingency Management*, *6*(3), 14–26. doi:10.4018/IJRCM.2017070102

Li, J., Sun, W., Jiang, W., Yang, H., & Zhang, L. (2017). How the Nature of Exogenous Shocks and Crises Impact Company Performance?: The Effects of Industry Characteristics. *International Journal of Risk and Contingency Management*, *6*(4), 40–55. doi:10.4018/IJRCM.2017100103

Lopez-Fernandez, M., Perez-Perez, M., Serrano-Bedia, A., & Cobo-Gonzalez, A. (2021). Small and Medium Tourism Enterprise Survival in Times of Crisis: "El Capricho de Gaudí. In D. Toubes & N. Araújo-Vila (Eds.), *Risk, Crisis, and Disaster Management in Small and Medium-Sized Tourism Enterprises* (pp. 103–129). IGI Global. doi:10.4018/978-1-7998-6996-2.ch005

Mahajan, A., Maidullah, S., & Hossain, M. R. (2022). Experience Toward Smart Tour Guide Apps in Travelling: An Analysis of Users' Reviews on Audio Odigos and Trip My Way. In R. Augusto Costa, F. Brandão, Z. Breda, & C. Costa (Eds.), *Planning and Managing the Experience Economy in Tourism* (pp. 255-273). IGI Global. https://doi.org/10.4018/978-1-7998-8775-1.ch014

Malega, P. (2017). Small and Medium Enterprises in the Slovak Republic: Status and Competitiveness of SMEs in the Global Markets and Possibilities of Optimization. In M. Vemić (Ed.), *Optimal Management Strategies in Small and Medium Enterprises* (pp. 102–124). Hershey, PA: IGI Global. doi:10.4018/978-1-5225-1949-2.ch006

Malewska, K. M. (2017). Intuition in Decision-Making on the Example of a Non-Profit Organization. In V. Potocan, M. Ünğan, & Z. Nedelko (Eds.), *Handbook of Research on Managerial Solutions in Non-Profit Organizations* (pp. 378–399). Hershey, PA: IGI Global. doi:10.4018/978-1-5225-0731-4.ch018

Maroofi, F. (2017). Entrepreneurial Orientation and Organizational Learning Ability Analysis for Innovation and Firm Performance. In N. Baporikar (Ed.), *Innovation and Shifting Perspectives in Management Education* (pp. 144–165). Hershey, PA: IGI Global. doi:10.4018/978-1-5225-1019-2.ch007

Marques, M., Moleiro, D., Brito, T. M., & Marques, T. (2021). Customer Relationship Management as an Important Relationship Marketing Tool: The Case of the Hospitality Industry in Estoril Coast. In M. Dinis, L. Bonixe, S. Lamy, & Z. Breda (Eds.), Impact of New Media in Tourism (pp. 39-56). IGI Global. https://doi.org/doi:10.4018/978-1-7998-7095-1.ch003

Martins, P. V., & Zacarias, M. (2017). A Web-based Tool for Business Process Improvement. *International Journal of Web Portals*, *9*(2), 68–84. doi:10.4018/IJWP.2017070104

Matthies, B., & Coners, A. (2017). Exploring the Conceptual Nature of e-Business Projects. *Journal of Electronic Commerce in Organizations*, *15*(3), 33–63. doi:10.4018/JECO.2017070103

Mayer, V. F., Fraga, C. C., & Silva, L. C. (2021). Contributions of Neurosciences to Studies of Well-Being in Tourism. In A. Perinotto, V. Mayer, & J. Soares (Eds.), *Rebuilding and Restructuring the Tourism Industry: Infusion of Happiness and Quality of Life* (pp. 108–128). IGI Global. https://doi.org/10.4018/978-1-7998-7239-9.ch006

McKee, J. (2018). Architecture as a Tool to Solve Business Planning Problems. In M. Khosrow-Pour, D.B.A. (Ed.), Encyclopedia of Information Science and Technology, Fourth Edition (pp. 573-586). Hershey, PA: IGI Global. doi:10.4018/978-1-5225-2255-3.ch050

McMurray, A. J., Cross, J., & Caponecchia, C. (2018). The Risk Management Profession in Australia: Business Continuity Plan Practices. In N. Bajgoric (Ed.), *Always-On Enterprise Information Systems for Modern Organizations* (pp. 112–129). Hershey, PA: IGI Global. doi:10.4018/978-1-5225-3704-5.ch006

Meddah, I. H., & Belkadi, K. (2018). Mining Patterns Using Business Process Management. In R. Hamou (Ed.), *Handbook of Research on Biomimicry in Information Retrieval and Knowledge Management* (pp. 78–89). Hershey, PA: IGI Global. doi:10.4018/978-1-5225-3004-6.ch005

Melian, A. G., & Camprubí, R. (2021). The Accessibility of Museum Websites: The Case of Barcelona. In C. Eusébio, L. Teixeira, & M. Carneiro (Eds.), *ICT Tools and Applications for Accessible Tourism* (pp. 234–255). IGI Global. https://doi.org/10.4018/978-1-7998-6428-8.ch011

Mendes, L. (2017). TQM and Knowledge Management: An Integrated Approach Towards Tacit Knowledge Management. In D. Jaziri-Bouagina & G. Jamil (Eds.), *Handbook of Research on Tacit Knowledge Management for Organizational Success* (pp. 236–263). Hershey, PA: IGI Global. doi:10.4018/978-1-5225-2394-9.ch009

Menezes, V. D., & Cavagnaro, E. (2021). Communicating Sustainable Initiatives in the Hotel Industry: The Case of the Hotel Jakarta Amsterdam. In F. Brandão, Z. Breda, R. Costa, & C. Costa (Eds.), *Handbook of Research on the Role of Tourism in Achieving Sustainable Development Goals* (pp. 224-234). IGI Global. https://doi.org/10.4018/978-1-7998-5691-7.ch013

Menezes, V. D., & Cavagnaro, E. (2021). Communicating Sustainable Initiatives in the Hotel Industry: The Case of the Hotel Jakarta Amsterdam. In F. Brandão, Z. Breda, R. Costa, & C. Costa (Eds.), *Handbook of Research on the Role of Tourism in Achieving Sustainable Development Goals* (pp. 224-234). IGI Global. https://doi.org/10.4018/978-1-7998-5691-7.ch013

Mitas, O., Bastiaansen, M., & Boode, W. (2022). If You're Happy, I'm Happy: Emotion Contagion at a Tourist Information Center. In R. Augusto Costa, F. Brandão, Z. Breda, & C. Costa (Eds.), *Planning and Managing the Experience Economy in Tourism* (pp. 122-140). IGI Global. https://doi.org/10.4018/978-1-7998-8775-1.ch007

Mnjama, N. M. (2017). Preservation of Recorded Information in Public and Private Sector Organizations. In P. Jain & N. Mnjama (Eds.), *Managing Knowledge Resources and Records in Modern Organizations* (pp. 149–167). Hershey, PA: IGI Global. doi:10.4018/978-1-5225-1965-2.ch009

Mokoqama, M., & Fields, Z. (2017). Principles of Responsible Management Education (PRME): Call for Responsible Management Education. In Z. Fields (Ed.), *Collective Creativity for Responsible and Sustainable Business Practice* (pp. 229–241). Hershey, PA: IGI Global. doi:10.4018/978-1-5225-1823-5.ch012

Monteiro, A., Lopes, S., & Carbone, F. (2021). Academic Mobility: Bridging Tourism and Peace Education. In J. da Silva, Z. Breda, & F. Carbone (Eds.), *Role and Impact of Tourism in Peacebuilding and Conflict Transformation* (pp. 275-301). IGI Global. https://doi.org/10.4018/978-1-7998-5053-3.ch016

Muniapan, B. (2017). Philosophy and Management: The Relevance of Vedanta in Management. In P. Ordóñez de Pablos (Ed.), *Managerial Strategies and Solutions for Business Success in Asia* (pp. 124–139). Hershey, PA: IGI Global. doi:10.4018/978-1-5225-1886-0.ch007

Murad, S. E., & Dowaji, S. (2017). Using Value-Based Approach for Managing Cloud-Based Services. In A. Turuk, B. Sahoo, & S. Addya (Eds.), *Resource Management and Efficiency in Cloud Computing Environments* (pp. 33–60). Hershey, PA: IGI Global. doi:10.4018/978-1-5225-1721-4.ch002

Mutahar, A. M., Daud, N. M., Thurasamy, R., Isaac, O., & Abdulsalam, R. (2018). The Mediating of Perceived Usefulness and Perceived Ease of Use: The Case of Mobile Banking in Yemen. *International Journal of Technology Diffusion, 9*(2), 21–40. doi:10.4018/IJTD.2018040102

Naidoo, V. (2017). E-Learning and Management Education at African Universities. In N. Baporikar (Ed.), *Management Education for Global Leadership* (pp. 181–201). Hershey, PA: IGI Global. doi:10.4018/978-1-5225-1013-0.ch009

Naidoo, V., & Igbinakhase, I. (2018). Opportunities and Challenges of Knowledge Retention in SMEs. In N. Baporikar (Ed.), *Knowledge Integration Strategies for Entrepreneurship and Sustainability* (pp. 70–94). Hershey, PA: IGI Global. doi:10.4018/978-1-5225-5115-7.ch004

Naumov, N., & Costandachi, G. (2021). Creativity and Entrepreneurship: Gastronomic Tourism in Mexico. In J. Soares (Ed.), *Innovation and Entrepreneurial Opportunities in Community Tourism* (pp. 90–108). IGI Global. https://doi.org/10.4018/978-1-7998-4855-4.ch006

Nayak, S., & Prabhu, N. (2017). Paradigm Shift in Management Education: Need for a Cross Functional Perspective. In N. Baporikar (Ed.), *Management Education for Global Leadership* (pp. 241–255). Hershey, PA: IGI Global. doi:10.4018/978-1-5225-1013-0.ch012

Nedelko, Z., & Potocan, V. (2017). Management Solutions in Non-Profit Organizations: Case of Slovenia. In V. Potocan, M. Üngan, & Z. Nedelko (Eds.), *Handbook of Research on Managerial Solutions in Non-Profit Organizations* (pp. 1–22). Hershey, PA: IGI Global. doi:10.4018/978-1-5225-0731-4.ch001

Nedelko, Z., & Potocan, V. (2017). Priority of Management Tools Utilization among Managers: International Comparison. In V. Wang (Ed.), *Encyclopedia of Strategic Leadership and Management* (pp. 1083–1094). Hershey, PA: IGI Global. doi:10.4018/978-1-5225-1049-9.ch075

Nedelko, Z., Raudeliūnienė, J., & Črešnar, R. (2018). Knowledge Dynamics in Supply Chain Management. In N. Baporikar (Ed.), *Knowledge Integration Strategies for Entrepreneurship and Sustainability* (pp. 150–166). Hershey, PA: IGI Global. doi:10.4018/978-1-5225-5115-7.ch008

Nguyen, H. T., & Hipsher, S. A. (2018). Innovation and Creativity Used by Private Sector Firms in a Resources-Constrained Environment. In S. Hipsher (Ed.), *Examining the Private Sector's Role in Wealth Creation and Poverty Reduction* (pp. 219–238). Hershey, PA: IGI Global. doi:10.4018/978-1-5225-3117-3.ch010

Obicci, P. A. (2017). Risk Sharing in a Partnership. In *Risk Management Strategies in Public-Private Partnerships* (pp. 115–152). Hershey, PA: IGI Global. doi:10.4018/978-1-5225-2503-5.ch004

Obidallah, W. J., & Raahemi, B. (2017). Managing Changes in Service Oriented Virtual Organizations: A Structural and Procedural Framework to Facilitate the Process of Change. *Journal of Electronic Commerce in Organizations*, *15*(1), 59–83. doi:10.4018/JECO.2017010104

Ojo, O. (2017). Impact of Innovation on the Entrepreneurial Success in Selected Business Enterprises in South-West Nigeria. *International Journal of Innovation in the Digital Economy*, *8*(2), 29–38. doi:10.4018/IJIDE.2017040103

Okdinawati, L., Simatupang, T. M., & Sunitiyoso, Y. (2017). Multi-Agent Reinforcement Learning for Value Co-Creation of Collaborative Transportation Management (CTM). *International Journal of Information Systems and Supply Chain Management*, *10*(3), 84–95. doi:10.4018/IJISSCM.2017070105

Olivera, V. A., & Carrillo, I. M. (2021). Organizational Culture: A Key Element for the Development of Mexican Micro and Small Tourist Companies. In J. Soares (Ed.), *Innovation and Entrepreneurial Opportunities in Community Tourism* (pp. 227–242). IGI Global. doi:10.4018/978-1-7998-4855-4.ch013

Ossorio, M. (2022). Corporate Museum Experiences in Enogastronomic Tourism. In R. Augusto Costa, F. Brandão, Z. Breda, & C. Costa (Eds.), Planning and Managing the Experience Economy in Tourism (pp. 107-121). IGI Global. https://doi.org/doi:10.4018/978-1-7998-8775-1.ch006

Ossorio, M. (2022). Enogastronomic Tourism in Times of Pandemic. In G. Fernandes (Ed.), *Challenges and New Opportunities for Tourism in Inland Territories: Ecocultural Resources and Sustainable Initiatives* (pp. 241–255). IGI Global. https://doi.org/10.4018/978-1-7998-7339-6.ch014

Özekici, Y. K. (2022). ICT as an Acculturative Agent and Its Role in the Tourism Context: Introduction, Acculturation Theory, Progress of the Acculturation Theory in Extant Literature. In C. Ramos, S. Quinteiro, & A. Gonçalves (Eds.), *ICT as Innovator Between Tourism and Culture* (pp. 42–66). IGI Global. https://doi.org/10.4018/978-1-7998-8165-0.ch004

Pal, K. (2018). Building High Quality Big Data-Based Applications in Supply Chains. In A. Kumar & S. Saurav (Eds.), *Supply Chain Management Strategies and Risk Assessment in Retail Environments* (pp. 1–24). Hershey, PA: IGI Global. doi:10.4018/978-1-5225-3056-5.ch001

Palos-Sanchez, P. R., & Correia, M. B. (2018). Perspectives of the Adoption of Cloud Computing in the Tourism Sector. In J. Rodrigues, C. Ramos, P. Cardoso, & C. Henriques (Eds.), *Handbook of Research on Technological Developments for Cultural Heritage and eTourism Applications* (pp. 377–400). Hershey, PA: IGI Global. doi:10.4018/978-1-5225-2927-9.ch018

Papadopoulou, G. (2021). Promoting Gender Equality and Women Empowerment in the Tourism Sector. In F. Brandão, Z. Breda, R. Costa, & C. Costa (Eds.), Handbook of Research on the Role of Tourism in Achieving Sustainable Development Goals (pp. 152-174). IGI Global. https://doi.org/ doi:10.4018/978-1-7998-5691-7.ch009

Papp-Váry, Á. F., & Tóth, T. Z. (2022). Analysis of Budapest as a Film Tourism Destination. In R. Baleiro & R. Pereira (Eds.), *Global Perspectives on Literary Tourism and Film-Induced Tourism* (pp. 257-279). IGI Global. https://doi.org/10.4018/978-1-7998-8262-6.ch014

Patiño, B. E. (2017). New Generation Management by Convergence and Individual Identity: A Systemic and Human-Oriented Approach. In N. Baporikar (Ed.), *Innovation and Shifting Perspectives in Management Education* (pp. 119–143). Hershey, PA: IGI Global. doi:10.4018/978-1-5225-1019-2.ch006

Patro, C. S. (2021). Digital Tourism: Influence of E-Marketing Technology. In M. Dinis, L. Bonixe, S. Lamy, & Z. Breda (Eds.), *Impact of New Media in Tourism* (pp. 234-254). IGI Global. https://doi.org/10.4018/978-1-7998-7095-1.ch014

Pawliczek, A., & Rössler, M. (2017). Knowledge of Management Tools and Systems in SMEs: Knowledge Transfer in Management. In A. Bencsik (Ed.), *Knowledge Management Initiatives and Strategies in Small and Medium Enterprises* (pp. 180–203). Hershey, PA: IGI Global. doi:10.4018/978-1-5225-1642-2.ch009

Pejic-Bach, M., Omazic, M. A., Aleksic, A., & Zoroja, J. (2018). Knowledge-Based Decision Making: A Multi-Case Analysis. In R. Leon (Ed.), *Managerial Strategies for Business Sustainability During Turbulent Times* (pp. 160–184). Hershey, PA: IGI Global. doi:10.4018/978-1-5225-2716-9.ch009

Perano, M., Hysa, X., & Calabrese, M. (2018). Strategic Planning, Cultural Context, and Business Continuity Management: Business Cases in the City of Shkoder. In A. Presenza & L. Sheehan (Eds.), *Geopolitics and Strategic Management in the Global Economy* (pp. 57–77). Hershey, PA: IGI Global. doi:10.4018/978-1-5225-2673-5.ch004

Pereira, R., Mira da Silva, M., & Lapão, L. V. (2017). IT Governance Maturity Patterns in Portuguese Healthcare. In S. De Haes & W. Van Grembergen (Eds.), *Strategic IT Governance and Alignment in Business Settings* (pp. 24–52). Hershey, PA: IGI Global. doi:10.4018/978-1-5225-0861-8.ch002

Pérez-Uribe, R. I., Torres, D. A., Jurado, S. P., & Prada, D. M. (2018). Cloud Tools for the Development of Project Management in SMEs. In R. Perez-Uribe, C. Salcedo-Perez, & D. Ocampo-Guzman (Eds.), *Handbook of Research on Intrapreneurship and Organizational Sustainability in SMEs* (pp. 95–120). Hershey, PA: IGI Global. doi:10.4018/978-1-5225-3543-0.ch005

Petrisor, I., & Cozmiuc, D. (2017). Global Supply Chain Management Organization at Siemens in the Advent of Industry 4.0. In L. Saglietto & C. Cezanne (Eds.), *Global Intermediation and Logistics Service Providers* (pp. 123–142). Hershey, PA: IGI Global. doi:10.4018/978-1-5225-2133-4.ch007

Pierce, J. M., Velliaris, D. M., & Edwards, J. (2017). A Living Case Study: A Journey Not a Destination. In N. Silton (Ed.), *Exploring the Benefits of Creativity in Education, Media, and the Arts* (pp. 158–178). Hershey, PA: IGI Global. doi:10.4018/978-1-5225-0504-4.ch008

Pipia, S., & Pipia, S. (2021). Challenges of Religious Tourism in the Conflict Region: An Example of Jerusalem. In E. Alaverdov & M. Bari (Eds.), *Global Development of Religious Tourism* (pp. 135-148). IGI Global. https://doi.org/10.4018/978-1-7998-5792-1.ch009

Poulaki, P., Kritikos, A., Vasilakis, N., & Valeri, M. (2022). The Contribution of Female Creativity to the Development of Gastronomic Tourism in Greece: The Case of the Island of Naxos in the South Aegean Region. In M. Valeri (Ed.), *New Governance and Management in Touristic Destinations* (pp. 246–258). IGI Global. https://doi.org/10.4018/978-1-6684-3889-3.ch015

Radosavljevic, M., & Andjelkovic, A. (2017). Multi-Criteria Decision Making Approach for Choosing Business Process for the Improvement: Upgrading of the Six Sigma Methodology. In J. Stanković, P. Delias, S. Marinković, & S. Rochhia (Eds.), *Tools and Techniques for Economic Decision Analysis* (pp. 225–247). Hershey, PA: IGI Global. doi:10.4018/978-1-5225-0959-2.ch011

Radovic, V. M. (2017). Corporate Sustainability and Responsibility and Disaster Risk Reduction: A Serbian Overview. In M. Camilleri (Ed.), *CSR 2.0 and the New Era of Corporate Citizenship* (pp. 147–164). Hershey, PA: IGI Global. doi:10.4018/978-1-5225-1842-6.ch008

Raghunath, K. M., Devi, S. L., & Patro, C. S. (2018). Impact of Risk Assessment Models on Risk Factors: A Holistic Outlook. In K. Strang, M. Korstanje, & N. Vajjhala (Eds.), *Research, Practices, and Innovations in Global Risk and Contingency Management* (pp. 134–153). Hershey, PA: IGI Global. doi:10.4018/978-1-5225-4754-9.ch008

Raman, A., & Goyal, D. P. (2017). Extending IMPLEMENT Framework for Enterprise Information Systems Implementation to Information System Innovation. In M. Tavana (Ed.), *Enterprise Information Systems and the Digitalization of Business Functions* (pp. 137–177). Hershey, PA: IGI Global. doi:10.4018/978-1-5225-2382-6.ch007

Rao, Y., & Zhang, Y. (2017). The Construction and Development of Academic Library Digital Special Subject Databases. In L. Ruan, Q. Zhu, & Y. Ye (Eds.), *Academic Library Development and Administration in China* (pp. 163–183). Hershey, PA: IGI Global. doi:10.4018/978-1-5225-0550-1.ch010

Ravasan, A. Z., Mohammadi, M. M., & Hamidi, H. (2018). An Investigation Into the Critical Success Factors of Implementing Information Technology Service Management Frameworks. In K. Jakobs (Ed.), *Corporate and Global Standardization Initiatives in Contemporary Society* (pp. 200–218). Hershey, PA: IGI Global. doi:10.4018/978-1-5225-5320-5.ch009

Rezaie, S., Mirabedini, S. J., & Abtahi, A. (2018). Designing a Model for Implementation of Business Intelligence in the Banking Industry. *International Journal of Enterprise Information Systems, 14*(1), 77–103. doi:10.4018/IJEIS.2018010105

Richards, V., Matthews, N., Williams, O. J., & Khan, Z. (2021). The Challenges of Accessible Tourism Information Systems for Tourists With Vision Impairment: Sensory Communications Beyond the Screen. In C. Eusébio, L. Teixeira, & M. Carneiro (Eds.), *ICT Tools and Applications for Accessible Tourism* (pp. 26–54). IGI Global. https://doi.org/10.4018/978-1-7998-6428-8.ch002

Rodrigues de Souza Neto, V., & Marques, O. (2021). Rural Tourism Fostering Welfare Through Sustainable Development: A Conceptual Approach. In A. Perinotto, V. Mayer, & J. Soares (Eds.), *Rebuilding and Restructuring the Tourism Industry: Infusion of Happiness and Quality of Life* (pp. 38–57). IGI Global. https://doi.org/10.4018/978-1-7998-7239-9.ch003

Romano, L., Grimaldi, R., & Colasuonno, F. S. (2017). Demand Management as a Success Factor in Project Portfolio Management. In L. Romano (Ed.), *Project Portfolio Management Strategies for Effective Organizational Operations* (pp. 202–219). Hershey, PA: IGI Global. doi:10.4018/978-1-5225-2151-8.ch008

Rubio-Escuderos, L., & García-Andreu, H. (2021). Competitiveness Factors of Accessible Tourism E-Travel Agencies. In C. Eusébio, L. Teixeira, & M. Carneiro (Eds.), *ICT Tools and Applications for Accessible Tourism* (pp. 196–217). IGI Global. https://doi.org/10.4018/978-1-7998-6428-8.ch009

Rucci, A. C., Porto, N., Darcy, S., & Becka, L. (2021). Smart and Accessible Cities?: Not Always – The Case for Accessible Tourism Initiatives in Buenos Aries and Sydney. In C. Eusébio, L. Teixeira, & M. Carneiro (Eds.), *ICT Tools and Applications for Accessible Tourism* (pp. 115–145). IGI Global. https://doi.org/10.4018/978-1-7998-6428-8.ch006

Ruhi, U. (2018). Towards an Interdisciplinary Socio-Technical Definition of Virtual Communities. In M. Khosrow-Pour, D.B.A. (Ed.), Encyclopedia of Information Science and Technology, Fourth Edition (pp. 4278-4295). Hershey, PA: IGI Global. doi:10.4018/978-1-5225-2255-3.ch371

Ryan, L., Catena, M., Ros, P., & Stephens, S. (2021). Designing Entrepreneurial Ecosystems to Support Resource Management in the Tourism Industry. In V. Costa, A. Moura, & M. Mira (Eds.), *Handbook of Research on Human Capital and People Management in the Tourism Industry* (pp. 265–281). IGI Global. https://doi.org/10.4018/978-1-7998-4318-4.ch013

Sabuncu, I. (2021). Understanding Tourist Perceptions and Expectations During Pandemic Through Social Media Big Data. In M. Demir, A. Dalgıç, & F. Ergen (Eds.), *Handbook of Research on the Impacts and Implications of COVID-19 on the Tourism Industry* (pp. 330–350). IGI Global. https://doi.org/10.4018/978-1-7998-8231-2.ch016

Safari, M. R., & Jiang, Q. (2018). The Theory and Practice of IT Governance Maturity and Strategies Alignment: Evidence From Banking Industry. *Journal of Global Information Management*, *26*(2), 127–146. doi:10.4018/JGIM.2018040106

Sahoo, J., Pati, B., & Mohanty, B. (2017). Knowledge Management as an Academic Discipline: An Assessment. In B. Gunjal (Ed.), *Managing Knowledge and Scholarly Assets in Academic Libraries* (pp. 99–126). Hershey, PA: IGI Global. doi:10.4018/978-1-5225-1741-2.ch005

Saini, D. (2017). Relevance of Teaching Values and Ethics in Management Education. In N. Baporikar (Ed.), *Management Education for Global Leadership* (pp. 90–111). Hershey, PA: IGI Global. doi:10.4018/978-1-5225-1013-0.ch005

Sambhanthan, A. (2017). Assessing and Benchmarking Sustainability in Organisations: An Integrated Conceptual Model. *International Journal of Systems and Service-Oriented Engineering*, *7*(4), 22–43. doi:10.4018/IJSSOE.2017100102

Sambhanthan, A., & Potdar, V. (2017). A Study of the Parameters Impacting Sustainability in Information Technology Organizations. *International Journal of Knowledge-Based Organizations*, *7*(3), 27–39. doi:10.4018/IJKBO.2017070103

Sánchez-Fernández, M. D., & Manríquez, M. R. (2018). The Entrepreneurial Spirit Based on Social Values: The Digital Generation. In P. Isaias & L. Carvalho (Eds.), *User Innovation and the Entrepreneurship Phenomenon in the Digital Economy* (pp. 173–193). Hershey, PA: IGI Global. doi:10.4018/978-1-5225-2826-5.ch009

Sanchez-Ruiz, L., & Blanco, B. (2017). Process Management for SMEs: Barriers, Enablers, and Benefits. In M. Vemić (Ed.), *Optimal Management Strategies in Small and Medium Enterprises* (pp. 293–319). Hershey, PA: IGI Global. doi:10.4018/978-1-5225-1949-2.ch014

Sanz, L. F., Gómez-Pérez, J., & Castillo-Martinez, A. (2018). Analysis of the European ICT Competence Frameworks. In V. Ahuja & S. Rathore (Eds.), *Multidisciplinary Perspectives on Human Capital and Information Technology Professionals* (pp. 225–245). Hershey, PA: IGI Global. doi:10.4018/978-1-5225-5297-0.ch012

Sarvepalli, A., & Godin, J. (2017). Business Process Management in the Classroom. *Journal of Cases on Information Technology*, *19*(2), 17–28. doi:10.4018/JCIT.2017040102

Saxena, G. G., & Saxena, A. (2021). Host Community Role in Medical Tourism Development. In M. Singh & S. Kumaran (Eds.), *Growth of the Medical Tourism Industry and Its Impact on Society: Emerging Research and Opportunities* (pp. 105–127). IGI Global. https://doi.org/10.4018/978-1-7998-3427-4.ch006

Saygili, E. E., Ozturkoglu, Y., & Kocakulah, M. C. (2017). End Users' Perceptions of Critical Success Factors in ERP Applications. *International Journal of Enterprise Information Systems*, *13*(4), 58–75. doi:10.4018/IJEIS.2017100104

Saygili, E. E., & Saygili, A. T. (2017). Contemporary Issues in Enterprise Information Systems: A Critical Review of CSFs in ERP Implementations. In M. Tavana (Ed.), *Enterprise Information Systems and the Digitalization of Business Functions* (pp. 120–136). Hershey, PA: IGI Global. doi:10.4018/978-1-5225-2382-6.ch006

Schwaiger, K. M., & Zehrer, A. (2021). The COVID-19 Pandemic and Organizational Resilience in Hospitality Family Firms: A Qualitative Approach. In A. Zehrer, G. Glowka, K. Schwaiger, & V. Ranacher-Lackner (Eds.), *Resiliency Models and Addressing Future Risks for Family Firms in the Tourism Industry* (pp. 32–49). IGI Global. https://doi.org/10.4018/978-1-7998-7352-5.ch002

Scott, N., & Campos, A. C. (2022). Cognitive Science of Tourism Experiences. In R. Augusto Costa, F. Brandão, Z. Breda, & C. Costa (Eds.), Planning and Managing the Experience Economy in Tourism (pp. 1-21). IGI Global. https://doi.org/ doi:10.4018/978-1-7998-8775-1.ch001

Seidenstricker, S., & Antonino, A. (2018). Business Model Innovation-Oriented Technology Management for Emergent Technologies. In M. Khosrow-Pour, D.B.A. (Ed.), Encyclopedia of Information Science and Technology, Fourth Edition (pp. 4560-4569). Hershey, PA: IGI Global. doi:10.4018/978-1-5225-2255-3.ch396

Selvi, M. S. (2021). Changes in Tourism Sales and Marketing Post COVID-19. In M. Demir, A. Dalgıç, & F. Ergen (Eds.), *Handbook of Research on the Impacts and Implications of COVID-19 on the Tourism Industry* (pp. 437–460). IGI Global. doi:10.4018/978-1-7998-8231-2.ch021

Senaratne, S., & Gunarathne, A. D. (2017). Excellence Perspective for Management Education from a Global Accountants' Hub in Asia. In N. Baporikar (Ed.), *Management Education for Global Leadership* (pp. 158–180). Hershey, PA: IGI Global. doi:10.4018/978-1-5225-1013-0.ch008

Sensuse, D. I., & Cahyaningsih, E. (2018). Knowledge Management Models: A Summative Review. *International Journal of Information Systems in the Service Sector, 10*(1), 71–100. doi:10.4018/IJISSS.2018010105

Seth, M., Goyal, D., & Kiran, R. (2017). Diminution of Impediments in Implementation of Supply Chain Management Information System for Enhancing its Effectiveness in Indian Automobile Industry. *Journal of Global Information Management, 25*(3), 1–20. doi:10.4018/JGIM.2017070101

Seyal, A. H., & Rahman, M. N. (2017). Investigating Impact of Inter-Organizational Factors in Measuring ERP Systems Success: Bruneian Perspectives. In M. Tavana (Ed.), *Enterprise Information Systems and the Digitalization of Business Functions* (pp. 178–204). Hershey, PA: IGI Global. doi:10.4018/978-1-5225-2382-6.ch008

Shaqrah, A. A. (2018). Analyzing Business Intelligence Systems Based on 7s Model of McKinsey. *International Journal of Business Intelligence Research, 9*(1), 53–63. doi:10.4018/IJBIR.2018010104

Sharma, A. J. (2017). Enhancing Sustainability through Experiential Learning in Management Education. In N. Baporikar (Ed.), *Management Education for Global Leadership* (pp. 256–274). Hershey, PA: IGI Global. doi:10.4018/978-1-5225-1013-0.ch013

Shetty, K. P. (2017). Responsible Global Leadership: Ethical Challenges in Management Education. In N. Baporikar (Ed.), *Innovation and Shifting Perspectives in Management Education* (pp. 194–223). Hershey, PA: IGI Global. doi:10.4018/978-1-5225-1019-2.ch009

Sinthupundaja, J., & Kohda, Y. (2017). Effects of Corporate Social Responsibility and Creating Shared Value on Sustainability. *International Journal of Sustainable Entrepreneurship and Corporate Social Responsibility*, *2*(1), 27–38. doi:10.4018/IJSECSR.2017010103

Škarica, I., & Hrgović, A. V. (2018). Implementation of Total Quality Management Principles in Public Health Institutes in the Republic of Croatia. *International Journal of Productivity Management and Assessment Technologies*, *6*(1), 1–16. doi:10.4018/IJPMAT.2018010101

Skokic, V. (2021). How Small Hotel Owners Practice Resilience: Longitudinal Study Among Small Family Hotels in Croatia. In A. Zehrer, G. Glowka, K. Schwaiger, & V. Ranacher-Lackner (Eds.), *Resiliency Models and Addressing Future Risks for Family Firms in the Tourism Industry* (pp. 50–73). IGI Global. doi:10.4018/978-1-7998-7352-5.ch003

Smuts, H., Kotzé, P., Van der Merwe, A., & Loock, M. (2017). Framework for Managing Shared Knowledge in an Information Systems Outsourcing Context. *International Journal of Knowledge Management*, *13*(4), 1–30. doi:10.4018/IJKM.2017100101

Sousa, M. J., Cruz, R., Dias, I., & Caracol, C. (2017). Information Management Systems in the Supply Chain. In G. Jamil, A. Soares, & C. Pessoa (Eds.), *Handbook of Research on Information Management for Effective Logistics and Supply Chains* (pp. 469–485). Hershey, PA: IGI Global. doi:10.4018/978-1-5225-0973-8.ch025

Spremic, M., Turulja, L., & Bajgoric, N. (2018). Two Approaches in Assessing Business Continuity Management Attitudes in the Organizational Context. In N. Bajgoric (Ed.), *Always-On Enterprise Information Systems for Modern Organizations* (pp. 159–183). Hershey, PA: IGI Global. doi:10.4018/978-1-5225-3704-5.ch008

Steenkamp, A. L. (2018). Some Insights in Computer Science and Information Technology. In *Examining the Changing Role of Supervision in Doctoral Research Projects: Emerging Research and Opportunities* (pp. 113–133). Hershey, PA: IGI Global. doi:10.4018/978-1-5225-2610-0.ch005

Stipanović, C., Rudan, E., & Zubović, V. (2022). Reaching the New Tourist Through Creativity: Sustainable Development Challenges in Croatian Coastal Towns. In M. Valeri (Ed.), *New Governance and Management in Touristic Destinations* (pp. 231–245). IGI Global. https://doi.org/10.4018/978-1-6684-3889-3.ch014

Tabach, A., & Croteau, A. (2017). Configurations of Information Technology Governance Practices and Business Unit Performance. *International Journal of IT/Business Alignment and Governance*, *8*(2), 1–27. doi:10.4018/IJITBAG.2017070101

Talaue, G. M., & Iqbal, T. (2017). Assessment of e-Business Mode of Selected Private Universities in the Philippines and Pakistan. *International Journal of Online Marketing*, *7*(4), 63–77. doi:10.4018/IJOM.2017100105

Tam, G. C. (2017). Project Manager Sustainability Competence. In *Managerial Strategies and Green Solutions for Project Sustainability* (pp. 178–207). Hershey, PA: IGI Global. doi:10.4018/978-1-5225-2371-0.ch008

Tambo, T. (2018). Fashion Retail Innovation: About Context, Antecedents, and Outcome in Technological Change Projects. In I. Management Association (Ed.), Fashion and Textiles: Breakthroughs in Research and Practice (pp. 233-260). Hershey, PA: IGI Global. https://doi.org/ doi:10.4018/978-1-5225-3432-7.ch010

Tantau, A. D., & Frăţilă, L. C. (2018). Information and Management System for Renewable Energy Business. In *Entrepreneurship and Business Development in the Renewable Energy Sector* (pp. 200–244). Hershey, PA: IGI Global. doi:10.4018/978-1-5225-3625-3.ch006

Teixeira, N., Pardal, P. N., & Rafael, B. G. (2018). Internationalization, Financial Performance, and Organizational Challenges: A Success Case in Portugal. In L. Carvalho (Ed.), *Handbook of Research on Entrepreneurial Ecosystems and Social Dynamics in a Globalized World* (pp. 379–423). Hershey, PA: IGI Global. doi:10.4018/978-1-5225-3525-6.ch017

Teixeira, P., Teixeira, L., Eusébio, C., Silva, S., & Teixeira, A. (2021). The Impact of ICTs on Accessible Tourism: Evidence Based on a Systematic Literature Review. In C. Eusébio, L. Teixeira, & M. Carneiro (Eds.), *ICT Tools and Applications for Accessible Tourism* (pp. 1–25). IGI Global. doi:10.4018/978-1-7998-6428-8.ch001

Trad, A., & Kalpić, D. (2018). The Business Transformation Framework, Agile Project and Change Management. In M. Khosrow-Pour, D.B.A. (Ed.), Encyclopedia of Information Science and Technology, Fourth Edition (pp. 620-635). Hershey, PA: IGI Global. https://doi.org/ doi:10.4018/978-1-5225-2255-3.ch054

Trad, A., & Kalpić, D. (2018). The Business Transformation and Enterprise Architecture Framework: The Financial Engineering E-Risk Management and E-Law Integration. In B. Sergi, F. Fidanoski, M. Ziolo, & V. Naumovski (Eds.), *Regaining Global Stability After the Financial Crisis* (pp. 46–65). Hershey, PA: IGI Global. doi:10.4018/978-1-5225-4026-7.ch003

Trengereid, V. (2022). Conditions of Network Engagement: The Quest for a Common Good. In R. Augusto Costa, F. Brandão, Z. Breda, & C. Costa (Eds.), *Planning and Managing the Experience Economy in Tourism* (pp. 69-84). IGI Global. https://doi.org/10.4018/978-1-7998-8775-1.ch004

Turulja, L., & Bajgoric, N. (2018). Business Continuity and Information Systems: A Systematic Literature Review. In N. Bajgoric (Ed.), *Always-On Enterprise Information Systems for Modern Organizations* (pp. 60–87). Hershey, PA: IGI Global. doi:10.4018/978-1-5225-3704-5.ch004

Vargas-Hernández, J. G. (2017). Professional Integrity in Business Management Education. In N. Baporikar (Ed.), *Management Education for Global Leadership* (pp. 70–89). Hershey, PA: IGI Global. doi:10.4018/978-1-5225-1013-0.ch004

Varnacı Uzun, F. (2021). The Destination Preferences of Foreign Tourists During the COVID-19 Pandemic and Attitudes Towards: Marmaris, Turkey. In M. Demir, A. Dalgıç, & F. Ergen (Eds.), *Handbook of Research on the Impacts and Implications of COVID-19 on the Tourism Industry* (pp. 285–306). IGI Global. https://doi.org/10.4018/978-1-7998-8231-2.ch014

Vasista, T. G., & AlAbdullatif, A. M. (2017). Role of Electronic Customer Relationship Management in Demand Chain Management: A Predictive Analytic Approach. *International Journal of Information Systems and Supply Chain Management, 10*(1), 53–67. doi:10.4018/IJISSCM.2017010104

Vieru, D., & Bourdeau, S. (2017). Survival in the Digital Era: A Digital Competence-Based Multi-Case Study in the Canadian SME Clothing Industry. *International Journal of Social and Organizational Dynamics in IT, 6*(1), 17–34. doi:10.4018/IJSODIT.2017010102

Vijayan, G., & Kamarulzaman, N. H. (2017). An Introduction to Sustainable Supply Chain Management and Business Implications. In M. Khan, M. Hussain, & M. Ajmal (Eds.), *Green Supply Chain Management for Sustainable Business Practice* (pp. 27–50). Hershey, PA: IGI Global. doi:10.4018/978-1-5225-0635-5.ch002

Vlachvei, A., & Notta, O. (2017). Firm Competitiveness: Theories, Evidence, and Measurement. In A. Vlachvei, O. Notta, K. Karantininis, & N. Tsounis (Eds.), *Factors Affecting Firm Competitiveness and Performance in the Modern Business World* (pp. 1–42). Hershey, PA: IGI Global. doi:10.4018/978-1-5225-0843-4.ch001

Wang, C., Schofield, M., Li, X., & Ou, X. (2017). Do Chinese Students in Public and Private Higher Education Institutes Perform at Different Level in One of the Leadership Skills: Critical Thinking?: An Exploratory Comparison. In V. Wang (Ed.), *Encyclopedia of Strategic Leadership and Management* (pp. 160–181). Hershey, PA: IGI Global. doi:10.4018/978-1-5225-1049-9.ch013

Wang, J. (2017). Multi-Agent based Production Management Decision System Modelling for the Textile Enterprise. *Journal of Global Information Management, 25*(4), 1–15. doi:10.4018/JGIM.2017100101

Wiedemann, A., & Gewald, H. (2017). Examining Cross-Domain Alignment: The Correlation of Business Strategy, IT Management, and IT Business Value. *International Journal of IT/Business Alignment and Governance, 8*(1), 17–31. doi:10.4018/IJITBAG.2017010102

Wolf, R., & Thiel, M. (2018). Advancing Global Business Ethics in China: Reducing Poverty Through Human and Social Welfare. In S. Hipsher (Ed.), *Examining the Private Sector's Role in Wealth Creation and Poverty Reduction* (pp. 67–84). Hershey, PA: IGI Global. doi:10.4018/978-1-5225-3117-3.ch004

Yablonsky, S. (2018). Innovation Platforms: Data and Analytics Platforms. In *Multi-Sided Platforms (MSPs) and Sharing Strategies in the Digital Economy: Emerging Research and Opportunities* (pp. 72–95). Hershey, PA: IGI Global. doi:10.4018/978-1-5225-5457-8.ch003

Yaşar, B. (2021). The Impact of COVID-19 on Volatility of Tourism Stocks: Evidence From BIST Tourism Index. In M. Demir, A. Dalgıç, & F. Ergen (Eds.), *Handbook of Research on the Impacts and Implications of COVID-19 on the Tourism Industry* (pp. 23–44). IGI Global. https://doi.org/10.4018/978-1-7998-8231-2.ch002

Yusoff, A., Ahmad, N. H., & Halim, H. A. (2017). Agropreneurship among Gen Y in Malaysia: The Role of Academic Institutions. In N. Ahmad, T. Ramayah, H. Halim, & S. Rahman (Eds.), *Handbook of Research on Small and Medium Enterprises in Developing Countries* (pp. 23–47). Hershey, PA: IGI Global. doi:10.4018/978-1-5225-2165-5.ch002

Zacher, D., & Pechlaner, H. (2021). Resilience as an Opportunity Approach: Challenges and Perspectives for Private Sector Participation on a Community Level. In A. Zehrer, G. Glowka, K. Schwaiger, & V. Ranacher-Lackner (Eds.), *Resiliency Models and Addressing Future Risks for Family Firms in the Tourism Industry* (pp. 75–102). IGI Global. https://doi.org/10.4018/978-1-7998-7352-5.ch004

Zanin, F., Comuzzi, E., & Costantini, A. (2018). The Effect of Business Strategy and Stock Market Listing on the Use of Risk Assessment Tools. In *Management Control Systems in Complex Settings: Emerging Research and Opportunities* (pp. 145–168). Hershey, PA: IGI Global. doi:10.4018/978-1-5225-3987-2.ch007

Zgheib, P. W. (2017). Corporate Innovation and Intrapreneurship in the Middle East. In P. Zgheib (Ed.), *Entrepreneurship and Business Innovation in the Middle East* (pp. 37–56). Hershey, PA: IGI Global. doi:10.4018/978-1-5225-2066-5.ch003

About the Contributors

Thivashini B. Jaya Kumar is a Lecturer at the School of Management & Marketing, Taylors Business School, Taylor's University, Malaysia. She was awarded Bachelor of Business from Victoria University, Australia and Master in Management from Taylors University. Prior to entering academia, she was a business analyst with 3+ years of experience. She holds a PhD in Business with a research interest in service marketing, consumer behavior, international business and entrepreneurship. Currently she teaches service marketing and international business modules.

Oluwabunmi Bakare-Fatungase is an Information Professional/Researcher in the Department of Information Management, Faculty of Communication & Information Sciences, Lead City University. Her research interest covers emerging technologies, digital & virtual libraries, information use and user communities, bullying and mobile bullying, etc. She is passionate about emphasizing the significant roles of Librarians in solving different societal issues with the arsenal of information at their disposal. She is a fellow of the Council for the Development of Social Science Research in Africa and a Queen Elizabeth Scholar in the Advanced Scholars West Africa (QES-AS-WA) program, Carleton University, Canada

Isik Cicek is an assistant Professor of Management and Strategy at the Faculty of Aviation Management, Necmettin Erbakan University, Turkey. His research interests human resources management, strategic management, and organizational behavior. He obtained his PhD degree of Management Engineering at İstanbul Technical University. He teaches courses in management and organization, strategic management, organizational behavior, business management, entrepreneurship

Iris-Panagiota Efthymiou is a Lecturer at the University of East London and the University of Greenwich. Executive, results-driven, multi-talented enterprise, and institutional director, author, and keynote speaker with over 20 years of experience in entrepreneurship, international affairs, and executive leadership roles. Possesses a solid foundation in research, management, consultancy, and strategic development. Iris has worked as a college director and created her own Public Affairs consultancy. She worked with politicians, Diplomats, entrepreneurs, academics, and journalists, and spoke at the UN Headquarters in Geneva. She is a Board Member of HAPSc, and a Scientific Associate of the LabHEM, of the University of Piraeus. She published over 15 books, 30 articles, and Book chapters in peer-reviewed journals. She is the Chief Editor of the Journal of Politics and Ethics in New Technologies and AI. Iris has a PhD in Behavioural Economics (summa cum laude), a Master's in Health Economics and Management, and Bachelor's in Economics. She believes in equal opportunities, uniqueness, and the normality of imperfection!

Ozlem Erdas Cicek is currently an Assistant Professor at the Department of Computer Engineering, Necmettin Erbakan University in Turkey. She obtained her Ph.D. in Computer Science from Middle East Technical University in Turkey. Her areas of interest include Machine Learning and Deep Learning. She has interdisciplinary studies in Pharmaceutical Sciences, Energy Engineering, Architecture, and Management.

Feranita Feranita is a Senior Lecturer at the Faculty of Business and Law, Taylor's University, Malaysia. She is also the founding Director of International Family Enterprise Centre (IFEC) at Taylor's University. She received her PhD from Lancaster University, UK. Prior to that, she obtained a Master of Research in Management Sciences from ESADE Business School, Spain, and an MBA from Nanyang Business School, Singapore. Primarily focusing on qualitative research method, her research centres around family business, entrepreneurship, innovation, and university-industry collaborations. She has published in journals such as British Journal of Management, R&D Management, and Journal of Family Business Strategy. Her publications also include family business cases in SAGE Business Cases, book chapters in entrepreneurship and social entrepreneurship, as well as media articles. As a certified professional coach, she coaches startups and business families.

J. Piet Hausberg is a Senior Consultant at Cassini Consulting in Hamburg and holds the Chair of Technology and Innovation Management at the University of Osnabruck, Germany. He holds a PhD from LUISS Guido Carli University, Rome. His research interests include business incubation and acceleration, crowdfunding, and open innovation. He published in top tier international journals like R&D Management, Journal of Technology Transfer, International Journal of Innovation Management, and Journal of Small Business Management.

Tobias D. Herbst is the Head of Process Data Technology at Avacon Netz GmbH (part of E.ON SE) and former Director of Business Development & Key Account Management of the Business Unit Rail at Schaeffler Technologies AG & Co. KG. He holds a PhD from Osnabrück University, Germany, Chair of Technology and Innovation Management at the School of Business Administration and Economics. His research areas are Digital Transformation and Corporate Governance and Development. He published in top-tier international journals like the International Journal of Innovation Management.

Lin Woon Leong is a senior lecturer at Taylor's University, Malaysia, which is recognized as the top-ranked private university in Southeast Asia and currently stands at #284 in the QS World University Rankings 2023, placing it among the top 1% of influential universities worldwide. Lin specializes in the Faculty of Business and Law and holds a Ph.D. from Universiti Putra Malaysia and an MBA from East Anglia University in the UK. His research interests span various areas, including business ethics, sustainability, corporate social responsibility, corporate political strategy, and the circular economy. Additionally, Lin has recently expanded his research to include the field of blockchain. Lin embarked on his academic journey in 2019 upon the completion of his Ph.D. Subsequently, on January 1, 2023, he was promoted to the position of associate professor, recognizing his exceptional contributions to his field. Furthermore, in June 2023, Lin assumed the prestigious role of Head of Research for the Faculty of Business and Law, a testament to his expertise and leadership capabilities in the academic realm. Lin Woon Leong has made significant contributions to academic publishing, with an impressive publication record of over 37 articles in reputable journals. You can find his publications listed in the following link: Google Scholar Profile. His work has been acknowledged and indexed by prestigious organizations such as ABS, Thomson Web of Science (SSCI), and Scopus, reflecting their recognition in the academic community. Lin's research has gained substantial attention, evident from his H-index of 14 on Google Scholar as of June 26, 2023. Furthermore, his publications have garnered over 1,009 citations since 2018, illustrating their impact and influence on scholarly discourse. Lin 's significant presence in academic publishing highlights his expertise and valuable contributions to his field. Lin's research covers a wide range of topics, contributing to various fields of study. Notable areas of focus include investigating the impact of clean energy and technological innovation on economic growth in Asian countries, exploring the role of sustainability and natural resources management in enhancing environmental quality, and examining the effectiveness of green growth, governance, and green technology innovation in achieving the Sustainable Development Goals within G7 countries. Additionally, Lin's research delves into the role of entrepreneurial education in preparing future entrepreneurs in Malaysia and analyzing the consequences of the COVID-19 pandemic on the ASEAN tourism industry. Lin has successfully secured a total of 9 research grants from various institutions. These grants have allowed for the exploration of diverse research areas and the development of innovative solutions for sustainable development. The institutions involved in supporting Lin's research endeavors include Taylor's University, as well as national and international institutions. Currently, Lin serves as the primary supervisor for 8 Ph.D. students, guiding and mentoring them in their research pursuits. The focus areas of their research cover a wide range of topics including sustainability, ethical leadership, circular economy, ethical marketing, corporate environmental responsibility, and family business and entrepreneurship. Additionally, Lin also acts as a co-supervisor for 4 Ph.D. students, supporting their research in these areas. Lin's supervision of these Ph.D. students demonstrates their commitment to fostering academic excellence and contributing to the development of knowledge in these important fields. Through his multidisciplinary approach, Lin Woon Leong demonstrates his commitment to addressing pressing issues in fields such as business, economics, sustainability, and societal challenges. His extensive publication record and the widespread citation of his work highlight his expertise and valuable contributions to the academic community.

Sudetu Oseni is an Office/Information Management Professional/Researcher in the Department of Office Technology and Management, School of Information and Communication Technology, Auchi Polytechnic, Auchi. Her research interest covers emerging technologies in office and information management, digital, virtual and mobile offices, social network communication etc. She is particularly concerned about Office Managers' roles in the present digital world. She belongs to numerous Professional Bodies including a Fellow of the Institute of Policy Management Development (IPMD), Nigeria.

Thanuja Rathakrishnan is currently employed as a Lecturer at Taylor's University in Malaysia. She successfully completed her doctoral studies in Business Economics at Universiti Putra Malaysia (UPM). Prior to her PhD, she pursued a Master of Business Administration degree from Putra Business School, UPM, Malaysia. She also holds a bachelor's degree in Communication and Management from Upper IOWA University, USA. Throughout her career, Dr. Thanuja has focused on various areas such as entrepreneurship, entrepreneurship education, family businesses, SMEs, and tourism projects, which has expanded her interest in entrepreneurial tourism management. She has also been actively involved in consultancy projects with both government and non-government organizations. Apart from her academic commitments, Dr. Thanuja contributes to the scholarly community in other capacities as well. She serves as an esteemed member of the Editorial Review Board for the

Journal of Responsible Tourism Management. Additionally, she volunteers as a Local Virtual Volunteer for AIESEC, an international non-profit organization that offers leadership development and cross-cultural exchange opportunities to young people.

Ayşe Aslı Yilmaz received her MS in Management and Organization from Inonu University in 2009. In 2011 she was assigned as the course director and instructor on Peace Support Operations(PSO), Cultural awareness in Multinational Environments, Strategic Communication, Civil Military Cooperation and Gender Awareness in PSOs in Partnership for Peace Training Center as well as different UN and NATO affiliated agencies and training centers. She is currently studying Ph.D. in Business Administration (English prg.), Social Sciences Institute at Atılım University.

Index

M

N

O

P

Q

R

S

V

W

www.ingramcontent.com/pod-product-compliance
Lightning Source LLC
LaVergne TN
LVHW081323300926
849161LV00008B/1862
9781799887973